YELLER-BELL

To Rina

with every good wish

John Rhodes

March 2009.

YELLER-BELLY YEARS
Growing up in Lincolnshire 1930–50
'Remember'd with Advantages'

John Rhodes

Extracts have earlier appeared in the *Scunthorpe Telegraph* and
The Lincolnshire Poacher and on *www.briggensians.net*

Some photographs by courtesy of the *Scunthorpe Telegraph* and
John and Valerie Holland.

Front cover photograph: the author, aged eight.

Designed and typeset in Palatino by Postscript Communications Ltd
www.post-comms.co.uk

Further copies are available from:
John Rhodes
13 Hill Rise
St Ives
Cambridgeshire PE27 6SP
Email: jarivo@gmail.com

To my Mother and Father and all other Rhodes,
major and minor,
as well as Yeller-bellies everywhere

CONTENTS

Acknowledgements..i

1. The First Ten Years..1

2. The Square..17

3. Further Afield...27

4. My Early Schooling...37

5. High Days and Holy Days...51

6. Culture, Comics and Books...63

7. Church, Cubs and the Cinema...67

8. My War 1939–45...77

9. Brigg Grammar School 1941–48...93

10. Initials and Nicknames...127

11. Potato-picking Sixty Years Ago..135

12. Leisure and Pleasure...143

13. Lindsey Blind...159

14. Teenage Angst and the Sap Rising....................................175

15. Ashby County Primary School..183

Epilogue...203

ACKNOWLEDGEMENTS

This retirement project started as an attempt to answer my grandchildren's question: *'What was it like when you were young, Grandpa?'* Sections have been written at different times over several years. However, it has been finished with encouragement from my wife Sheila and our children, Ruth, Tim and Jonathan. Sheila has been particularly patient and long-suffering, having been dispossessed of her dining room table for long periods, as I collated my thoughts in longhand, and driven out of her sewing room, so I could laboriously tap them out on the computer keyboard with two index fingers. She muffled her ears when whole sections inexplicably disappeared into cyberspace and were irrecoverable, while I fumed and questioned the lineage and quality of my computer.

I should also like to thank those who were my contemporaries during my Yeller-belly Years in Brigg for their companionship, and hope that neither they nor their heirs feel I have maligned them. As Shakespeare's Henry V said of the feats done at Agincourt, I have tried to show my very ordinary early life *'remember'd with advantages'*.

I owe a great debt of gratitude to Postscript Communications Ltd, who have made my dream a reality. I give thanks to Éloïse Varin, who was responsible for the impressive design work, and especially to Matthew Cann who, in addition to being a close friend of my younger son and a former student at St Ivo School (where I was Headmaster for twenty years), was the midwife to this venture. By his careful diligence in copy-editing and proofreading my text and in overseeing the book's production, which has seen fine images emerging from the most dog-eared of snaps taken on cheap cameras of pre-war vintage as well as more formal photos taken by local professionals in the 1940s, he has produced a volume that is pleasing to me.

As an English teacher for over forty years I expended miles of red ink in highlighting grammatical and orthographical errors. I am sure my colleagues, students and friends will search for such errors in this book. And I have to admit that should they find any errant commas, misplaced apostrophes, spelling mistakes or errors of fact, the fault is mine, all mine.

Finally, a note on this book's title. 'Yeller-belly' is a term used to denote a person from Lincolnshire. Traditionally it is thought to derive from the yellow waistcoats worn by the Lincolnshire Regiment in pre-khaki days. The term does not suggest cowardice but staunchness for Queen and Country.

John Rhodes, August 2007

1
THE FIRST TEN YEARS

I was born in 1930, the first son of my parents and born into a family firmly fixed in the lowest levels of the lower middle class. My father was Frank Edgar and had been born in Caistor in 1898; my mother was Minnie (*née* Peck) and had been born in Bigby. Both places are within nine miles of my own birthplace, Brigg – or, to give it its full title, Glanford Brigg. From later family researches I don't think either side of the family had moved out of Lincolnshire for over four hundred years, so I was a confirmed 'Yeller-belly' on both counts.

Until comparatively recent years I had thought my family to be the epitome of the lowest stratum of middle-class morality – to the best of my knowledge no-one had been in prison, no-one had run off with someone else's wife or husband, no-one had been bankrupt and no-one had been the town drunkard or village idiot. I thought the family had a most conventional, ordinary background – in fact I thought we Rhodeses and Pecks were rather a dull lot. However, on my retirement I engaged in some genealogical research and came across several lurid surprises: there are a number of skeletons clanking in the family cupboard. It was only through my independent, strong-minded and unmarried paternal grandmother that I bear the surname I do. But in my Yeller-belly Years I was blissfully unaware of all this. If only I had been interested enough to ask the right questions…

In 1930 my father, after a brief flirtation with a job in the iron and steel industry at Scunthorpe (which was supposed to offer higher wages in the post-war years of the mid-twenties), was now firmly established in the retail trade. He worked for Lacey and Clark's, a drapery business that had pretensions to being a small departmental store, whose premises were situated at a corner of the Market Place between the Angel and the Lord Nelson. Father both served in the shop and was their travelling salesman over an area of some fifteen miles' radius of Brigg. My mother, having worked for Eccles the tailors in Wrawby Street before her marriage, was now immersed only in domestic duties. It was very rare for any wife to work in the thirties and anyway the unemployment rate was abnormally high. We never had much money, even though my father progressed and changed jobs, becoming a local government officer with the Lindsey Blind Society. He never earned more than £1,100 pa over the next thirty years, and for most of the time less than half that, but we had enough. I was always dressed in good quality clothes, always had shoes, never went hungry and certainly did not consider myself to have a deprived childhood. I was comfortable, content and cherished, but inevitably not spoiled.

My earliest memories are rather blurred and fragmentary, focused by remembered snippets of conversation years later. We were not a demonstrative family and my parents rarely talked about family matters and relationships, even when I was in my twenties. In fact I was in my late twenties before I learned that I had been a twin, but that my sibling had not survived.

The family album contains photographs of me, sitting up in a black, deep-bellied pram with small, seven-inch-diameter wheels. Plenty of good, fresh air was strongly recommended for growing babies and I was duly pushed out by my mother to draw lungfuls of clean Lincolnshire air. Her especial friend, Lil Rands, lived two doors away at no. 31 Central Square and she too had had a baby boy some three weeks before I arrived. Min and Lil would push their prams for miles. These excursions were as regular as clockwork – on Tuesday afternoons after the ironing had been completed in the morning and on Friday afternoons after the morning's baking. The other days of the week all had their allotted tasks: Monday was always wash day and Mother prided herself on having the first lot out on the line by 7am; Wednesday was half-day closing and Father might be back for the afternoon; Thursday was market day and the weekly order had to be placed with the grocer. Saturday (when Father was working) was for visiting my grandparents down Riverside, where we also called on a Thursday. But come rain or shine John Rands and I were pushed out on long perambulations – on Tuesday as far as 'Black House', which stood at the corner where the road to Scawby branched off from the A15 to Lincoln, some three and a half miles from Central Square. On Fridays we were pushed the other way to Wrawby, then down what was called Wrawby Tunnel to join the Barton road and so back home, another six miles or so. Such was the importance of fresh air that inclement weather was not allowed to impede our twice-weekly treks and I was sheltered behind a storm sheet against the elements.

I well remember going to Rowbottom's, the grocers in Bigby Street, where I would be taken out of my pram and perched somewhat precariously on a high stool while my mother gave her weekly order, which would then be delivered in the early evening by a grocer's boy on an ancient delivery cycle. This was a most sturdy machine with a small front wheel able to accommodate a huge metal basket, which could contain the weekly orders of about half a dozen families. The bacon was cut to order, the sugar was weighed out and then slithered into blue paper bags and the butter and lard was hacked from huge mounds on either marble or wooden platters. The tea was sold loose and the coffee was a strong brown liquid in a bottle whose label fascinated me. It showed a Scottish soldier resplendent in kilt, white spats, white sporran and red tunic with a bushby at his side, being served coffee by a suitably servile coloured servant in a turban. 'Camp' coffee contained a high proportion of chicory, but I didn't realise this and it was twenty years before I tasted real coffee. My night-time drink was Horlicks (which I disliked because it was supposed to do me good) and I was pleased when Mother switched to Bournvita, both sweeter and nicer. A particular treat at the grocer's was to crawl or totter to the display of biscuits rising from floor level to about four foot high in an array of twelve-inch tins in serried ranks, each rank with a glass cover. This would be lifted up and I would be presented with a usually slightly broken biscuit. Custard creams were my favourite.

Having placed the order, which was laboriously written out in longhand in the grocer's order book with a carbon copy underneath, Mother and I made our way to Lacey and Clark's, where she would occasionally order material or try on a new dress. On special occasions we might have tea and a cake in the café, and sometimes I was allowed to explore the carpet department, clambering or crawling over the new carpets with their powerfully exotic smell and their dense pile, which I delighted in stroking. Then it was down to Riverside.

My maternal grandparents, Charles and Betsy Peck, lived there with my 'Aunt' Elsie in what was a 'tied' house (now long demolished) on the banks of the River Ancholme between Spring's jam factory and the gasworks. It had few facilities: the water had to be obtained in a bucket from an outside tap and any hot water heated on the fire. I can't remember Gran Peck using a gas ring (though the house was lit by gas from the adjacent gasworks) but only the oven at the side of the coal fire. Grandad Peck looked after the horses belonging to Brigg Urban District Council and when they were made redundant with the arrival of refuse lorries, he swept the streets.

The front door of their house opened onto the path along the riverbank, but this door was hardly ever used. We always approached from the Market Place under the arch between EH Smith's and Curry's, down the road to the Cattle Market and then past part of Spring's factory to the Council yard and so arrived at the back door of my grandparents' rather gloomy house and that of the adjoining house, where lived the Watkins family. 'Prim' Watkins was the Council foreman and renowned for a fiery temper. Across the yard were sheds that housed the various Council carts and over in the corner backing onto the gasworks were the stables and a barn where straw was kept. In my early years the Council had some five or six horses, of which my favourite was 'Daisy', a large black shire horse with enormous white feathery feet, even though she pulled the 'dilly-cart', but more of that later.

If I needed to go to the loo while I was there, it meant going across the yard past the stables to an outhouse containing a communal toilet with two smoothly worn holes in an expanse of wood under which two large metal buckets collected the excreta. I was always instructed to use the seat on the left-hand side, because the other one was Prim's throne, although I can never remember having to use the facilities at the same time as anyone else. If you were lucky, rectangles of newspaper, skewered together in a pile, hung from string attached to a nail on the back of the toilet door. There was no light at all in that loo and only a dire emergency would draw my feet across the yard, especially on a dull winter's afternoon. It was most unnerving to sit in a somewhat smelly darkness and hear the loud snuffles and the erratic noise of dragging chains as the horses in their nearby stable ate their oats and mash. Each was partially attached to its feeding trough by a chain, one end of which was clipped to the bridle while from the other end hung a stone ball. This chain tethered the horse close to its trough while allowing it considerable freedom of movement, but whenever it moved its head there was an eerie, drawn-out clanking of chains.

I sometimes helped my grandfather to feed the horses, almost falling into the large metal feed hopper in my eagerness to collect oats on the wooden-handled scoop. I became used to walking among the horses in their individual stalls in the dark, dilapidated building which was rarely illuminated when I was there. A little later on it was a privilege to go with Grandad Peck and the horses when he took them in pairs along the riverbank to their field near the sewage works. Very occasionally I was allowed to ride on Daisy's back. When he brought them to the field, he would slip their bridles and these large shires would lumber off to the large, galvanised iron tank, which contained their water supply. Back in the Council yard, while the adults were making their farewells, I would go exploring among the four carrying carts, the malodorous dilly-cart and sometimes the tar-spraying vehicle in which the tar was heated and kept molten. In one corner of the yard was a large, raised container that was kept full of water. It was as big as the tank of a modern petroleum tanker and a long chain hung down, which you pulled to deliver copious water through a rubber chute. I seem to remember the fire brigade kept the tank filled: 'Prim' Watkins was a prominent member of the Brigg Fire Brigade.

✦✦✦

Grandad Rhodes lived with his daughter, Aunt Ethel, at no. 20 (now no. 49) Grammar School Road, the first in a terrace of some twenty houses, owned by a private landlord and rented out. My grandmother on my father's side had died some two years before I was born: she had been an Annie Wilson and came from the Caistor area like my grandfather. Like my other grandparents, he lived in one room, a sort of living room cum kitchen, and like theirs the 'front' room was used possibly once a year at Christmas time. I have stated he was born in Caistor (just after the time of the Crimean War), and for him Caistor was still the finest place on earth.

He even wrote published poetry about it in his eighties. He had been a skilled wheelwright in his time and retained a real carpentry expertise and a wide selection of ancient tools of his trade. He was over seventy when I was born and in retirement had been the caretaker of Brigg Reading Room near the bridge. My father played billiards or snooker there regularly before I was born, but my arrival seems to have seriously curtailed his visits, though later I occasionally accompanied him there when I was very young. I can vaguely recall the cues being chalked and the vast, lighted canopies that hung over the green-baized tables – and the smoke-laden atmosphere. My father had smoked quite heavily before I arrived, but sacrificed his habit to accommodate me: he couldn't afford both of us! Thus I was brought up in a smoke-free atmosphere and had little desire to become a smoker later on.

The one smoker in the family was Grandad Rhodes, who was always dragging on an old briar pipe, which he used to fill with St Bruno for preference. His white, walrus moustache was stained an orangey brown and he had an aroma unlike any of my other relatives. He had been a keen and expert fisherman and kept his rods in their bamboo containers alongside his landing net in the lean-to scullery. He was also addicted to westerns and I remember, when I was still comparatively young, going up Grammar School Road to Jack Clark's shop, opposite the eponymous Grammar School, to seek out the latest Zane Gray from the public-lending library (twopence per book per week), run as part of his general store by the ex-naval man I was to know well later. I was also entrusted with a further sum to purchase two ounces of thick Robin twist, I think – St Bruno was a rarer treat.

Grandad Rhodes had a long, narrow garden that my father tried to give some time to, but I remember it as being overgrown in parts. However, it did have some fine raspberry canes amongst the long grass and these offered mouth-watering berries in the summer. At the bottom of the garden there was a ramshackle brick building that was divided in two and served my grandfather and his next-door neighbour. Grandad Rhodes kept his tools here and did occasional carpentry jobs: he made me a fine sledge there when he was nearly eighty.

Two outhouses were attached to the back of his house. One was a wash-house with a brick-encased copper and a fire-grate beneath. I can't remember the fire ever being lit, but Grandad preferred to shave there rather than in the cramped quarters of the scullery, even though the scullery was part of the house and you had to cross a backyard to reach the wash-house. Next to the wash-house was the lavatory – again the facilities consisted of a large wooden board with a smooth hole over a capacious zinc bucket and again it was unlit. You took a candle if you had to go and yet again squares of newspaper did the business, whereas at our house we had Izal toilet rolls. These were impregnated with an antiseptic solution that rubbed off on your fingers and they were comparatively stiff and rough compared with the luxuriously soft tissues of today.

It was at Grandad Rhodes's house that I met Mrs Playfoot, whom I held in great awe for her supposed supernatural powers. She was a small, rather wizened, widowed lady with white hairs protruding from her chin. She was invariably clad in a flowered wrap-around apron and was of a similar age to my grandfather. Mrs Playfoot had a particular gift: she read teacups and thus foretold the future. If we had had high tea, prepared by Aunt Ethel, at no. 49, then the teacups with their dregs had to be carefully saved. Sometimes Mrs Playfoot, who lived further down the terraced row in Grammar School Road, came along to no. 49 if she hadn't already been a guest at tea and sometimes we would traipse down to her house. It was important that you drank as much of the tea as possible without getting the leaves in your mouth: otherwise you could wash out all the tea leaves from the cup. For with due ceremony you had to move your used cup three times in a circle and then hastily invert the cup over the saucer. After a moment or two Mrs Playfoot would recover the cup and gaze intently at the interior. To me as I anxiously looked first at the cup and then at Mrs Playfoot, the haphazard pattern of tea leaves as they adhered to the bottom and sides of the cup signified nothing. But Mrs Playfoot could detect all sorts of facts about the future from the shape of an individual leaf or of clusters of leaves and from their relative positions within the cup. She would pore over the cup and stare intently with long pauses and with the occasional apprehensive sucking noise through gaps in her stained teeth. I would hold my breath in fearful anticipation until she had read the runes and was ready to make her pronouncements: the postman would bring a parcel within three days; I would be confined to bed with an illness in the next six months; or I would sail on a ship on the sea soon. If it was summer and we were going as usual to Scarborough, then the latter was almost inevitably true, for a high spot of our annual holiday was a two-hour cruise up the Yorkshire coast on the dear old *Coronia* – as she very well knew. I can never remember if that mysterious and eagerly anticipated parcel ever arrived or if I was confined to bed, but when you contracted chicken pox or measles then that is where you always found yourself.

◆◆◆

Sweets were important to me as a young child – and their importance grew in proportion to their scarcity in 1940. At no. 24 Central Square lived the Stephensons, an elderly couple with one grown-up son. Mrs Stephenson offered a variety of home-made sweets, which she sold out of her front room. From a very early age I would clutch my penny or twopence firmly in my hand and go along the street to no. 24. Here there was a fabulous array of clear and twisted peppermints, stripy humbugs and coconut ice in virulent green and pink together with at least three different kinds of sticky toffee. They were arranged in glass jars or on shallow metal trays. Although the coconut ice was delicious, you didn't get many squares for your twopence and so that was a rare, special treat. Usually I chose the peppermints for their sweet distinctive taste and for their long-lasting qualities. If Mother came along with me, then she might buy toffee, usually with bits of Brazil nut in it, since that was Father's favourite – and I was sure to have some too. The other local source of sweets was Mrs East's shop, which was a medium sized wooden building (constructed by her husband) adjoining their house at the very end of Woodbine Avenue, next to the stream that played an important part in my childhood and across from Glebe Road School. Mrs East's shop was an Aladdin's cave adorned with large metal sheets advertising Reckitt's Blue and Colman's Mustard as well as Stephenson's Ink. She sold everything and was a useful source if Mother ran out of sugar or an extra loaf was needed in a hurry. (Our bread was usually delivered by van from Lyon's bakery near the junction of Glebe Road and Grammar School Road.) From Mrs East I purchased fizzy kay-li, sherbet dabs and liquorice in shapes varying from coiled circles covered in hundreds and thousands to shoelace lengths, from thick, hard, slabby bars that challenged your teeth to liquorice shaped like a pipe with red hundreds and thousands covering the bowl. On Saturdays I made a fortnightly visit to Mr Binns's shop with my father. This was in Wrawby Street and was a specialist sweet shop as well as being a tobacconist's. Here I remember row upon row of different delicacies in large glass jars and display cabinets with all manner of chocolate bars and beribboned chocolate boxes. There were fruit jellies and fruit pastilles, tins of golden Parkinson's humbugs, Cadbury's and Fry's chocolate bars, some cream-filled, Bluebird toffees, dolly mixtures, jelly babies and soft mushroom-shaped sweets covered with desiccated coconut. My favourites were, however, allsorts from Bassett's and an anonymous jar containing boiled sweets in various fish and fruit shapes that had a lingering pear-drop taste. Beech-Nut chewing gum was available in small paper packets containing five or six small pieces of gum covered in a hard white shell, but made no appeal to me at that time. Later I occasionally bought a packet so I could chew along with my teenage peers, but the results of my masticulatory efforts were unrewarding and I never indulged the habit. Nowadays it is one of my strongest aversions to see the pavements bespattered so foully and liberally with discarded gobbets of gum.

◆◆◆

During my childhood I had two spells in hospital – both in Lincoln, which was some 25 miles away. When I was three, I broke my leg and then complicated matters by contracting scarlet fever in hospital. My injury occurred as a result of an accident in what was in those days something of a rarity – a road accident. I can't remember much about it, but we were on our way back from Hull (still a foreign and despised place to true-born Briggites). Apparently one Wednesday early closing day, my parents had decided to take me to see Father Christmas at a Hull departmental store and we were returning along the narrow country roads between the New Holland ferry and Brigg. My father was driving an Austin Seven van used to make some of Lacey and Clark's deliveries. I was sitting in front on my mother's knee: seat-belts were, of course, then undreamed of. It was dark and there was some winter fog from the Humber, when rounding a corner my father was confronted by a large traction engine. Neither would have been going very fast, but a collision seemed inevitable until my father took evasive action and drove into the ditch by the side of the road. I was thrown off my mother's knee and through the windscreen. I ended up in a hedge with a broken leg and a cut face, on which faint scars are still visible some seventy years later. Presumably an ambulance at last arrived and I was taken to Lincoln hospital over thirty miles away. For sixteen weeks I was there, first in traction at the General Hospital and then later in isolation at wherever they segregated scarlet fever patients, for I had contracted that disease during my convalescence in hospital in Lincoln. The dangers of cross-infection are nothing new. Lincoln was also to me foreign territory, but not despised – rather admired as the county town for us 'Yeller-bellies'. However, it was difficult to get to, even with the aid of The Lincolnshire Road Car Company, and so my parents were reduced to Sunday afternoon visits and the occasional visit on early closing day by courtesy of Lacey and Clark's same Austin Seven: the van had escaped much more lightly than I had. Of course, when I was in the isolation hospital all my parents could do was to stare forlornly from a distance and from behind a glass window.

My second spell in hospital was considerably shorter and remarkable only for one vivid memory. At the age of seven or eight I had my tonsils out – a common and fashionable occurrence at the time. All I can remember was waking up in a hospital cot bed and lying on a rust-brown rubber sheet in a pool of blood that issued from my mouth. I can also recall rice puddings that Mother made regularly on my return home, puddings made even more palatable by the addition of a spoonful of raspberry jam or a knob of butter. This practice she continued at least once a week for years afterwards and we follow the custom from time to time today. The extraction of my tonsils enabled me to drink swiftly and copiously (which came in useful when 'sconced' at Wadham in the 1950s) and the scarlet fever left me with perforated eardrums.

Our doctor was Dr Frith when I was a child and he brought me into the world in my parents' bedroom at no. 29, because home confinements were then the norm. He had his surgery in Bridge Street, which was a long trek from Central Square. I had the usual childhood ailments of mumps, measles and chicken pox, all of which necessitated in those days an absence from school of between two and four weeks. I remember two things in particular – the itchiness of the spots and the luxury of having a fire in my bedroom at the height of my attack of mumps. My mother brought up live coals, taken from off the kitchen fire, on a shovel together with paper and sticks – a rather dangerous and smoky operation. To my continuing surprise I was circumcised when I was a baby: it must have been deemed either medically desirable for some reason or else fashionable, for my parents would not have wished me to be deprived. As far as I can ascertain there has been no Jewish influence in our family for over four hundred years. I was also vaccinated a little later and still bear the circular array of needle-points on my arm.

◆◆◆

My earliest playground was the garden where my father spent a considerable proportion of his spare time – until bowls occupied many of his leisure hours after the war. We had medium sized lawns back and front and at the back a trellis, surmounted on a rustic fence and covered in Paul Scarlet roses during the summer, separated my play area from the vegetable plot, measuring some twelve yards by fifty. Here my father grew potatoes and carrots (well suited to the sandy soil), peas and onions. He erected a substantial bean row and we fed on salted runner beans for much of the winter. He also grew cabbages and cauliflowers and one of my jobs at a relatively early age was to scrape caterpillars and their eggs off the leaves and souse them in a water-filled jam jar before swilling them down the drain. I can still see my fingers in green sanguinary slime and smell the distinctive odour of damp cabbage leaves. The white wings dappled with greys and blacks of the redoubtable Cabbage Whites were a very familiar sight in early summer and they seemed to be particularly addicted to our particular piece of garden.

The back lawn was where I learned to catch balls, at first gently lobbed by my parents but later caught on the rebound after being hurled forcefully against the wall of the house. I also played French cricket with Johnny Rands and other friends and here too I learned to turn head over heels, though I could never do handstands against the side of the house as others did with apparent ease. Ellen Thacker from next door could stand on her hands unaided and unsupported, with her dress tucked carefully into her navy blue knickers – and she was two years my junior. We also made a tent in summer out of Mother's clothes horse with an old sheet draped over and an old blanket on the floor. It was essential that the sheet was large enough to cover both the sides and to drape over the front and the back, because the interior had to be suitably gloomy – another blanket covered the sheet at the height of summer – and it had to be private. As I grew older the clothes horse proved too small to accommodate three or more people and we had to devise larger structures involving bigger sheets, wooden poles, an old fireguard and my brother's pram.

It was not until the late 1940s that we acquired a garden shed, but the Randses had one. We were forbidden to play in it, but their shed provided the setting for one intriguing Sunday morning episode. Rats had made their home under the shed, lured there by neighbours who dumped vegetable peelings and stale bread on their gardens. The rats became prolific and a menace so a friend of a neighbour who lived elsewhere in the small town (at least half a mile away and hence a stranger to me) was invited to bring his two dogs along, terriers and peerless ratters. Much to our disgust and disappointment John Rands and I were kept inside with our mothers and had only a very restricted view of the proceedings from the kitchen window of no. 31. There was much activity, considerable barking, conflicting advice from the various adults gathered around and I think at one point a ferret had to be fetched. After what seemed to be an interminably dull and uninteresting period there was a sudden maelstrom of feverish activity. Dogs growled and worried, men waved and hit out with sticks and then what appeared to be several carcasses were put in a sack and taken away. It was potentially the most exciting event for years, but we had been deliberately excluded and we were far from gruntled.

Mice were much more predictable and regular pests. I think over the years we had a mixture of house and field mice, for we were only 250 yards from the nearest farmer's fields. After the telltale signs of a mouse's presence had been noticed, a trap was prepared. This had a small wooden base surmounted by shaped wire and a powerful spring. The cheese was baited on two metal prongs from which a hoop extended. You then forced the neck-breaking wire back against the stiff spring until it was held in place by the wire that extended from its anchor point at the back of the wooden base and was inserted into the hoop. You had to ensure that the slightest tug at the cheese would release the spring and bring the metal bar down forcefully on the offending mouse's neck. It was a work of art to balance the trap finely and there was a danger that your fingers would be caught in the trap going off unexpectedly as you placed it strategically in the pantry. If your fingers were caught, they would throb painfully for at least half an hour and sucking did little to alleviate the pain.

It was safe to play in the streets in those days, for cars and lorries were infrequent and horse and carts only marginally more frequent along the tree-lined street that ran between Central Square and Woodbine Avenue. Mr Williamson came round with his large barrow selling fruit and vegetables and Mr Pieroni pushed his ice-cream cart around the Square on summer evenings. Some years later the Sergeants' horse-drawn wagon came from Hibaldstow: their ice-cream made from a still secret recipe was delicious and to have one of their ices as a once-a-week treat in the immediate post-war years relieved the drabness of that utility marked period. (From 1945 to 1947 you would never have imagined that we had actually won the war.) Sergeants' hand bell had a distinctive note and made my mouth water in anticipation, just as it did for my own elder children in the early sixties when the horse had been superseded by a van and the hand bell by an electric carillon.

As children, my contemporaries and I played all manner of games in their due season. Hoops came out in early March and we trundled them along and learned how to put back-spin on them so that they came racing back. Most hoops were wooden and so was mine at first, but then my father had a blacksmith friend in one of the local villages make a large iron hoop for me together with a metal device for keeping its momentum going. This instrument was hooked at one end with a ring for grasping firmly at the other. You were supposed to slot the hook round the moving rim low down and by pulling upwards help accelerate its forward propulsion considerably. However, I never did master this device and instead contented myself with keeping my beloved hoop trundling along simply by manual contact like all my friends.

Some time about Easter (on a day that seemed to be subliminally agreed), whips and tops came out. There were traditional turnip-shaped tops of coloured wood with a metal stud at the base, but once we had mastered these we graduated to 'cracker-jacks', slim toadstool-shaped tops. These not only revolved more swiftly but could also be made to leap up to twenty yards if we made the correct contact with our whips. You could buy whips with a coloured wooden stock and a leather thong threaded through a small hole in the top and knotted in place. However, sticks or old pieces of dowelling with thick string or thin rope wrapped round the top were just as good – and didn't cost sparse pocket money. To satisfy our incipient aesthetic tastes we used to draw patterns in coloured chalks on the upper surface of the tops and rejoiced in the whirligig of their multi-hued gyrations. We would spend hours in early spring whipping our tops and having races with them along the street.

In a slack period with no time-honoured particular game to play, we could fall back on hide-and-seek, counting rapidly up to a hundred in fives and then yelling *'Coming!'* The first one to be tagged on their precipitous way back to 'block' (usually the base of a lamppost or the telegraph pole) was the next 'seeker'. But as we grew older we played football and cricket – the same old tennis ball was used for both. At football, jerseys were discarded and placed in the road to act as goalposts – to be hastily recovered if a lorry or a horse came along. The latter seemed to take especial pleasure in defecating along our street and their deposits were hastily seized upon by Miss Stringer for her roses. My father would often tell me that our roses needed the same horse dung sustenance, but I never dared outface Miss Stringer. In cricket the telegraph pole near our front gate served as an admirable set of stumps, even though the square-leg boundary was a mere two paces from the wicket. We carefully chalked three stumps and bails on the pole and many were the fierce arguments about whether you were 'in' or 'out', especially if the ball seemed to strike the pole high up or at its extreme edges. The altercations were sometimes so furious that we came to blows. The bowling crease was at the nearest lime tree, some twelve yards away. It was six and out if you hit the ball into a neighbour's garden and it meant that our cover drives were our strongest strokes.

We also played competitively with cigarette cards at school, in the street and against the house wall. I was at a disadvantage, as my father had given up smoking when I arrived – he couldn't afford us both, as I have said. John Rands's father smoked 'Kensitas', which came in large packets and had distinctive cards featuring a bald-headed boy called Henry. However, these cards were square and no good for 'playing ciggies'. Nevertheless we both managed to acquire sufficient cards to play through bartering and swapping, which were the same methods we used to make up sets of cigarette cards, which we collected avidly. There were various forms of competition in playing ciggies for between two and six players. 'Far-ee' could be played by any number, because you had to see how far you could propel your card by holding it between thumb and forefinger and flicking the wrist. The one whose card flew furthest collected all the other cards. We played this on our way to school. Another game was to place a stone or a small coin down in the road and from a largish circle flick your cards to try to cover the object. If you succeeded, you collected all the other cards. My favourite 'ciggy' game involved propping a card up against the side of the house or the school wall and from a distance of some eight or nine yards flicking the cards in an effort to knock the upright card down. Again the successful player collected all the cards that had been flicked in vain.

In early autumn we played conkers. We used to collect horse chestnuts and then, having pierced a hole through them with a metal auger or a heated steel knitting needle, would keep them on a long string. My father used to bring me conkers from Louth, but locally the best came from the avenue of chestnut trees leading to the detached villa on the way to Wrawby. The landowner hated any trespassers and it was a brave lad who ventured past the lodge at the gate to snatch a handful or two. Sometimes we had more than a hundred on strings, because rivalry extended to numbers of conkers as well as the one that had 'conkered' most challengers. We prepared our conkers carefully before competition by heating them in the family oven and / or immersing them in vinegar for a few days. We even kept some from last year in a bedroom drawer, hoping that age might toughen the conker, even if it did look wizened and shrivelled. Rules about not cooking conkers or using preservatives were largely ignored. You strung your conker on a piece of string some two and a half feet long. You and your opponent then took it in turns to strike each other's conker. If you deliberately flinched and moved your conker, then your opponent had three extra goes. Again there were furious arguments about what constituted such movement: *'You moved it!' – 'I didn't.' – 'You did!' – 'Didn't!' – 'Did, so there!'* And another bout of fist-waving and wrestling would ensue. You were entitled to examine your opponent's conker in mid-contest for signs of fracture, but if you tried to widen a crack with your thumbnail, further blows were inevitable. Different people had different techniques. You could vary the length of the string by wrapping it round your knuckles and this could be crucial. A full-length strike from a long swing would deliver more force, but a shortened length was more accurate, especially when you had gauged the distance by nearly touching your opponent's conker. The slightest contact would mean that you had to forfeit your turn. The street was littered with cracked, broken and discarded conkers during late September and early October: the game mysteriously disappeared for another year by the October half-term.

In December we always hoped for snow and ice and in most winters we were rarely disappointed. Global warming was not an issue in the thirties and forties. We would fashion slides, sometimes as much as thirty yards long, in the school playground or on the street – and no safety-conscious caretaker came to spoil them with sand or salt. As we wore shoes and boots that had been liberally studded to give longer wear, we made loud clashing sounds as we sped down the slides and we struck sparks as we first launched ourselves on our way. In the school playground we queued up and often the queue would exceed a hundred people. Falls were frequent, but I can't remember anyone breaking a limb. Most of us had sledges, but Lincolnshire is far from ideal for tobogganing. It was hard to find a suitable incline: the nearest was at Wrawby sandpits and that was too long a hike to be really useful. So we took it in turns to pull each other around the Square or down Glebe Road. It was particularly exhilarating to be dragged at speed onto a slide and then cast adrift with a final tug to spin the sledge so that you went whirling round and round in an uncontrollable skid. However, the biggest thrill came when my father would allow me to fasten my sledge to the back of the Lindsey Blind van and he would drive off down to the garage in Grammar School Road with me and a favoured friend precariously clutching each other on the sledge that had no sides. He never drove above fifteen miles per hour, but we seemed to be travelling at supersonic speeds on a Cresta run.

The streets around Central Square, like the houses, were lit by gas in the mid-thirties: electricity was for us definitely post-war. An employee of the gas company would cycle around at both dusk and dawn to light or extinguish the gas mantles in the glass beacons. Often he would have a ladder over his shoulder to replace broken mantles, for naughty boys would sometimes throw stones at the gas lights to break the glass and the delicate filaments within.

We also had nightly visits along the street from the dilly-cart (ironically named from the nursery rhyme, *Lavender's blue, dilly-dally*), which collected what was quaintly referred to as 'night soil'. Apparently none of the residents in Woodbine Avenue needed to evacuate their bowels during the hours of daylight! We residents of Central Square with our internal, flushing toilets considered ourselves superior to the unfortunates in Woodbine Avenue and East Parade who, until about the time of the Silver Jubilee of George V, had to have their waste products collected daily by the night-soil men in their stained clothes and rubber aprons. Nevertheless we were fascinated by the horse-drawn dilly-cart and regularly followed the slow progress of the cart down the street at a safe distance with our fingers pinching our noses. Well, it was a distraction on an otherwise boring evening: you could get tired of hide-and-seek.

Sometimes we were rewarded with another curious spectacle. The shire horse that pulled the dilly-cart would suddenly become immobile and its sinews would stiffen. The front legs would be forward and the rear legs stretched back. Then from beneath the belly of the horse would descend and unfurl a thick proboscis, seemingly two foot long and the size of a fire-hose nozzle that connected to a hydrant. Suddenly there would issue forth an explosive jet of hot, amber urine that rebounded from the tarmac surface in splattering showers before surging down the gutter to the nearest drain in a steaming, spume-bubbling, ammonia-smelling mass. We were awestruck by this amazing phenomenon and deeply impressed by the size of the horse's member. Later I was to witness similar occasions whilst potato-picking.

Once or twice I can remember the Council workers coming to Central Square to resurface the road. This took much longer than it would nowadays, because the technology was primitive. A horse would drag the heavily encrusted tar-spraying vehicle up to our end of the town from the Council yard at Riverside. Lorries would deliver large piles of gravel chippings, which were dumped on the grass verge between the lime trees. 'Prim' Watkins would arrive with an enlarged gang of workers, complete with barrows and tar-smothered, leather aprons. The tar-spraying machine was a cylinder on wheels with a chimney at one end. The bottom quarter of the cylinder was a coal-fired furnace, which heated the bitumen lumps into a bubbling, molten mass. After the old surface of the road had been scratched and gouged by hand-tools to afford better adhesion, the head tar-sprayer in large leather gauntlets, leather apron, sou'wester-like headgear and wearing large, darkened goggles would release a tap. Out would come black, bubbling liquid tar, fountaining up from a nozzle, resembling a large garden spray. The sprayer would direct the tar onto a section of the road and his colleagues from barrows filled with gravel chips would scatter these on the tar in shovelsful. By this time the behemoth we had all been longing for had arrived. We had heard it long before we saw it, as its approach was heralded by a loud and clonking sound that could be heard in the Square as it trundled along Wrawby Road, seriously delaying what traffic there was on the main Grimsby road. The steamroller was an impressive sight. The forward roller was some five feet in diameter and the steam-boiler amidships was about the same size. The two rear wheels were even larger, measuring about six foot six inches – bigger than my father. The driver stood high up in his cab, surrounded with all kinds of pipes, pistons and levers. He would roll forward and back, forward and back over the newly laid chippings and a few square yards at a time a new surface would be steamrollered in place. It seemed to take several days to do just our side of the Square, but for weeks afterwards loose chippings were a hazard to motorists and pedestrians alike. However, they were an even bigger danger to us cyclists. If we came off our cycles (as happened all too frequently) onto this new surface, grazed knees became a much more serious and painful problem. The torn knee would be probed for minute particles of granite and, after cleansing with soap and water, copious stinging iodine would be applied.

And so my tenth birthday found me at ease in a small North Lincolnshire market town. I had slowly resigned myself to having a sibling rival in the family and even pushed him out in his pram on rare occasions. David must have been a well-ordered and contented baby, for I cannot recall any nights when my slumbers were shattered by his cries, even when he was teething. We never had to share a bedroom. He moved into the front third bedroom from our parents' room once our evacuee, the egregious Brian J, had returned to Hull and I retained the larger one at the back. The war had been in progress for a year, but we were still in the phoney war stage and it had made relatively little impression on me then. Sweets were rationed, yet I was fed, watered and generally contented. I was adequately clothed, warm and, I have to admit, coddled. I could cope at school and I had Cubs and choir to cater for my outside interests. It was a humdrum, ordinary existence, but nonetheless agreeable for all that.

Mrs East's shop, Woodbine Avenue, Brigg

2
THE SQUARE

I think the Square deserves a chapter to itself, because for a number of years it circumscribed my life. It was part of a new development in council house building after the First World War – homes fit for heroes. Brigg's main building firm was RM Phillips and this contract established them: the complex comprised Woodbine Avenue, East Parade, Central Square and West Square, though the latter consisted of only three pairs of semi-detacheds in a straight line. At least we in Central Square had four sides.

No. 29 was a small semi-detached and I was born in the main bedroom: home births were the norm. It was virtually unheard of for a mother to go to a maternity hospital in those days; anyway, the nearest one was at Scunthorpe and that was some nine miles away – definitely foreign country. Dr Frith attended my mother and for some ten days after the birth we had a maiden lady, who came in 'to oblige'. This was probably Miss Markham who lived not far away in East Parade and who would return home once my father had come in from work – at least that was the procedure when my brother was born eight years later.

Not until I was in my mid-twenties did I learn that I came into the world as a result of fratricide. I was a twin, but my brother (I think) was stillborn because I had more than my fair share of what was on offer within the womb. My mother only vouchsafed this revelation to my wife Sheila when she was expecting our first child in the course of a woman-to-woman gossip over the washing-up. When Sheila reprimanded me for not telling her I had been a twin, I was dumbfounded as it was certainly news to me. My parents, like many in the 1930s, were very reticent about matters involving sex and birth and I was completely uninterested until my mid-teens. I am still not sure whether my brother went full term or whether he terminated naturally midway, but I do remember feeling a dark shadow over me and for weeks I sensed the mark of Cain.

No. 29 Central Square was in the form of a stunted, reversed L-shape that adjoined no. 28 as a mirror image at the 'room'. This was not a sitting room, nor a dining room, nor a lounge: it was the sole living room, measuring some fourteen square feet with two small-paned windows front and back in a roughly N–S line. There was a fireplace and an in-built cupboard on one side of it and at the other a small recess into which the room door opened. The front door to the house opened directly into a small hallway. Immediately on the left was the door to the room and immediately behind the opened front door was a door to the cupboard under the stairs. The stairs were between this cupboard and the bathroom. Well it had a large cast-iron bath and a flushable toilet, but not until after the Second World War did we have a washbasin and not until this time did we have hot running water on tap. Still we felt superior, for many of the other houses had outside loos. At the end of the five-pace hall there was a rack with hooks for coats. Opposite the bathroom door was the door to the kitchen. This was small and had a rear window and an open coal fire, which fed an adjoining oven. Beneath the rear window was a stone sink with a cold-water tap and in the recess between the oven and the back wall was a draining board and a shelf on which sat a gas ring. There was a space under the shelf to store some pots and pans and cleaning materials. The back door was halfway along the wall opposite the fireplace and two small areas were bricked off on either side of the back door: one was a walk-in pantry and the other was the coal-house. One step into the pantry and you came up against a stone slab at breast height and to the right there was a series of short shelves for storage. A small cabinet with a perforated zinc mesh to keep out flies stood under the slab and in this Mother kept meat and bread. Milk stood on the stone slab. The coal-house wall was demolished in the mid-forties to provide more living space in the kitchen and the coal was transferred to a galvanised tin coal bunker at the rear of the house until about 1950, when the Council did some renovations and installed a minimum central heating system fed off a gas fire and serving the ground floor only. It was not until the late forties that we had hot water on tap and for years my father had to boil a kettle for his morning shave.

Up the stairs, which curved back on themselves, there was a small landing about six foot square, from which the doors to three bedrooms led as well as the door to the airing cupboard on the top of the stairs. My parents' room was the largest and was both over and the same size as the living room. It had windows front and back. My bedroom was over the kitchen and the third bedroom was over the bathroom. Each bedroom had a fireplace, but you had to be seriously ill in bed for a fire to be lit therein. I can remember having a fire in my bedroom at the height of my attack of mumps and chicken pox, which in those days necessitated between two and four weeks off school – two weeks for a mild attack of measles and four weeks for a nasty bout of mumps. It was a perilous procedure having a fire in your bedroom. Live coals were heaped on a fire shovel from the fire in the kitchen and then my mother would negotiate her way up the stairs with one hand holding the burning shovel and the other the firewood and paper. All the while there would be acrid smoke billowing from the shovel. The fire was always allowed to die out before it was time for me to go to sleep.

The garden was quite large by comparison with the house. There was a front lawn about twenty feet by thirty feet in which was a circular flowerbed, later made rectangular on a whim of my father. In front of the front door there was a small flower area, which extended to the front door of no. 28. The shared front path led up from a small front gate towards the two houses and then separated to go to both the front and back doors of each of the houses. The gate, about a metre wide, was set in thick privet hedges, which extended along most of our side of the Square. A footpath ran along the front hedges and was separated from the road by a four-foot grass verge into which trees were interspersed and outside our gate was a telegraph pole. This was a social totem, because for ten years from 1938 we had the only private telephone in the Square, installed by the County Council when my father began to work for the Lindsey Blind Society. There was a public box around the corner, but it was often not working.

The back garden was some eighty feet in length and tapered slightly. Concrete posts with wires ran up the sides of each back garden in the Square, but there seemed to be a no-man's land in the very middle. Our rear garden backed onto the garden of a house on the opposite side of the Square but the limits were not clearly defined. However, I can't remember any significant territorial disputes. Our garden was carefully tended and provided us, my grandparents and some neighbours with substantial supplies of fresh vegetables throughout the thirties and the war.

Central Square consisted of thirty-two houses, some semi-detached and some in blocks of four, all looking outwards, rather like a square of British redcoats making a last stand before assailing Zulus. Some of the houses like ours were rough-coated and snowcemmed, others were all red brick. Woodbine Avenue faced the Square along its southern side and half its western side. East Parade extended from Wrawby Road along the eastern and northern sides and further along past the back gardens of the six houses of West Square. The houses in East Parade and Woodbine Avenue differed slightly in design from those in Central Square, but they were all three-bedroom council houses put up in the twenties. My mother and father moved into no. 29 Central Square as newlyweds in 1925/26 and lived there until their deaths in 1975 and 1969 respectively.

People moved relatively rarely up to the 1950s and for the first twenty years I lived at no. 29 I doubt if more than 15% of the tenants of all these council houses changed. I can remember something about almost every family who lived in the thirty-two houses of the Square and something about most of the residents in East Parade and Woodbine Avenue, for they were an integral part of my life. Each section of the Brigg council estates had an in-built conviction regarding their status in the town, partly based on the age and design of the houses and partly upon the perceived quality of the tenants. Of course, Central Square was the pick of the bunch. East Parade was slightly better than Woodbine Avenue, which was on a par with Mill Lane on the other side of the town across the river, and all were superior to Hawthorn Avenue, which contained probably a hundred houses northwest of Central Square beyond East Parade. Those who lived in Hawthorn Avenue considered themselves superior to those who had the misfortune to live in Newlands. It is difficult to imagine now how petty were the snobberies of the council estates in the 1930s. Of course, tenants of private landlords considered themselves superior to us – and as for those who owned their own homes, they were in the social stratosphere.

The residents of Central Square were particularly well known. At no. 1 lived Miss Stringer, a maiden lady who was a schoolteacher and also took in fee-paying piano pupils, mostly girls. Elsie Stringer was of ample proportions and was a formidable school-ma'am of whom I stood in awe when I was a seven-year-old in her class at Glebe Road. She had Eton-cropped hair and whiskers sprouting from her chin. Next door were the Winterbottoms (whose surname fascinated my imagination). They had an attractive daughter some years older than me. Then the Easts: he played in Brigg Town Prize Band and there were two girls, Christine and Valerie, a bit younger than me, who went to the Convent for their education. After a gap came the Dentons' house, which started a block of four. Mr Denton was a town councillor and worked for a firm of auctioneers. Tall and rangy, Bill Denton was our local ARP warden during the war. He was a member of the bowls club like my father and I think he may have been a football referee in local leagues. It was he who acquired for me my first grown-up two-wheeler through his work at the auctioneers when during the war cycles were difficult to come by. It had a large frame and twenty-eight-inch wheels and was a three-speed, much too big for me and completely unsuitable. But it was a big-boy's bike – a very big boy! – and there wasn't a choice, so I prevailed upon my father to buy it. I wobbled around on it erratically for a couple of years. The Dentons had a daughter, Muriel, a little older than myself, and an even older son, who for years played football for Brigg Town.

The next two houses I am not sure about – I think one was called Petch – but they were childless couples with whom I did not come in contact. These were the two inside houses of four, but in the final house on the eastern side of the Square lived the Cairns, one branch of a Scottish family that had at least three offshoots in Brigg.

Beginning the northern side were the Thorpes, who had one or two Convent-educated daughters. Then came the Sennett family, where there were two sons, Geoff and John. The latter was a year older than me but we sometimes played together and remained in touch all the way through

Grammar School. Mr Sennett worked for Messrs EH Smith and Sons, the ironmongers in the Market Place – a cheerful figure in his brown smock. Next came the Whitties, who had two vivacious daughters, Stella and Monica, and probably an elder brother; and then came the Parkers, who had two boys, both younger than me, and an even younger daughter, who I seem to remember had the rather aristocratic name of Eleanor. The Parkers' garden adjoined ours at the back and occasionally the boys would throw stones in my direction when I was doing some chore in the garden like collecting caterpillars from the cabbage leaves. I was older and didn't deign to retaliate; anyway, they never could throw far enough. Mr Parker worked for a men's outfitter in the town and usually held his nose at an alarmingly acute angle.

After this block of four there was another gap and then a second block of four, which comprised the northern side. First came the Lofthouses. Mr Lofthouse had contracted a terminal illness, which was unnamed at that time but is now the big C, and was a sick man. I remember a wan, invalid figure on a couch in the living kitchen, far different from the efficient manager he had once been. He died during the war years, leaving a widow and three girls and a boy. Margaret and Anne were older than me, Olga was about the same age and Peter was two years junior to me at school. They were all quite brainy and a close-knit family with little cash to spare. (Remarkably, these last two houses are occupied today by the children I knew seventy years ago and thus provide a link between the thirties and this brave new century. What changes they must have seen!)

Then came the Fowlers, a childless couple. Mr Fowler worked for the Council as a handyman and with his mate did repair jobs around the council estates. His mate was an eccentric called 'Wild Harry' Neale and both he and Mr Fowler were also part-time firemen, which was an ample reason for never seeming to finish jobs they were on. 'Wild Harry' had a reputation as a somewhat slapdash workman, but he was in his element haring off to fight the fortunately infrequent fires in his burnished helmet and smart blue uniform. He was also reported to engage in semi-professional wrestling matches at Scunthorpe at weekends, but I could never verify this. The Smiths lived next door with their two boys, Derek and Colin. Derek was in the same class as me for most of our schooldays and he later became a librarian. We used to swop comics in the early forties – my *Adventure* for his *Wizard*. Finally in the block came the Whitehands, who had relatives to stay during the war from some city likely to be blitzed. One of these 'foreigners' was Cecil Taylor, who was older than me and was the Ancholme House Captain at Brigg Grammar School. He was looked up to, because he was very good at sports for both the School and the House as well as being very intelligent: he won an Open Scholarship and went on to study at Imperial College,

London. 'Cec' had two younger brothers, so their house must have been the most crowded in the Square.

In the northwest corner of the Square were the Sabertons, whose two sons went on to play their cornets in Brigg Town Prize Band. Next lived the Shorts, but I can't remember much about them. Then came the Hughes family with two daughters, the elder of whom, Margaret, was in the same class at Glebe Road and with whom I cavorted round the maypole one year. I think Mr Hughes served in the navy during the war. Their house was linked to the Robinsons, just as we were linked to the Sedgwicks. There was an older daughter, Peggy. Mr Robinson worked at the gasworks or possibly at the boiler house for Spring's jam factory. I can remember a figure in greasy, grubby overalls with oil-stained hands and face, striding purposefully from his house to Riverside. I think he was the engineer charged with keeping our gas supply going, for it was not until after the war that electricity came to Central Square. Our homes, like our streets, were lit by gas and a supply of gas mantles had to be kept readily available. Neighbours frequently came asking if we had a spare mantle. If I were sent to purchase one or more, probably from Mrs East's corner shop, I had to be careful not to drop or knock the mantle with its flimsy filament.

Then came the Rimmingtons, who were distantly related on my mother's side of the family through the wife, Fanny. Her husband, Harry, was a large man with an unpredictable temper, who was a local referee up to Midland League status. Michael Rimmington, their son, was a couple of years younger than me with a tendency to throw stones and be a 'cheeky monkey'; there were also two girls, Kathleen and Ann. The Morrisons next door had nautical connections. Mr Morrison had spent many years at sea and I think his son served in the merchant navy during the war. There were also twin girls about my age who went to the Convent, because the Morrisons were one of the two Catholic families in the Square.

At the start of our southern side came the elderly couple, the Stephensons. He was retired, having been – I vaguely recall – a gravedigger. His wife used to make home-made sweets before the war: it was a decided treat to go with a penny or twopence for some of Mrs Stephenson's humbugs or peppermints. I didn't buy coconut ice very often, because it didn't last a tenth of the time that the peppermints did, but this was delicious and really my favourite. Sometimes I was invited to collect remnants off the coconut ice plate with a dampened finger – ah, what bliss! She had some old-fashioned brass scales and polished 2oz weights: if she were in a benevolent mood the pointer would swing well past the 2oz mark. The Stephensons had a son, Lewis, much older than me and he was one of the few active servicemen from the Square during the war: he was an LAC in the RAF. Next door were the MacKails, who had grown-up children. Both girls were in London during the war and worked as receptionists in hotels. Towards the end of the war, or just after, the owner of one of these hotels came to stay for a week with the MacKails in consecutive years. He was a small, well-dressed man with spats and a dapper Homburg hat and of Italian descent. His name was Mr Tonga and was the first London gentleman I ever met, so exotic he could as well have come from Mars.

I grew to know him quite well, because on his visits he regularly called to use our telephone in order to keep in touch with events at his hotel. Nobody else made calls to London. He was undoubtedly an eccentric. He had a pronounced accent and was a health fetishist, believing we could all vastly improve our circulation and general health by exercising in a cold bath. At some time he was pictured extensively in a centre spread of the *Daily Mirror* performing these exercises, clad in a minute pair of swimming trunks – most men when necessary wore woollen one-piece bathing costumes then – and looking gravely determined. I was conscious only of a potbelly protruding from the water when the MacKails proudly showed us the article in the paper. There was also a boy, Billy, who trained as a pilot in Rhodesia, although I don't think he saw any active service, but I avidly scrounged the Rhodesian stamps from his letters home.

Then came the Meltons, the other Catholic family, who gave themselves airs, or at least the wife did. Mrs Melton was a semi-invalid, who walked with the aid of a crutch and sprouted pronounced facial hair. Her husband was a printer and cycled four times daily to and from the press in the centre of Brigg. He helped publish the weekly *Brigg Star* at Caldicotts. There were two children: Kathleen, the elder and a very attractive girl, and Anthony, who was the apple of his mother's eye. Neither child was ever allowed to play in the street like the rest of us, although they were somewhat older than us. They were brought up to be refined young persons.

The Meltons' house was connected physically to the Piggots, a much more harum-scarum family and who must have caused Mrs Melton many a shudder. Mr Piggot worked in the steelworks at Scunthorpe on shifts, so often Mrs Piggot would raucously order us to make less noise when we were playing in the street. There were two girls, probably twins, Barbara and Anne, who used to go out with servicemen, sometimes Americans. They wore the first nylons that I ever saw on their shapely legs. Their brother Alan was a year older than me and we went to each other's birthday parties in the period pre-war. He left school at fourteen and soon stories abounded about how he was earning a fortune in London. Much of it was hearsay and after the war on his infrequent visits home there were tall stories but little evidence of great wealth. I think he was probably a spiv or a conman in the early fifties and may even have served time. He also served for a very short period in the Grenadier Guards and he appeared in Central Square in smart uniform, standing tall and with his peaked cap touching his nose and obscuring his vision. He left the Guards in rather dubious circumstances, but he was a colourful contemporary even if black-sheepish.

At no. 28 the first family that I can remember were the Thackers, who had a pretty, fair-haired daughter called Ellen. Her blue eyes were the first to tug my heartstrings at the age of six. She would have been a year younger than me and a family photograph shows she was allowed to share a tent that John Rands and I had constructed in our back garden out of my mother's clothes horse and an old blanket. Then about the outbreak of war they left to go to Scunthorpe and the Sedgwicks arrived from the northeast, obviously newcomers with strange-sounding accents. Arthur came from Sunderland and Nan from Newcastle. At first Arthur was in a reserved occupation as a gas-fitter and engineer, but he was later called up and served in Burma.

He told me stirring stories of Sunderland FC, to whom he was addicted, and I often used to go into the town on a Saturday night to purchase a *Green 'Un* for him, so he could savour an account of the latest match of his beloved team. He was also a useful opening bat, playing for the sugar factory after the war in local leagues. He was noted for strong left-wing views and in 1946/47, after he'd been demobbed, he was regularly visited by the 'Red Doctor', a Dr McCready, who was a red-haired Scot and a convinced Communist. McCready did his utmost to gain 'Sedgy' as an adherent to the cause, but in the end he went away empty-handed. The Sedgwicks were childless until they adopted Michael, who was some years younger than my brother, David. It is worthwhile noting that in the 1950s all three of us went up to Oxford University from this semi-detached pair of council houses via Brigg Grammar School: that must be some kind of a record.

Next door to us on the other side were first the Oldhams, a childless couple who moved to Scunthorpe early in the war because Mr Oldham worked in the steelworks. (Or did he die early and she move away? I can remember little about them.) Then came the Daubneys with their son, Ted, a few years older than my brother David. Tom Daubney worked at the sugar factory and spent much time at the Britannia or the Queen's Head, though I never recall him fighting drunk. He was a stalwart of Brigg Town FC as trainer with the magic sponge. He was in awe of his wife, who was always encased in a wrap-around pinafore and retained an outmoded twenties hairstyle, straight and cut short. Then came the Rands, who were my parents' especial friends. I called them Auntie Lil and Uncle Alf and their son, John, born three weeks before me, was my best boyhood friend. We were in the same class at infant school and at Glebe Road until Johnny went on to the prep department of Brigg Grammar School, where his father had been educated. By the time I went to the Grammar School I found myself a year ahead of him, although he was three weeks my senior. Uncle Alf was the office manager at WA Sass's, the garage by the Monument. He played in Brigg Town Prize Band, like his father, and he was a gifted amateur photographer who developed his own films.

He and my father were both keen members of Brigg Bowling Club and often Dad was treasurer and Uncle Alf secretary, until he had a fatal heart attack one night at band practice. They lived at no. 31. The final house in the Square was attached to Miss Stringer's no. 1 and was set at an angle, facing up to Wrawby Road. No. 32 had more successive occupants in my time than any other in the Square. For a year or two the Plowrights lived there, though I have no distinct memory of them. Mr Plowright became editor of the *Scunthorpe Evening Telegraph* and they moved there. Their daughter, Joan, became Lady Olivier and a celebrated actress in her own right; their son became an executive TV producer. I came in contact with Joan Plowright years later when we were both temporary and unqualified teachers at Ashby County Primary School.

I have clearer memories of the next family living there, the Cottons, because their daughter Margaret was an early object of my affections in her crisp green gingham dress. She went to Miss Lyne's private school, where the children of upwardly mobile parents were sent to avoid contact with the rough children at the County Infant School and Glebe Road. That family moved on and were followed by the Hooks, who returned to Grimsby after the war. They had no children and Mr Hook was in insurance. They were followed within my timescale by the recently married Broomes.

◆◆◆

It is curious how these names, families and individuals remain fixed in the memory after nearly seventy years. I certainly could not enumerate my current neighbours with anything like the same knowledge or accuracy. Back in the thirties people seemed more neighbourly and certainly had more time for each other. They used to talk outside their back doors or across the double-strand wire fence that separated the pairs of houses. They left doors and windows open and unlocked regularly, but I cannot recall a single burglary nor sneak thief prowling. News spread quickly: slightly malicious gossip was gleefully retailed. Bad news brought genuine commiseration and shared grieving, just as good news was greeted with enthusiasm, unless it involved financial gain when the applause was tinged with envy, but in Central Square no-one was likely to come into a fortune. A win on the Brigg-owned Grand National winner, Sheila's Cottage, brought several windfalls, however. Now we shelter behind hedges of Leylandii in our detached homes, made as impregnable against thieves and callers as we can.

Central Square, Brigg, c. 1925 (the Rhodes family home is third from the right)

Market Place, Brigg

3
FURTHER AFIELD

Not only was it safe to play in the street, but we could also wander further without any adult supervision or accompaniment. We would walk towards Wrawby along the footpath by the side of the A18, the main road to Grimsby. Crossing at the fork to Barton, we would walk into the village and veer off to the old sandpits, which from time to time became our playground. Or we could turn down Brickyard Lane at Barton Road End. My earliest memory of exploring further afield was when three or four of us went down Brickyard Lane and entered one of Farmer Hill's fields of growing corn not long before harvest time, so it must have been one day in the summer holidays. I can't have been older than six and we pushed our way into the cornfield, pretending it was the jungle and we were pursuing lions.

Somehow I became separated from the others and I found myself surrounded by cornstalks considerably taller than myself, alone in a strange greeny-amber light, completely disorientated. I panicked and began blundering about trying to locate the edge of the field. I don't suppose I was more than fifteen yards within the field, but I could have been in the middle of an Amazonian forest. I remember thistles and poppies amid the dense cornstalks, as I thrashed about looking for a way out. I yelled and yelled until I at last heard an answering shout. I stumbled my way through the seemingly impenetrable stalks and finally pushed through to the edge of the field, some twenty yards from where my friends were calling and looking anxiously around. I was mightily relieved to find myself back in the open: my heart was still racing madly and I furtively dashed what might have been tears from my eyes. We went home quite subdued, but I never told my parents about my nasty experience and moments of blind panic in the cornfield.

The tenant of the land that stretched from the back gardens of East Parade to the fields bordering Brickyard Lane was Farmer Hill. Much of this land has been the new Brigg Recreation Ground for more than fifty years, but in my childhood it was part of a mixed arable farm. This meant there were a few pastures for a small herd of cows, but most was given over to cereals and vegetables. There were also about three horses to pull the various carts. The farmhouse itself and the outbuildings of barns, sheds, cow byre and stables were not far from East Parade. In my late teenage years I was to play tennis on Brigg Urban District Council's new grass courts created in front of the old farmhouse, but in the thirties it was a meadow stretching to Wrawby Road and facing the cemetery. This meadow was a fine place to play, but it was also dangerous: Farmer Hill had an almost pathological dislike of small boys from the adjacent council estate playing on his land. Stories abounded among my contemporaries about being chased off by Farmer Hill and of dire punishment meted out if you were caught.

On one unforgettable occasion my particular friend, John Rands, and I were caught. There would have been a small group of us playing at the cemetery end of the meadow and we always kept a careful eye on the farmhouse some two hundred yards away. If Farmer Hill appeared, we would hurriedly scarper over the fence covering a break in the hedge and run swiftly to home and safety. But this time he was cunning: he made his way out of the back of his house into East Parade and came behind us from the road. He suddenly appeared, climbing over the fence behind us. We all scattered in panic, but John Rands and I weren't quick enough. We were grasped firmly by the arm by the enraged farmer and dragged off towards the farm buildings. We were pushed into a barn and Farmer Hill snarled, *'You can stay there for an hour.'* A key turned in the lock. It was dark in the barn, with only faint illumination from small holes in the roof and around the eaves.

It was also sweet-smelling, because hay and oats were stored here, but we were next to the stable and a door was open into the darkness from which hideous sounds of clanking chains and puffing noises emanated. John Rands was probably more alarmed than I was, because I was used to stable noises from time spent with my grandfather in the stables down Riverside. We calmed our fears eventually and John stifled his sobs when I assured him that the horses were firmly tethered by their chains and couldn't get at us. So we sat down in the hay and listened to the horses clanking their chains and snuffling their fodder. At last we heard the key turn in the lock. Evening sunlight streamed in and a menacing Farmer Hill told us to clear off and keep off his land in future. I don't think we told our parents of this episode until years afterwards and I feel they would probably have thought we deserved the punishment for trespassing. I can't believe that our fathers would have gone storming up to the farmhouse to have it out with Farmer Hill and threaten legal proceedings as many modern parents might in these litigious days.

It probably wasn't the last time we ever played in his fields, but we more often contented ourselves with the area we called 'The Brook'. This was an odd triangular piece of land behind Woodbine Avenue that bordered the playing fields of both the Girls' High School and the Boys' Grammar School. A stream ran along the Grammar School side and this proved the main attraction. The land was far too uneven and in parts too overgrown to be much use for football or cricket. However, we could make islands and bays along the stream; we could introduce dams and stepping stones. We could sail imaginary boats in the form of twigs or pieces of thicker branches and we could bring roughly fashioned boats from home and paddle with them down the shallower areas as long as we had on our 'wellies'. In the spring we would collect frogspawn and later tadpoles. The frogspawn we placed in jam jars and took home to watch the transition to tadpoles and later frogs. Mother refused to allow such jam jars in the house, but they could be kept outside. Later we chased frogs and in early summer we fished for sticklebacks and tiddlers either with our hands or in nets saved over from our annual holiday.

We climbed over and along the wooden palisade that spanned the stream at the Wrawby Road end of the area and explored the overgrown banks and deeper waters on the far side. Here we would often go over the tops of our wellington boots and have to return home with sopping feet. We also crossed the stream and pushed our way through the hedge that was the boundary of the Grammar School field. There were venerable trees just inside the field and these were ideal for climbing or swinging on ropes that had been attached to thick lower branches. The senior boarders took exception to our playing in the school field and made regular sallies to drive us off. They couldn't catch us by coming directly over the field, so they tried strategy and would go round by Glebe Road and come at us from the rear. However, we posted lookouts and always had plenty of prior warning if the boarders were making a hot incursion. We would take shelter in an adjoining garden, belonging to one of our number, and each side contented itself by hurling insults at 'snooty Grammar-gogs' on the one hand and 'smelly council house oiks' on the other.

The Brook was really a small piece of waste ground, but there was some two hundred yards of water along which we could play; in some parts it was two to three inches in depth, but in others two to three feet. It was jumpable in most of its length. However, the main designated play area was the recreation ground on the outskirts of the town by the level crossing on Bigby High Road. This had a set of swings, a seesaw and a roundabout, as well as a largish corrugated iron shed with seats for people to shelter in inclement weather. The 'Rec' was quite a large expanse, capable of holding a full-sized football pitch, and there was a steep bank down from the road to the level of the football pitch and swings. Moreover, adjacent was a vastly overgrown area behind the billboards, which faced the road and the railway line. This area was crowded with elder bushes and large weeds including beds of stinging nettles and was a stimulating playground. At first I was taken to the swings by my mother on our pre-school afternoon perambulations, but later when I was seven or eight we would go in a group of half a dozen from our council estate by ourselves, even though it was a mile away and it meant crossing a main road or two. We were allowed to go by ourselves, because traffic wasn't a major hazard in the thirties. We had many a thrilling game of cricket and football, depending not on the season but rather on our whim and the availability of a cricket bat. Soccer games ended in astronomical scores, more in line with modern basketball than Premier League results. We could play hide-and-seek in the adjacent rough ground. We could also race out of the Rec to the fence by the railway line to wave to the carriages of passenger trains or to count the number of trucks and containers pulled by the goods trains, or to watch the occasional shunting in the sidings. All we had to do was watch the signal or listen for the warning bell at the level crossing.

One of our more exciting escapades involved a home-made slide arranged down the side of the quite precipitous bank. The shed to provide shelter fell into disuse and disrepair and Brigg children gave it a helping hand. This meant it was quite easy to dismantle some of the corrugated iron sheets, which measured some eight feet by three. These we could lie down the bank and along the grass floor, overlapping to form a serviceable slide. We then took another piece of corrugated iron sheeting, placed it on the slide, aligning the grooves, and gravity did the rest. We could crowd up to half a dozen onto the sliding piece. We would be given a helping shove and go careering down the bank for some twenty-five yards, holding on to our neighbour and screeching with exhilaration. I can't remember any severed fingers, but that must have been a danger.

Even further afield were Wrawby sandpits and Scawby Park. I was introduced to the disused sandpits when I was a Cub, for we spent an evening there on organised activities. Thereafter we made the occasional foray by ourselves to this wild terrain where coarse grass grew on the top and great gouges had been made in the hillside to excavate the sand. We fought imaginary battles with pirates and swung over cliffs on tree-ropes and dropped to the soft sand below. But it was a tiring two-mile walk to the sandpits and the suggestion to go there to play was not always greeted with enthusiasm. Scawby Park was even further away and I should have been older before I went there to play.

◆◆◆

Up to the age of ten I didn't often travel outside a five-mile radius of Brigg, but the family annual week's holiday was the exception. As members of the lowest orders of the middle classes, it was expected that we should go off for a week's holiday in the summer and we would look down on and pity any schoolmate who had had to stay at home because of lack of money. My parents had been to Skegness for their honeymoon and on one occasion before my arrival had been to the Isle of Man with Alf and Lil Rands: there were some fine photographs of Laxey Wheel taken by Uncle Alf to prove it. There is also a photographic record of a joint family holiday with the Randses to Llandudno just before I was three years old. I am standing on the sandy beach, clad in a woollen bathing suit and some waterproof apron, in copious floods of tears. There are two buckets of sand at my side and in the album the caption to the snap was *'And two buckets too!'*, which suggests that I had fallen out with John Rands over the use of sand and pails. However, I can't remember anything of Llandudno, nor of the occasion our family alone went to Southport, because my father wanted to visit the famous Flower Show. Possibly the joint holiday with children by the Rhodes and Rands families wasn't an unqualified success as I can't remember going on holiday together again. The Rands went south to Eastbourne, the Isle of Wight and Hastings; we regularly went north to our beloved Scarborough.

Memory is prompted by the family album, for I can't remember too many details, but from 1935 to 1938 we went each year and stayed in a boarding house in Queen Street run by Mrs Terry, of whom no visual trace lingers in the memory. Queen Street was in central Scarborough near Boyes departmental store, so there were no sea views. Mrs Terry provided breakfast and a high tea with a late evening drink and a biscuit (singular). We were regular and favoured guests and I am told I was made much of.

On the evenings when my parents went to performances at the Open Air Theatre (Sir Edward German's *Merrie England*) or to the Floral Hall (a recital by Richard Tauber in person), Mrs Terry kept an eye on me. From Queen Street we could go with equal facility to either the North Bay or the South Bay. In the thirties the North Bay was considered the more select and hence less lively. I preferred the south side where you could see them making rock and where families with exotic Italian names made scrumptious ice-cream. Here also was the harbour crowded with working trawlers, fishing boats and pleasure craft: it was here that you boarded the *Coronia*, which to me had all the allure of a blue riband, transatlantic *Queen*. There was also an amusement park (Corrigan's?) at one end of the sweeping bay and the dark, mysterious Gala-Land at the other end, where a very clever man with sharp scissors cut out the most perfect silhouettes of people and animals.

But the biggest attraction to me on the south side were the donkeys. I was fascinated by them. I took as many rides as my parents could afford and when there was no more, I followed the group of donkeys up and down the chosen route, to and fro and back again for hours. How I envied the youths brandishing sticks and uttering cries of *'Whoosh!'* and *'Git on!'*, nominally in charge of the animals. I say 'nominally', because nothing could shake the donkeys out of their time-hallowed routine of slowly plodding on the outward journey and breaking into a reluctant canter on the way back. Though they had commonplace and often asexual names, such as *Blackie* or *Brownie*, *Freda* and *Tommy*, they were to me fabulous steeds. I anticipated most eagerly throughout the dogged, outward plod, the turn and then the bumpy, rollicking canter back to base. Then I was a warrior on his charger at Waterloo or knight in shining armour at the lists.

Watching speedboats out in the bay from the tortuous climb up to the Grand Hotel was another enjoyable pastime, more acceptable than walking to the famous Spa or wandering through the noted Italian Gardens on the South Cliff. I never went in an actual speedboat because of the expense, but one of my father's skills was to dig out a speedboat in the sand in which I could sit and steer by the small spade stuck in the dashboard. I loved this experience and spent hours each holiday in the various craft my father sculpted. If I found a friend, then the seat could be enlarged to take two. I used to make sand speedboats for my own children and I am pleased to say that the skill has passed down to a third generation.

Another favourite spot was Peasholm Park with its gardens, the boating lake, the striking Chinese pagoda and the exciting water chute across the road near the Open Air Theatre. You could also take the miniature train from here and head off into uncharted territory; even the prosaic Scalby Mills took on a fascinating allure when seen from this train. Alone in the family I have never learned to swim, being hydrophobic and seemingly to have a congenital dislike of being wholly immersed in water, so I never ventured into the huge, open-air swimming pool. Nostalgia suggests blue skies and hot sunshine, but I remember clearly a chalked notice outside the North Bay Pool with the legend *54*, indicating a pool temperature of a none-too-inviting 54°F. However, I felt safe in the paddling pool/boating lake in Peasholm. I had a fairly large yacht, which was annually crammed into the cheap cabin trunk that accompanied us to Scarborough. It took my father all his time to lift let alone carry this trunk, so that on arrival at Scarborough station (for pre-war we always travelled by train and had to change twice) we had to have a taxi. This was a very rare occurrence in the travels of the Rhodes family and even today I blench at the thought of having to hire a taxi at an airport or station. Back to my yacht: it had a duck egg blue bottom and three adjustable sails. It didn't sail all that well to tell the truth and would sometimes become becalmed in the middle of the boating lake, sails feebly drooping. If I were dressed up, say on a Sunday when I could sail my boat but not don my swimsuit, then I had to exhort another boy in the pool with the boats to give mine a push shorewards. But on a sunny weekday morning I was allowed to put on my stripy, woollen bathing costume and be in the water with the boat myself. Together we made some fabulous voyages.

Scarborough remains for me the premier English seaside resort and we returned there for family holidays after the war. We even had a family holiday there with my parents and our own two elder children, staying at Read's Hotel with its varied facilities, stunning sea views and ready access to the Cricket Festival – a far cry from Mrs Terry's boarding house. However, I never fully recaptured the magic of those Scarborough family holidays of my childhood.

The other seaside place that I visited quite regularly before the war was Cleethorpes, but it was local and could in no way compare with Scarborough. We only went there on day outings. Just occasionally it would be a family outing as a special treat, but more often I was part of an organised group and not with my parents. It was to Cleethorpes we went on the annual Cubs' outing and on the choirboys' summer trip, but more of this later. Cleethorpes had a pier and it had Wonderland, and most importantly for me it had Shetland ponies as well as donkeys on which you could take rides. The ponies were small and tubby, but they could outstrip the donkeys on the bouncy, galumphing gallop back to base. Later Thelwell's drawings were to bring back vivid memories of these pony rides on the Cleethorpes sands. I say 'sands', but this was no golden beach: it was the Humber estuary and more mud than sand. It was difficult to make sandcastles on this beach. The water seemed colder and was more sullen, washing the Lincolnshire coast: Andrew Marvell's words about 'Humber flood' always had a special resonance and he was born across the river in Hull, so he should know. Often we enjoyed the train ride more than the day at the coast, though it was here that I had my first taste of candyfloss, sticky pink and sugary.

However, Cleethorpes did have its numerous admirers. In summer at weekends and during wakes weeks, thousands of people from South Yorkshire would travel there. There were special trains by the dozen and we could stand at the Wrawby Road junction with East Parade and count twenty, thirty, forty or more red buses from Yorkshire Traction making their way to Cleethorpes in convoys. The day was often grey and dismal-looking, but the Yorkshire folk waved and cheered at us in mid-morning and waved and sang at us on their way back in the evening.

❖❖❖

In the mid-thirties the year's main cycle was a division between term time and school holidays. I don't remember time hanging heavily during the holidays, but beyond the annual week away there was little of importance or excitement. However, one day does remain firmly in the memory. I would have been eight coming up to nine at the time. John Rands and I had somehow become involved with a new friend, whom we knew at school. His name was Gordon Kitchen and he lived with his mother and grandparents in Glebe Road. We were probably all at a loose end and eagerly accepted Gordon's mother's suggestion that we should go and play in Grandfather Cheesman's orchard and she would pack us up some sandwiches.

Glebe Road was barely three hundred yards from Central Square and the orchard proved to be behind Jack Clark's shop in Grammar School Road, not very much further. Off we went without a care in the world. The orchard proved to be large, delightfully overgrown and best of all there was a small outhouse in the middle, complete with a fireplace and some very tattered seating. Our imaginations had free rein: we were Arctic explorers, highwaymen or pirates, or defended ourselves in the outhouse against hordes of marauding Red Indians, fearsomely black Zulus or fiendishly green Martians, as the fancy took us. We found combustible material and daringly lit a fire in the old grate, which caused much smoke to pother out and fill the room but lent a marvellously eerie and novel atmosphere to our adventures. We brewed tea and the unique smoky taste remains. Time passed blissfully and it was only when the food had long been consumed and our stomachs told us that it must be near teatime that we decided to go home, still uncertain of the time. We saw Gordon home, thanked his mother and grandparents for a wonderful day and went off tired but happy to Central Square.

Here I was greeted by a completely unexpected and furious response. My mother had been beside herself with worry and, though I did not know it, she was some three months pregnant with my younger brother. When we hadn't returned for our midday dinner, she and Auntie Lil had spent the afternoon searching and enquiring after us. Even now my father was looking for us down the riverbank, thinking we might have gone visiting my grandparents down Riverside. He had just decided to alert the police and they were looking too. It was eight o'clock and I was in serious trouble. When my father returned, the tirade continued and out of sheer relief I was subject to corporal punishment – that didn't happen very often in our house. He used the back of a long-handled clothes brush on my backside, accompanying the blows with dire warnings about what would happen if I ever again disappeared for the day without telling anyone. Then I was dispatched early to bed, supperless. The next morning the storm had blown over and life resumed its normal tenor. However, I have always retained a sense of deep injustice. Not at the punishment itself, but when I discovered later that day as we compared notes that John Rands had been duly reprimanded but then told to lie down on the sofa in the front room: no beating, no bed and he had had a full supper. Life can be so unfair. However, I don't think I went AWOL again for several years after that.

When John Rands was away on holiday, I can remember playing with another schoolfriend, Roy Firmedow, who lived in the end house of East Parade, no. 40. His father drove Esso tankers out of the depot between the two bridges and later did office work there. My father filled up with British Petroleum at Sass's and Roy and I often fell out over the virtues of the two brands of petrol. Roy had an elder sister, Doreen, and this was one of the rare occasions I played with girls – I must have been desperate. Doreen was the usual bossy, elder sister and we meekly followed her suggestions. She was supported by another girl, my age nearly, Peggy Bevans, who lived a few doors away in East Parade and whose father also worked in the petroleum industry. As Doreen decreed, we played mothers and fathers. I was nearly nine at the time and was quite happy to fall in with her ideas, when being grown-up involved smoking, an unknown but enticing vice. The disused and empty wash-house next to the outside lavatory was our joint home, which we furnished with boxes and crates for a table and chairs. A cloth was spread over the table and illumination (when the door was shut) was provided by a nightlight in a saucer. Our smoking consisted of cutting lengths of string about three centimetres long and lighting them from the nightlight. The lit and smouldering end could be made to glow and wisps of smoke to rise if you took an extra large intake of breath. Unlike President Clinton, I did inhale and it made my eyes water! We talked what we imagined adult talk to be – about the weather, neighbours and the recently abdicated king. We ate imaginary meals and puffed on our pieces of string. We went to bed, but there was no hint whatsoever of intimate relations: we simply put our head down on the table and closed our eyes – just as we had done on our desks at infant school. However, I think Roy and I had to give our 'wife' a dutiful peck on the cheek before leaving for work. This was after going to the 'lav' next door, as firmly instructed by Doreen, following her mother's daily instructions to her, for you didn't want to have to go to those dreadful school loos and they were probably no better in the workplace. Such mixed playtimes were extremely rare: I was usually in a group of four or five boys, if John Rands and I weren't playing on our own.

Such was my humdrum and rather constricted existence in those days. There was little affluence and no consumer society to emphasise what I was missing and to raise false longings. There was no television to bring the big, bad world into our living rooms and show lavish lifestyles to cause envy. What I saw on the silver screen about Hollywood stars was another world altogether. I was generally content and savoured the odd excursions from the norm.

Nowadays it is impossible to play in the street and few parents would allow their children to wander as we did at an early age. Play has been over-organised by adults and health and safety regulations have further circumscribed such activities. Today children both physically and imaginatively have never been so 'cabined, cribbed, confined'. The main conduit of their imaginations seems to be PlayStation 3.

Tears at the seaside:
on the beach at Llandudno

4
MY EARLY SCHOOLING

There were no pre-school groups or nursery classes for me. More affluent families sent their tots to the kindergarten attached to Miss Lyne's Preparatory School, but my education started somewhat peremptorily in September 1935. I didn't think I had much choice in the matter and accepted it as in the natural sequence of events, rather like whooping cough. I can't remember feeling outraged like Laurie Lee when told to wait outside for the present, so I was never disappointed when the gift did not duly materialise. Like most of my contemporaries I attended the infant school in Grammar School Road near the junction with Colton Street. It consisted of one low wooden hut, containing three classrooms, cloakrooms and an office for the headmistress, Miss Hodson, a stout, bespectacled lady, who had a formidable reputation. This office was also probably the staffroom. The other teachers were Miss Kennington, Miss Elwood and Miss Kenning. The first lived in a large house just over the bridge. She taught elocution privately and later opened a short-lived preparatory school in her home. Some years later she turned to selling perfumery and jewellery. Throughout her life she retained an interest in amateur dramatics and I even appeared in some of the plays she produced and presented on the High School stage in my late teens. She had the reception class in my time and Miss Elwood and Miss Kenning must have shared the other two classes with Miss Hodson taking different classes at different times. Miss Kenning was the strictest and as she lived on Wrawby Road and passed by our house regularly, I hid myself at her approach up to the time I went to the Grammar School. I can't remember much about Miss Elwood except rather prominent teeth and a bicycle, necessary because I think she lived at Wrawby.

We entered the hut by means of wooden steps and first of all had to put our outdoor coat (almost always a dark blue gaberdine raincoat) on our peg and if the weather was wet take off our wellingtons and put on elasticated soft shoes called 'daps'. I half remember lines of cots in one room, but the memory is blurred. However, we certainly compelled to have an afternoon nap or at least close our eyes, for from the beginning we observed the normal infant school hours of nine to three with a lunch break. I suspect I was brought home for lunch and taken back, but I can't be certain. I have equally vague memories of early reading primers in heavy print with black and white pictures of little boys in sailor suits and knickerbockers, carrying hoops or sailing ships – completely alien to my mode of dress and way of life. We had slates and chalk and brought dusters from home to clean our slates. We copied letters and then simple words from the board onto the side of our slate that had white lines scored into it and on the other side we did sums. We gathered round our teacher for story-time just before we went home – here 'Florrie' Kennington was in her histrionic element – and on Friday afternoons we could bring games from home to play with. In Miss Kenning's class just before going up to the 'top' school in Glebe Road we were introduced to pens and ink and gloriously messy stuff it proved to be. I remember having read to me excerpts from *The Water-Babies* by Charles Kingsley and from JM Barrie's *Peter Pan*. We improvised and acted little scenes from the latter in which I was the dog, Nana, moping lugubriously in my kennel and barking furiously but ineffectually when Peter absconded with Wendy and the boys.

By some mysterious means of osmosis I must have assimilated spelling and reading skills as well as an ability to do sums, though I recall little of the process. Nevertheless by the time I was nearly eight I was deemed ready to face the big boys and girls at Glebe Road School, which was barely three hundred yards from my home. I could certainly read and write with some fluency, though I didn't know my tables as well I should have done.

Glebe Road School occupied a much larger site than the infant school. It fronted onto Glebe Road and its field extended past East Parade and Hawthorn Avenue almost to the bottom end of Grammar School Road. There were two separate entrances in Glebe Road – one for the boys (nearer to Central Square) and one for the girls: we were educated together, but everything was done to keep us socially segregated. There was a small border of shrubs behind the main fence and then came the front playground, in which a four-foot looped metal railing divided the girls' play area (which was larger) from the boys'. There was a playground at the back of the classroom block that was monopolised by the boys and behind this was the playing field. The buildings were in the form of an inverted three-sided square – the fourth side being open to the playground. On each side there were four classrooms with the girls' cloakroom at the end of the left-hand side and the boys' complementing it on the right. Across the top were a specialist Woodwork room and a specialist Cookery room. The staffroom was in the left-hand corner and the headmaster's room in the right. There was a raised veranda running within all three sides and this surrounded the grass area in the middle. The grass area was divided into four sizeable squares by paving slabs, which crossed at right angles. A tall flagpole, on which the Union Jack was raised on special occasions – including annually May 24th, Empire Day – was there somewhere, I think in the centre of the bottom end.

The classrooms had window walls on the veranda side and its opposite. The brick wall separating the classrooms could be used to display maps, pictures and sometimes children's work. I can remember only one class in each year group, consisting of forty children. Glebe Road was what was termed in the thirties an 'elementary' school, which catered for children of all abilities from seven or eight to fourteen, then the official school-leaving age. When we were eleven everyone took the 'scholarship exam', which determined those few who were to leave Glebe Road and progress either to the Grammar School (boys) or the High School (girls).

In September 1937 I found myself in the 'baby' class, as the seniors disparagingly called it, and under the direct control of Miss Stringer. Elsie Stringer had been born when Victoria had another decade or two to reign and she had taught generations of Brigg children. She lived some four doors from our family and knew my parents well, since they all belonged to Brigg Choral Society at some time, so I knew her well by sight and had already been subject to much of the mythology. She was an able pianist and for years taught private pupils in her front – and only – living room. We regarded with some sympathy the numerous young girls who trudged along Central Square at their appointed hour, carrying a leather music case. Very few boys were among her pupils and these were treated with derision: piano-playing was 'cissy'. In the summer months we could hear, as we played out in the street, faltering efforts in waltz time or in two-fingered easy exercises with Miss Stringer's rich contralto voice keeping time or urging out the rhythm. In the classroom she had a stern reputation as being a tartar and she had no difficulty in controlling her classes. The girls were cowed by her voice and so were most of the boys, but our attention and efforts were guaranteed by the application of a foot-ruler to our fingers. We sang our hearts out under her searching gaze and imperious piano-playing. We sang rounds based on 'Three Blind Mice' and 'London's Burning' and under her foot-ruler baton which occasionally rattled inattentive knuckles we learned to sing these tolerably well. I seem to remember we also sang folk songs and sea shanties, which whether appropriate or not Miss Stringer deemed should be part of our cultural heritage. I liked 'Bobby Shaftoe' for its rollicking tune, but felt he must have been a bit of a 'cissy', combing down his yellow hair, since certainly my short back and sides (still cut at this time by Miss Bell in Albert Street, for I hadn't as yet graduated to Harry Westcott Senior in Wrawby Street) would allow no such vanity. Nor could I summon up much enthusiasm for 'Oh no, John, no John, No!' or for 'The Lass of Richmond

Hill': I would much rather have had a five-shilling piece than have had to put up with a girlfriend.

In Miss Stringer's class we continued at first with slate and chalk, copying words and sums from the board. We were also introduced to the dubious delights of multiplication and division after much chanting of tables. Silent reading and story-time were my favourites still. However, it was with much trepidation that I approached the teacher's high desk when it was my turn to read the small allotted portion aloud, standing by the tall stool from which her ample posterior protruded at a level with my downcast eyes.

Handicraft lessons had little appeal: we cut out shapes in coloured paper and stuck them on card to make patterns. The scissors, dull and blunt, were counted out and back into their tin and woe betide us if one had been temporarily mislaid. On the rare occasion that a bright shiny new pair had been introduced into the tin, there was much squabbling to grab that pair. In due course we progressed to things of more practical application, such as French knitting by means of a cotton reel studded with thin tacks. This gurgitated yards of multi-hued, thick woollen strings with which we might tie things up if we wished or which might have been prototypes for the coloured bootlaces later beloved by Mary Quant and her ilk. However, one project did have a usable end-product when we were instructed in weaving. On a piece of card (about six by eight inches) we made small incisions top and bottom at regular half-inch intervals with the same blunted scissors and then stretched wool between them in continuous, taut parallel lines in front. Next, either with our fingers or with a large, safely rounded darning needle (I forget), we threaded the rest of a ball of wool back and forth, in and out, under and over, laterally through the wefts or the warps. We had a class wool-box, which contained all the leftovers and odds and ends we could scrounge from our mothers' home knitting. Thus the balls of wool were quite small and we needed a substantial number to complete our weaving. I had no eye for colour and no aesthetic sense, so I just grabbed the next ball near the top of the wool-box. In addition my knotting was not particularly neat, but in the end I had a Joseph-coat of woven material stretched over my cardboard frame. Miss Stringer did some snipping and sewing in of loose ends and to my delight I had a jazzy piece of weaving fashioned into the shape of a teapot or pan holder. It was used daily at home for some five years and was the first of only three handicraft/woodwork items of any use that I ever completed during my years of full-time education.

At first Physical Education was class-based and performed in whatever clothes we had worn to school, though in spring the girls might discard their cardigans and the boys their jerseys. Later the boys from two classes were amalgamated and similarly the girls were put through their paces separately, but initially we had unisex PE. Miss Stringer simply ambled around the yard and blew her whistle. We exercised on the spot in rigid lines; we bowled wooden hoops and caught tennis balls. We wore sashes in primary colours to denote our teams and grew excited as we indulged in various relay races. Each of the four teams would have about ten members and from behind a set line we would dash forward some twenty yards or so to touch the fence or school wall then dash back, slapping the next team member, who then set off on their dash: we enjoyed the slapping. The teacher chose the team leaders – one week girls, the next boys – and these then chose their teams. It was an embarrassing process. I was never one of the more athletic members of the class, but I was usually picked before the coal-merchant's daughter who for obvious reasons we nicknamed 'Fatty'. In my favourite relay there was little running. We stood about two feet behind each other in our teams, then first the football had to be channelled through our legs from front to back. The team member at the rear would seize the ball and run to the front of the line and so we would proceed until the team was back to its initial order, whereupon the ball would be passed back overhead in looping parabolas and the sequence repeated. In those days no girl wore shorts or trousers to school and they hitched up their dresses and stuffed them into their knickers, which were invariably navy blue but at that time carried no erotic frisson whatsoever.

After being in Miss Stringer's care for a year, we all passed up into Miss Clark's class. The curriculum didn't seem to change much, though the words may have become longer and the sums more complicated. The large map of the world on the back wall was as old and cracked in its oil-cloth surface as the last one. By this time we had forsaken our slates and chalk and were expected to pen our efforts with the minimum of smearing. It was a coveted position of honour to be the ink monitor and have responsibility for pouring ink from a large stone jar bearing Mr Stephenson's name into the white, usually crazed, china inkwells, which fitted into the appropriate holes in our sturdy iron-framed desks. There was a sliding brass square, which you moved in its slot to cover the inkwell when not in use. However, the inkwells often became clogged with a residue of dust and little pieces of blotting paper that had been used as ink-stained darts against our adversaries in the class: the inkwell was the handiest receptacle in which to hide the evidence. Each Monday we were issued with a fresh piece of blotting paper (about four by five inches), which had to last the ensuing week. A Friday afternoon chore was for volunteers to wash out the inkwells in the cloakroom and place them in wooden racks to dry. The inkwells were then filled by the ink monitor on Monday morning. The pens, provided by the Education Committee, were simple, small pencil-size cylinders of unvarnished wood from Messrs Brown of Hull with a tight metal clip about an inch long at one end. The bronze-coloured metal nib was inserted into the clip and held firmly. The teacher kept further nibs in a box in her desk, but they cost money and we were constantly adjured to look after our nibs. However, accidents did happen regularly when pens rolled off the desks onto the floor and wear and tear was heavy. The twin points of the nib became crossed and when you pressed down on them to straighten them out, the nib could easily disintegrate. Mind you, this left half the nib protruding from its shaft and having two stubby but sharp points at either side. These made admirable projectiles and at times when the teacher was absent we played a form of darts, aiming the broken pens at the underside of a raised desktop.

Boys were also selected to be milk monitors. Free milk was consumed each morning break through straws somewhat reluctantly. Crates of small milk bottles holding a third of a pint were left at the school gate by the Co-op dairy lorry. Senior boys collected these and according to the register number from the morning roll-call left a crate plus the correct number of sundries outside each classroom door on the veranda. The class milk monitors had to bring them within the classroom and give them out two to a desk. In winter there was always the chance the top of the milk would be frozen and in summer standing since dawn in the hot sun might have caused the milk 'to go off'. The girls took it in turn to be the straw monitor and give out the yellow, waxy straws. The bottles had waxed cardboard tops with a small circular perforation. It was difficult to pierce this hole and frequently impatient fingers pressing hard on the circular perforation ensured the whole top went into the bottle and its contents were flung up in an explosive spray all over. This did not please the teacher, but it did mean there was less milk that had to be consumed.

Miss Clark had her own methods of enforcing discipline. She did not use a ruler like Miss Stringer, but we feared her sharp tongue more. She used to slap boys' legs – just above the knee and below our short trousers if we were sitting and behind the knee if we were standing. However, she had one further method that was more effective, more insidiously embarrassing for the boys and horribly degrading – in retrospect – for one unfortunate girl. She was 'M'. None of the families in our class were affluent and none would have earned more than about £350 a year. But M was more underprivileged than any of us. She was one of a largish family living in substandard housing near the river down a lane off one corner of the Market Place. She was noticeably poorly dressed in unfashionable, patched hand-me-downs. This would not normally have mattered in the slightest, but M's hair (despite the periodic ministrations of the school nurse) was usually visibly infested.

Other girls were firmly instructed by their mothers: *'And don't you go playing with that M.'* We boys wouldn't anyway: girls were inferior species to be ignored and avoided. Thus M was a forlorn, solitary and withdrawn little figure, who sat alone in the double desk well at the front of the class, yet also well away from the teacher's desk. Miss Clark's most feared sanction (in which she seemed to take perverse pleasure) was to summon to the front some inattentive or mischievous boy whispering at an inappropriate moment after she had commanded silence. She would utter a firm reprimand and then point dramatically at the vacant seat beside M: *'Take your books and go and sit there for half an hour!'* Most reluctantly we would drag our feet back to our desk at the rear of the class, collect our things and slowly with many painful grimaces and ill-concealed noises of distaste return to the front and sit at M's desk. We sat at the furthest edge away from her on the single seat, with as much of our posterior overlapping into the gangway as possible. From time to time we would ease our position, utter under our breath further exclamations of disgust and do some furtive but obvious scratching. We would also turn round, when Miss Clark's eye was not upon us, and garner sympathetic looks from our friends at the back. Looking back, our behaviour was unpardonable, but at the time we boys felt we were the victims and we did nothing whatsoever to spare M's feelings. Miss Clark maintained a quiet classroom and I suppose we did somehow progress up our learning curve, but it was at unknown and untold cost. I never liked the woman.

That September I moved up and for the first time had a male teacher. This was Ted Booth, bluff, hearty and grey-haired. He also lived not far from us – in his own detached house at the junction of East Parade / Woodbine Avenue with Wrawby Road. In the curious social hierarchy of the time, he was superior to us who lived in the council houses of Central Square but did not rate as highly as the retired majors, doctors, headmasters, legal executives, bank managers and senior local government officials, who lived in their detached houses on lime-avenued Wrawby Road. Not that he showed any social arrogance, but he had his own house and as a teacher (non-graduate) earned considerably more than my own father and those of almost all my acquaintances at that time. Actually he and Dad were established friends and our family was one of his depositors. He supplemented his teaching salary by being an agent for the National Deposit Friendly Society. I remember we had an olive-grey book in which monthly deposits of five shillings were recorded. I am still not sure what the objective of it all was, but it was a definite rite of passage when some years later I was entrusted to take the contribution along to his house all by myself. The NDFS book was of superior quality because it had to last years, unlike the folded piece of card

– white and ruled on the inside, pink and printed on the outside – which was the rent book, kept in the sideboard cupboard next to the best and rarely used tea service, and renewed annually. A man from the Council came every Monday morning wash day to collect the rent. He would inscribe the figure (ten shillings and sixpence a week, I think, in the early years of the war) opposite the column with a printed *w.e.* and the date and initial in the adjacent column.

Ted Booth was also a dedicated and proficient angler and could be regularly seen cycling off to his favourite spot on the Ancholme, complete with big wellies, two or three rods in their bamboo cases and a collapsible net which fitted into his fishing basket, slung over his back gas-mask-style. The basket contained not only his food and a flask of cold tea but also his bait-tins of worms and maggots. He was a most successful angler too and once presented my mother with one of her more intractable problems. One morning she found that a large pike, some four feet long with large, cold and unanimated eyes and rows upon rows of small sharp teeth, had been hung on the knob of our back door the previous evening. Apparently Dad had done him a service and he repaid it in this way. I remember it put my mother in a terrible fluster, but somehow she contrived a method of cutting it up and cooking it. Its taste eludes me, but I do recall the numerous small and bothersome bones. I have curiously few memories of being taught by Ted. He affected a gruff manner in his teaching and relied on a round yardstick to emphasise points on the blackboard, and used the same stick on our knuckles and pates to implant these same points in our brains. There were no project-based, child-centred, information-gathering lessons in the thirties – at least not at Glebe Road. We copied sums from the board and tried to work them out. By this time we had progressed from adding, subtracting, multiplying and dividing mere numbers: we did it in tons, stones, pounds and ounces, in furlongs, yards, feet and inches and even in those mysterious measures, rods, poles and perches. It was also Ted Booth who plunged me into a new and incomprehensible world of DECIMALS. It took me ages to decide at which point in the numerical sequence arrived at after my multiplying or dividing to place that damned dot – and I usually got it wrong.

There were no out-of-school activities that I can remember, though the senior boys could stay after school to complete some woodwork item. Mr Armstrong looked kindly on keen carpenters, but I was not of an age to cross over the threshold of the woodwork room at Glebe Road. Those of us who left at eleven never gained access: woodwork was reserved for the top classes. However, there must have been a school concert occasionally, for I was once in a play based on the story of Brer Rabbit and the Tar Baby at a young age. It was performed not at school (which had no assembly hall) but in the Parish Hall, a ramshackle building with a corrugated iron roof in Elwes Street near JW White's 'pop' factory, which competed with Laws to quench our thirsts with lemonade. The Parish Hall became Brigg's British Restaurant during the Second World War and at some stage we were crocodiled down from school to have our lunch there – except we called it 'dinner', for at about midday we always ate our main meal of the day whether at home or not. Usually I went home at twelve for a cooked dinner. If my father was away on his rounds, as he frequently was, his portion was put out on a plate and then later heated up again over a pan of simmering water at about 6pm when he returned. If he were late, Mother had to watch that the pan did not boil dry. The reheated food had a particular smell that pervaded the whole house in the early evening. It also had a peculiar and never-forgotten taste. Whatever else happened Mother would prepare and cook the dinner in the morning and have it on the table for half past twelve.

Back to the Tar Baby. I was probably about eight at the time and our class's effort was one of a number of similar performances by other classes that were presented before parents and friends, sitting on individual cane or bent wood chairs in front of a makeshift stage. I think we must have had a narrator standing at the side of the stage, for though I had a speaking part it was not too long to remember. Margaret Brader was possibly the narrator reading all the connecting links, because she was the cleverest and the prettiest girl in the class. However, I can remember most of the other members of the cast: Don France was Brer Rabbit, Ronnie Winterbottom the non-speaking Tar Baby, Sylvia Steeper was Brer Coon and I was the thwarted Brer Fox. I wore voluminous trousers of orange sateen, elasticated at the waist and ankles, and a thick bushy tail was safety-pinned to my bum. I also wore a fox-face mask from Woolworths in lurid colours. It fastened over the ears with rubber bands and the eyeholes did not allow much lateral vision. I blundered onto the stage, half dazzled by the spotlights, and vainly tried to locate the character I was supposed to be addressing. The performance could hardly be hailed as having star potential, but fortunately the audience was benevolently sympathetic.

School hours at Glebe Road were nine to twelve and half past one to four with mid-morning and mid-afternoon breaks, each of fifteen minutes. At first during playtimes we congregated with classmates in the front boys' yard; we felt safer there and we gossiped and chased each other either at 'tig' or hide-and-seek. The boys' toilets in an unroofed block in the corner of the playground were scrupulously avoided. The urinals were often clogged with leaves or worse and smelled. The small cubicles for doing 'number twos' had curved pieces of wood about eight inches long fastened to either side of the toilet bowl with a metal chain hanging down from the cistern, all well above our heads. It was well nigh impossible to reach the chain or the piece of string used as a substitute when the chain went missing. There were no locks on the doors, rarely any toilet paper that had not been plunged into the bottom of the bowl and we feared we might be trapped in a defenceless position by a group of menacing older boys. Thus only in the direst of emergencies would we consider using the school toilets. Many were the mad dashes home at the dinnertime break, particularly when you remember that we were frequently dosed with a laxative to keep us 'regular', whatever that meant. It was with great difficulty and much nose-holding that I forced down senna-pod tea with its revolting smell that was even worse than the taste. What a relief it was when the much more palatable California Syrup of Figs came onto the market. Later this was replaced by the almost attractive, chocolate-like 'Ex-Lax', but by this time taking laxatives regularly had gone out of fashion.

In due season at playtime we played conkers and rudimentary cricket. We kicked and harried a small ball in opposing hordes and in summer we played cigarette cards, either against a single opponent or in groups of half a dozen. We rarely ventured into the back playground during our first two or three years at Glebe Road and the senior boys laid exclusive claim to the small grass field beyond this. For some years we ignored the girls playing hopscotch or carrying dolls in their adjacent front yard, but gradually our testosterone stirred and kicked in. Furtive conversations took place along the thin-arched metal fence that divided us. There was never any time for a protracted conversation with a girl that interested you and usually messages were conveyed via your supposed friends to the supposed friends of that girl: *'Tell Marion that John Rhodes likes her'*, whereupon they would double up in paroxysms of laughter.

Towards the end of our third year we would find ourselves lingering by the fence and watching the girls skipping. Individually they did this with rapt concentration, singing out weird runes at the same time as they carried out some complicated processes – crossing over their hands, skipping on one foot at a time or with both feet together, or passing the rope into one hand and then slashing the ground on either side vigorously in the right tempo. They sometimes skipped in pairs facing each other or, if they were especially adept, in trios with the tallest girl twirling the rope. We were undoubtedly impressed, but no boy would dream of bringing a skipping rope to school. However, there was one participation that occurred as a challenge of great daring, for staff were supposed to patrol the playground to ensure a strict segregation of the sexes. Occasionally the girls had a much longer piece of rope and two of the more hefty girls would stand some twelve yards apart and swing the rope so that some six or more girls could skip together. This was the opportunity for some daring boy, having ascertained that no teacher was visible, to dash into the girls' playground and duck under the swirling rope to join in for some dozen circulations and then dash back to the safety of the boys' playground. Such feats were highly regarded and folklore informed us that one hero had once managed fifty skips.

The one event at Glebe Road School that needed much preparation and to which parents and local notabilities were invited was the annual Crowning of the May Queen, which was always recorded in both the *Brigg Star* and the *Hull Times*. The whole school was involved, though it was far more appealing to the girls. Most of the boys, using their favourite adjective, dismissed it as 'cissyish', but the girls were wracked by jealousies and copious tears were shed when they failed to be selected as one of the Queen's attendants. The boys dreaded possible selection as a page. A girl from the top class of thirteen to fourteen-year-olds was chosen by the staff to be the May Queen: they had an unenviable task. The choice was always open to bitter recriminations and allegations of favouritism from parents, especially if the daughter of a town councillor were chosen. I can't remember if the Queen was crowned by her predecessor or by some local female notability such as Mrs Edith Burgess, the vicar's wife, but she was trailed around the interior courtyard of the school in a flower-bedecked chariot, constructed in the woodwork room and overhauled annually. The chariot was pulled by six senior boys and was accompanied by a considerable retinue. The May Queen was conveyed to her rather ornate throne, where she draped herself regally. She wore a long white dress and train under a white fur-trimmed cape. Her attendants were in white knee-length dresses with white ankle socks and a flowered headdress. There was a different floral theme each year – Queen Lilac, Queen Rose, Queen Jonquil: the flowers were usually real but could be artificially simulated if not in season.

The event was held on a Wednesday afternoon in May, because Wednesday was half-closing day and fathers who worked in shops could theoretically attend. However, the audience (which was seated partly under the veranda and partly in the playground out front) largely consisted of mothers – doting if their child had a starring role, hypercritical if their child were not prominent. The whole thing was feminine-orientated and we boys suffered for the most part in silence. We marched around the perimeter to the tunes of 'Men of Harlech' and 'Hearts of Oak', played on the piano by Miss Stringer, and senior boys performed gymnastic feats on the grass in the middle. More junior classes provided maypole-dancing groups. The maypole was a central attraction and was fixed firmly in a new, silvery galvanised dustbin. The maypole-dancing teams, comprising about twelve children, were of both sexes. The girls wore white dresses with a coloured sash, either tartan or matching the flower colour of the year; the boys wore immaculately white shirts and short grey trousers and grey knee-length socks. All had newly whitened sand shoes. We gathered our particular streamer-ribbon from the unfurled maypole and stood in a circle, facing each other in pairs. To lively playing from Miss Stringer, we skipped off nimbly in one direction or the other and weaved our primary-coloured pattern on the maypole. When we had covered some three-quarters of the pole, we turned round and unravelled all our hard work. Later we danced in pairs and this involved – oh, horror! – skipping along with our arm around a girl's waist. Even though this was most repugnant to every boy, we all wanted to dance with the most attractive girl in the class.

Other teachers at Glebe Road were Mrs Silverwood, Mrs Bratley, Miss Marrows and a Cookery teacher, but I was never taught by these. Your own class teachers remain more firmly in the memory, even than the headmaster, Mr Bratley, whose initials, 'EG', were regularly seen but never deciphered – Eric… Ernest… Edward… Edgar… I never knew. He held a sergeant's rank in the wartime Special Constabulary, in which my father also served, and through this he knew my parents well, but we were not social equals. He was always spoken of within the family respectfully as 'Mr Bratley'. (How the status of teachers and headmasters has fallen!) He was a tall, rather remote man, bespectacled and with a face like a superior ape. He only very occasionally entered our classroom and was known to deal firmly and painfully with persistent offenders. I was dealt with at a more immediate level and never had to go and wait outside Mr Bratley's door. He was also a churchwarden at St John's Parish Church and regularly read the lesson, so I saw him often out of school, especially when he came to count the collection in the vestry, which at that time accommodated the vicar, Canon Burgess, the lay reader, Horace West, and the numerous men and boy choristers.

In September 1940 I started my 'scholarship year'. Our teacher was Mrs Smith (I think) and she presumably worked us hard, though without recourse to stick and slapping. Dim memories suggest she was a kindly, maternal lady, who wore glasses and comfortable, unfashionable clothes like my mother. She lived along Kettleby top and pedalled to school on an ancient sit-up-and-beg bicycle. There can be no doubt that the Scholarship Examination, the precursor of the Eleven-Plus, was socially divisive, because I was never again – after the summer of 1941 – on easy social terms with many of my Glebe Road contemporaries and, curiously, our paths rarely seemed to cross, even in a small town like Brigg. After years of cat-calling and deriding the older and stuck-up 'Grammar-gogs' from a safe distance, I was about to become one of them.

My father obviously wanted me to go to the Grammar School, despite the added cost, because it would give me educational and other opportunities that he had never had, leaving school as he did at twelve and becoming a grocer's errand boy. I was not so sure of the advantages, yet I was never put under any intense pressure to pass the 'scholarship'. I had no private coaching for the three papers, though I think my father may have borrowed a past paper or two from Ted Booth to look over with me. One paper concentrated on arithmetic, one on English and I think the third had some pretensions to measure innate intelligence by recognising similarities in different shapes in different positions and by deciding that father was to nephew as mother was to niece and not mother-in-law, grandmother or sister. It all seemed rather arcane and remote from the life I was living. We took the scholarship examination in classrooms at Glebe Road singly in desks set at regulated intervals and under strictly timed and observed conditions. There was some feeling of relief when it was over and we got on with playing 'ciggies' against the school wall.

When the results eventually came back to Glebe Road, they were read out to the scholarship class by the headmaster, Mr Bratley. They were rather confusing, because only one girl, the incomparable Margaret Brader, had passed outright: about a dozen others had been selected for further interviews to secure admission to either the High School or the Grammar School. This was daunting because these interviews took place at the appropriate secondary school, which was unknown, intimidating and hitherto forbidden territory. I have only a partial memory of this interview, but there were numerous other interviewees from schools in the surrounding villages, from such faraway places as Worlaby and Hibaldstow. We were asked questions by three strange adults, though I don't know if they were County officials or teachers from the Grammar School. I remember we had to read a lengthy passage quietly and then were asked questions about it. One phrase sticks in my mind – 'in Indian file' – and I was asked to explain the meaning. Fortunately I knew the answer and am convinced that on such a thin thread hung my final success in the scholarship exam. Yet some weeks elapsed before the final list of those who had passed their scholarship was read out by Mr Bratley. There were only four further boys and five girls.

I was not bought a new bicycle as others had been promised: that was a luxury completely outside the family budget. However, Dad was pleased, but both my mother and I were apprehensive. The gate had been opened, but to a new and intimidating world in which we learned through mysterious and rampant rumour (embroidered further by our unsuccessful contemporaries) that new Grammar-gogs were taken into the toilets by older malevolent boys and, in an initiation ceremony, had their buttocks beaten with a stick and their head thrust into the toilet bowl that was then flushed. That September whey-faced new Grammar-gogs walked fearfully up the drive to Brigg Grammar School.

◆◆◆

July 1941 marked the end of my elementary education at Glebe Road and I have mainly happy memories of my time there. It was close to home and, in general, unthreatening. I had made friends with boys from the far side of town, from strange areas like Silverside and Mill Lane. I had somehow managed to acquire sufficient knowledge to pass the scholarship examination and I had also learned to adjust my view of life to allow that girls might have some important part to play in the fairly distant future. In the early 1940s this knowledge was an odd mixture of a faintly musky but undeniably non-masculine smell, of long hair in plaits and hair ribbons that always seemed to be coming undone, of white ankle socks and gingham dresses – and glimpses of navy blue knickers.

Crowning of the May Queen, Glebe Road School, Brigg

5
HIGH DAYS AND HOLY DAYS

In addition to the school/holiday cycle there passed too the annual cycle of the great festivals of the Church, Christmas and Easter, and the two Brigg notable events, 'Status' and Brigg Fair. In Lincolnshire (unlike South Yorkshire), Ascension Day and Whitsuntide had only a pale significance. We didn't get a holiday from school on Ascension Day, though we did on Whit Monday as it was an official Bank Holiday, but there were no street processions of young girls in white dresses headed by brass bands. Looking forward to Christmas presents and to Easter eggs was exciting.

At Easter I probably received some five Easter eggs before the war – one from Grandad Rhodes, or rather from Auntie Ethel, one from my grandparents and 'Auntie' Elsie, one from the Rands, one from my parents and sometimes one from Mrs Proctor at the bottom of Glebe Road, who went to church and had a soft spot for me, as she had once had for my father. The chocolate eggs were carefully broken into manageable pieces, which were made to last for at least two weeks.

Christmas was the time I was most likely to meet other members of my father's family, whom we did not see very often. In retrospect I think it must have been as a result of sibling disapproval of my father marrying the girl of his choice. My father had one brother and three sisters. There had been a fourth sister, Doris, but she like my paternal grandmother had died before I was born and I never knew them. In addition to Aunt Ethel, who lived with and looked after Grandad Rhodes, there was an elder sister, Lil, an older brother, Harry, and a younger sister, Effie. Uncle Harry, who lived in a large detached house at Ashby, some eight miles away, had a general grocery store at one of the Butterwicks as well as a small corn and meal delivery business. His wife, Aunt Ada, was a forbidding, strait-laced Edwardian lady, who acted the *grande dame*, bristling with disapproval and looking down on other sections of the family. They had one son, young Harry, who was some four or five years my senior and whom I rarely met and with whom I had little in common. Uncle Harry by himself would visit Grandad Rhodes and Aunt Ethel on a Sunday morning about twice a month and would call briefly on us at about half past twelve. He never stayed for Sunday dinner, as his lunch would be on the table in Ashby at 1.30pm precisely. At Christmas he would bring a 'stag' (a large rooster) he had reared at Butterwick. It would still have all its feathers and I would look with interest at its blood-red comb, its still bright beady eyes and its sharp, spurred feet twined together with string. It was hung in the pantry for a day or two by its feet, before my mother with some help from my father would begin the difficult job of plucking and disembowelling the large creature. This provided our usual Christmas dinner and in return Uncle Harry always received a bottle of sherry or port as his reciprocal gift. Some years later during rationing he was the welcome supplier of an occasional extra bag of sugar for Mother and a packet of sweets for David and me.

We had even less to do with the Stokes and the Goys. Aunt Lil had married a man called Stokes who worked in the steelworks and they lived in Scunthorpe. I went with my father on the odd occasion when he had Lindsey Blind business in Scunthorpe, but my mother never came with us. There was a Cyril Stokes who was four years ahead of me at Brigg Grammar School. Unlike me, he was an expert cross-country runner, but he belonged to despised Sheffield House and our paths rarely crossed at school. To the best of my knowledge I never visited the Goy family in Broughton where they lived and, except at my father's funeral, I don't think they visited us in Central Square. When I did see Aunt Effie and her daughter, Josephine, two years younger than myself, it was at no. 49 Grammar School Road. She was a rather unsettling lady with a distant look in her eye and some history of minor mental instability, but she did have a curious effect later on my life when I was at Brigg Grammar School. She was responsible for the nickname by which I was universally known in my last four or five years at the school.

◆◆◆

On Christmas morning I found my presents in a pillowcase at the bottom of my bed. This contained games, such as Ludo, Snakes and Ladders or Tiddlywinks, perhaps a mechanical toy – I remember a drumming monkey was a favourite – and some further farm animals, because Grandad Rhodes one year made a fine farmstead for me. There were always one or two annuals, such as *Chicks' Own*, the *Rainbow* and *Tiger Tim* when I was younger then *The Beano* and *The Dandy* later on. Inevitably there were some items of clothing – socks, gloves and a pullover, all hand-knitted – tins of toffees and other confectionery and several handfuls of monkey nuts in their shells. There was a strong element of predictability about the presents pre-war and a dearth of exciting novelties during it. The most memorable present came in 1938 and was a big Meccano set from my parents in a wooden box, specially made by Grandad Rhodes. I spent many happy hours with this and treasure the Sunday evenings spent with my father constructing a large model windmill whose sails were turned swiftly by a clockwork motor that was part of the set. My mother had gone to Evensong with Lil Rands and David was (usually) sleeping soundly upstairs. I think the incidence of the Meccano set was no accident: it was to compensate for the recent birth of my brother, which had had a traumatic effect in destabilising my little world.

Family Christmases followed a safe and predictable pattern. On Christmas Day my mother's family always came for tea, after we had sometimes had Auntie Ethel and Grandad Rhodes to share Christmas dinner. This was a two-course feast with Hull Brewery's Pale Ale and lemonade to drink. The main dish was Uncle Harry's rooster accompanied by forcemeat balls, bread sauce, Turner's sausages and home-grown vegetables. This was followed by the largest of the Christmas puddings that had steamed out the kitchen for days in late November. The arrival of our guests for tea depended on whether they were going to listen to the King's broadcast on their own wireless at home or were going to be with us before three o'clock. Usually the Pecks arrived about half past two and the Marrises, Uncle Cyril and Aunt Doris pushing their daughter Joyce in her pram, walked over from Mill Lane by four o'clock. Everything stopped for the King's Christmas broadcast: the washing-up had to be completed in time and even the children paused in playing with their new toys.

Christmas Tea – the capital 'T' is well deserved – was late, eaten about 6.30pm because we were still stuffed with the Christmas dinner and time was needed for it 'to go down'. The Tea was another feast over which Mother had laboured long. There was ham and tongue salad with any remnants of the rooster and plates of unnecessary bread and butter, one white and one brown. There were sausage sandwiches. There was a large home-made Christmas cake with a tired-looking robin attached by a wobbly spring (more and more precariously as the years went by) to a log stuck firmly into the icing. No self- respecting housewife would dream of offering a *bought* cake in the thirties, though it was permitted to have it iced and decorated by a more skilled neighbour. There were fairy cakes, coconut macaroons, lemon curd tarts, a chocolate log and iced buns. But the most eagerly anticipated item was the trifle, over which Mother lavished particular care and attention – sponge bricks at the bottom, generously dowsed with sherry, tins of several different types of fruit with some juice (but not too much, for it mustn't be runny), covered in jelly and topped with custard over which whipped cream (oh, the efforts required to reach just the right consistency) and flaked almonds were spread. In Lincolnshire a woman's culinary reputation often depended upon her ability to make a superior trifle. Christmas was one of the few times I ate tinned peaches: if I had them at other times it was as a treat after being in hospital or recovering from measles or mumps.

After the women had done the washing-up, we played guessing games, dominoes or Ludo and the adults later played cards – rummy and whist. I was introduced to the mysteries of these adult games when I was about ten. It was not a bibulous evening, though there was lemonade for the children and we were allowed a small shandy before bedtime. Before the guests went at about half past nine, the men would have a (singular!) beer, a bottle of Hull Brewery's Pale Ale, and the ladies would have a sherry or a port and lemon. Pre-war whisky, liqueurs and brandy were unheard of at no. 29 Central Square and it was 1950 before we had a bottle of wine in the house. No-one drank stout or Guinness – it was deemed suitable only for hardened drinkers and Irish navvies.

On Boxing Day it was the tradition that the Rhodes family visited the Randses at no. 31. Here, in addition to another Yuletide Feast, we would watch lantern slides and examine books of photographs, for Uncle Alf was a gifted photographer. He took the weekly magazine *Amateur Photographer* and had submitted entries for competitions that had won minor prizes and been exhibited in Lincoln. (It was in this magazine that I first saw naked ladies, all tastefully posed, of course!) There would be embarrassed shrieks from our mothers as the page turned to ancient snaps of their holiday in the Isle of Man and revealed them resplendent in cloche hats and flapper dresses of the twenties. John Rands and I would compete at Tiddlywinks or try to do one of the jigsaws he had received for Christmas, while the adults chatted and later played cards. We were later to join in, but it was only in the mid-forties that we were allowed to gamble pennies and halfpennies at Newmarket, while Mother and Aunt Lil became more animated as a result of their two port and lemons. The evening was memorable because it provided my one 'sleepover', as it would be called nowadays – and for breakfast Aunt Lil made the best fried bread I ever tasted.

Somehow in January return fixtures had to be dutifully fulfilled. There was a Sunday afternoon down Mill Lane with Uncle Cyril and Aunt Doris, which meant a long walk both ways. This was an occasion for their front room to be used, aired and heated, for they spent almost the whole of their time in the living kitchen. There was also a Sunday afternoon visit for special high tea at Riverside, when their other room had its annual airing and outing. This room fascinated me as it was stuffed with horsehair furniture, some in dark leather with many studs, and a bulky, uncomfortable sofa in uncut moquette. There were antimacassars on the chairs and the sofa, giving off a strong aroma of mothballs, and there was an aspidistra. The turn-of-the-century atmosphere was completed by chenille coverings on the small side table and behind the door. To me the biggest attraction was an old, jangly, upright piano with yellowing keys on which I was occasionally allowed to make discordant sounds. 'Auntie' Elsie could play the piano moderately well and there would be a short singsong just before we went. Dad would sing excerpts from *Merrie England* – '*Where are the bow men, the bow men of England?*' – and I would join in the choruses and in 'One Man Went to Mow' and 'Ten Green Bottles'. However, my party piece in the mid-thirties was 'Old MacDonald Had a Farm'. Then there was, of course, a return visit from the Randses and a reciprocal sleepover for John Rands. As it was by now term time, this visit tended to be on a Saturday, if up to about 1941 it hadn't been fixed for New Year's Eve.

New Year was never wildly celebrated by my parents and their friends and from the mid-forties both Uncle Alf and Dad were much involved in one of the high spots of the Brigg social calendar, the Annual New Year's Eve Dance of the Brigg Bowling Club, held in the Angel ballroom, so there was then even less family celebration. From 1946 John Rands and I attended the dance and our mothers were left to see the New Year in together, with one or possibly two port and lemons.

We did celebrate Guy Fawkes Night on November 5th in our garden before the war, often with the Randses. We gathered up all the garden rubbish with any broken off branches I could discover in scouring the area and any derelict furniture I could scrounge from the neighbours. Usually we managed to amass a considerable amount of combustible material, even if much dirty grey and black choking smoke was generated. There was a selection of fireworks that I had helped to choose, agonising over the respective merits of one big rocket or three mortar bombs. We never had a grand display, for there was not the money. The few rockets were stuck in milk bottles and ignited at intervals. They were accompanied by awed and excited '*oohs*' and '*aahs*' as they arched brilliantly over the back gardens of Central Square. Catherine wheels were nailed to a clothes post and we gasped as they whirred and whirled around. Jumping jacks caused moments of shock and mayhem, but my favourites were the Roman candles that gulped and plopped as they sent balls of fire into the air. The cone-shaped firework called 'Volcano', which had cost the most, proved to be the most disappointing. As a six-year-old, I can remember the initial apprehension and then the smiles of satisfaction as I waved my lit sparkler around in wildly gyrating patterns. It didn't finish with Guy Fawkes Night, for over the next two days we searched for all the carcasses of spent fireworks we could find.

Guy Fawkes Night calls to mind the dimly remembered 'Nita', a dog we had for just over a year and both the first and the last. She was a liver and white spaniel and on the evening of November 5th was taken down to stay with Grandad Rhodes in Grammar School Road, where there was less risk of being frightened by zooming rockets and coruscating Catherine wheels. This is the only clear memory I have of Nita – where did she acquire that name?

I should have been about five years old at the time, too young to take her for walks by myself. We weren't a 'cat' family either. The only pets I had later were a few rabbits and these were successively and individually reared to sell at Stennet's Auction Mart during the war years.

The White Horse paddock was the main venue for the two annual town events that are fixed firmly in the mind: 'Status' and Brigg Fair. Status with its short 'a' was probably a corruption of Statute or the legal document granting permission for a fair to be held over three days in May. The amusements were set up in the White Horse paddock between the Grand Cinema and the bowling green. I seem to remember *Franklin's Amusements* plastered on the sides of ancient lorries which seemed to be immortal, duly arriving year after year. One of the major rides was powered by a steamroller, belted and belching fumes, but most even in the thirties were electric-powered and yards of cable would snake from some point in the cinema or the White Horse. It was a time we had eagerly anticipated and even as seven-year-olds we were able to go to the Status by ourselves with sixpence to spend on the Saturday afternoon. On the Saturday night I went with my parents and was allowed to go on rides for a whole half-crown's worth (around 13p in modern currency) and Dad would always win a coconut for me.

I enjoyed going on the slot machines, especially the halfpenny ones where you got five large ball bearings about half an inch in diameter for your halfpenny. These you sent, one at a time, hurtling around an upright, circular track by pressing a spring-loaded lever before they ended up in a series of semi-circular cups, above which was inscribed either 'WIN' (green) or 'LOSE' (red). If it rolled into the 'WIN' cup you got your halfpenny back and a free go, so theoretically you could gain an unending stream of halfpennies from an initial stake of one halfpenny. However, we were convinced that magnets were located behind the 'LOSE' cups, because our ball bearings all too regularly disappeared into those receptacles and were swallowed up in the maw of the machine. We did occasionally get one into the 'WIN' cup and we could spin out our time on the machine to a pleasurable ten minutes. The other machine I liked cost a penny and was a form of roulette. You placed your penny stake in a red, green, black, yellow or white hole at the top of the machine. Red and Black paid out two old pennies; Green five, Yellow ten and White a fortune of twenty pennies – nearly a florin! Some adults put pennies in each of the coloured holes – and usually got two pennies back for their fivepence investment. I simply restricted myself to gambling one penny at a time. I had a system of backing Green after two consecutive Blacks, but it wasn't infallible. You pulled the lever vigorously or lightly as instinct told you and the coloured disc rotated furiously until it came to an abrupt halt – and then seemed to jerk back one space if it had landed on a winning colour. These machines certainly had minds of their own. You gazed at the top coloured square on the disc's circumference to which a red arrow pointed. If you had ventured your penny on Black and the arrow pointed to that colour, two pennies dropped down into a large cup below. They were simple but compelling joys compared with the all-singing, all-flashing cabinets of today.

Up to the age of seven I had to be content with the children's rides – in cars or buses on a hand-driven roundabout or in a 'chuggy' boat, which was one of four in a series of gondolas on a small frame that you propelled by pulling on tasselled cords and which then swung in a gentle arc. However, after seven I graduated, at first with my father behind, to the motorcycles on the adult roundabout, which circled at a rapid, undulating speed. This was thrilling stuff and its appeal lasted the next dozen years. In my teens I would nonchalantly lie back, holding on with one hand as the motorcycle reached its climactic speed, careering round to blaring music before the power cut out and we glided slower and slower to a halt. Occasionally an older, steam-powered roundabout with Golden Gallopers appeared. The gilded steeds were attached to twisted, sugarcane poles and the motion was up and down as well as forward – pure magic. Roundabouts I adored, swing boats I detested, having had a very frightening experience on my first and only excursion onto the adult swing boats. I went on with a friend and made the mistake of sitting facing the grey, pebble-dashed wall of the Grand Cinema. We mounted the high steps into the boat, the steps were removed and we were pushed off. We pulled vigorously on the ropes and the boat went faster and faster, higher and higher on its pendulum course. The swing boats were sited very close to the vast bulk of the cinema wall and at first as we got the boat going I didn't look up. When I did, it seemed to me that our boat was about to crash spectacularly into the wall and splinter with appalling loss of life. My stomach was already queasy with the unaccustomed motion and now I was terrified, notwithstanding the fact that my companion with his back to the wall would be the first to be dashed to pieces. I shut my eyes, but couldn't maintain them closed. Fear made me open them and look ashen-faced at the rapidly approaching wall. I had stopped pulling, but my friend pulled with redoubled vigour and we seemed to go faster and higher until the danger of going full circle (and dropping out of the boat) was added to fear of the impending crash and a wildly gyrating stomach. I was vastly relieved when I had my feet firmly on the paddock floor and had no broken limbs. I never again ventured on the swing boats, or the flying boats as they were otherwise well called. Nevertheless my memories of the Status are enjoyable and noteworthy for the fact that I was given an extra sixpence to spend by my maternal grandparents.

The White Horse paddock was the main site of the annual Brigg Fair that Delius had made internationally famous. At that time I had never heard of Frederick Delius, a most un-Lincolnshirelike name, which I should have immediately scorned had I known it. In the thirties Brigg Horse Fair was still a major event, attracting most local farmers and others from counties as far away as North Yorkshire and Norfolk. There were also many horse stockmen who brought up herds of ponies from the New Forest and elsewhere. But the most exotic characters were the Romanies and the gypsy horse dealers: they were lumped together and universally referred to as 'gyppoes', never 'travellers'. They came from all parts of the country and arrived over the preceding two weeks in gaily painted caravans drawn by one or two horses and usually trailing another three or four behind. In addition to the caravans there were light, two-wheeled carts that were drawn by the sprightliest steeds and these on the August Thursday of Brigg Fair would be forever dashing up and down Wrawby Street at alarming speeds with the driver, often standing up, cracking a whip and uttering piercing cries of encouragement to the horse as it showed off its paces. The gypsies took over Wrawby Street and their horses lined both sides of the road from near the police station to past Grammar School Road. Here was a scene far removed from the normal daily round and I would gaze fascinated by the galloping gypsy carts with the driver flashing his whip, as the pony raced up to the Monument and back. The gypsy, invariably brown with black hair (curly or ringletted), could have come out of the pages of my pirate book, except for his dress. He wore a brightly coloured neckerchief above his open-necked shirt over a tweed jacket, a fancy 'weskit' and often moleskin trousers. But many wore earrings and this made them even more piratical and intoxicating to my stimulated imagination.

However, the most exciting place was where the herds of horses congregated. This was in Cross Street and sometimes they spread into Garden Street. Drovers with scraps of red cloth attached to long sticks cut from hedges would wave these as they tried to control the herds of ponies that were forever circling, breaking and reforming when the drovers dashed into the *mêlée* to select some animal that a prospective buyer wanted to examine in more detail. That pony would then be taken into Bigby Street or the station approaches to trot its stuff. Again from the age of seven I was able to wander at will with my school friends amid this noisy, heaving and crowded scene. It was a thrilling experience to pass up Cross Street and walk closely by the milling herds, always wary of a sudden, skittering surge, which would send us scuttling to take shelter in a shop doorway or behind one of the trees lining the street.

It was a more sedate scene in the paddock itself, to which the massive shire horses of the farmers were largely confined. In addition to the horses there were several hundred sheep in pens, for at Brigg Fair both animals were in plentiful supply as well as carts, harness and other tack. I enjoyed passing up the aisles of closely packed sheep pens. Each pen contained up to seven sheep of all varieties. There were white-faced Leicesters, narrow-faced crossbreeds with distinguishing blobs of colour on their fleeces and most curious of all the mule sheep. As you would expect, there were many Lincoln Longwools and I loved to plunge my hands sensuously into their fleeces, grasping and pulling gently, before withdrawing them redolent with lanolin. The horses were lined up by the cinema wall and often tethered to a horsebox. They were of all colours, some dappled Pecherons, many straight-legged Suffolk Punches and more beribboned shires, with huge, feathery feet and polished, newly nailed hooves. At the bidding of putative buyers they would be paraded up and down and made to trot. Their fetlocks were examined, their mouths probed and their teeth counted. Bargaining was brisk and deals were struck by a handclasp after much spit had been expectorated on them. The auctioneer was the Davy part of Hett, Davy and Stubbs. He was a burly figure with a large and heavily jowled face and wore an ancient tweed suit and a battered hat that defied all description – not a trilby, not a pork-pie and not a derby, but a bit of all three. He auctioned all the sheep and those horses that hadn't been sold privately. He had a mesmerising, singsong patter that I much admired and at the end came a loud rap on the pen and the mention of the farmer who had made the successful bid, for he knew them all.

A kaleidoscope of milling, noisy animals, spattered with dust and mud spoiling their erstwhile pristine condition, the splattering sounds of defecating and urinating animals and the smells of perspiring, closely packed humans and bewildered, frightened animals are my abiding memory of Brigg Fair. I would arrive early after a hurriedly consumed breakfast and watch the late arrivals penned after being decanted from vehicles of all shapes and sizes, because on Fair day there would be no available transport within three counties. After this I would hasten to Cross Street about ten o'clock for the arrival of the last herds and relish being immersed in this whirling, swirling mass. Then I would wander through the gypsy enclave, gawping at the extraordinary sights and individuals therein, before going to the paddock where the sheep were being auctioned. Lunch was forgotten and foregone and in the afternoon I would watch the late bargains and the loading up of the animals as they were transported to the farms of their new owners or the holding fields of the mutton butchers. I sometimes added my shrill cries to those of the khaki-smocked loaders, as they whistled and waved their arms in coercing the sheep towards the desired truck. I always felt sorry for the few forlorn nags with drooping heads that hadn't found a buyer. They hung on till late afternoon and then were spirited away to what must have been an uncertain fate.

One year, probably 1938, I was given unexpected responsibility and earned my first payment from a stranger. After the auctioning was over, a farmer looked around and his eye (for want of a better prospect) fell on me. *'Here, lad, do you want to earn a tanner?'* I expressed my readiness, expecting to go to a shop for some item he needed, since he was holding a rope halter attached to which was a large shire horse. *'Just look after him for a bit – you can give him an apple.'* Before I knew what was happening, he had gone and I was holding two small apples in one hand and a rope in the other, while gazing apprehensively at my new charge. Memory may exaggerate in fixing him as an enormous shire, black and glistening with a white blaze in the middle of his forehead and four fine, feathery feet. But it was definitely a large equine quadruped and I was to look after him. I took my responsibilities seriously, although in some trepidation, despite my experience of Grandad Peck's stable. I walked him over to the nearest empty sheep pen, climbed up and perched my posterior on the top rail. The horse (whose name I never knew) was placid enough and grinding something in his teeth. As he chewed, his large, yellowing teeth were visible, as was his pink, moist tongue that appeared periodically between his soft, pouting lips. My imagination conjured up one of Uncle Alf's best photographs, entitled 'Three Hours to Load', which showed three men trying to haul a mighty shire into the back of a horse van. The horse was reluctant and had reared up on its two hind feet and two of the men were hanging on to the tether with great difficulty. The battle of wills had gone on for three hours at a previous Brigg Fair. However, my charge showed no sign of such independence and defiance. I held the rope loosely, he chewed amiably and methodically and I chatted to him in a soothing voice. After some time I palmed one of the apples and slipped off the fence to offer it to him. He nuzzled my hand, snuffling at the apple, and then closed his velvety mouth over the fruit and blew gently. I resumed my perch and ate the other apple, while he masticated noisily and saliva in long strings of spume dribbled from the sides of his mouth. The afternoon passed and the horse and I stared at each other, as I chattered aimlessly. At last the farmer reappeared – with a pronounced list to starboard and slurred speech, since he had spent a very happy hour in the Queen's Arms, which like all the other hostelries in the town was open all day and whose cellar stocks were being seriously depleted. I was duly offered my sixpence and took it gratefully, before parting with a penny of it to buy some chips at Morris's. It must have been five o'clock before I returned home after an exhausting but lucrative and enjoyable day.

Brigg Fair was a colourful, tumultuous episode in the town's somewhat humdrum calendar. Yet even in the thirties it was only a pale imitation of its earlier Victorian/Edwardian heyday, when labourers were hired as well as animals sold and Jack Taylor gave his rendering of an old folk song to Frederick Delius.

Christmas jigsaw: myself and John Rands, 1938

6
CULTURE, COMICS AND BOOKS

It seems most strange to me now how devoid of books my early childhood was and how few books were owned by my parents. We certainly had no need of any bookcases and even by 1945 there were probably fewer than thirty books in the house and most of them belonged to me. My mother did not have any cookery books and little time for novels when I was young. My father had a fat volume entitled *Mr Middleton's Book of Gardening*, but it was not until the mid-forties that to this was added a biography of Lord Wavell and his selection of *Other Men's Flowers* (both gifts from a High School teacher for services rendered – lifts to Louth). We had two prayer books and a copy of the Holy Bible, though not the Family Bible: this was an enormous tome with garish coloured plates kept at Riverside. There was also a small, leatherette-bound dictionary, a Pocket Gem, that was kept in the sideboard drawer with the rent book and the Friendly Society deposit book and which I consulted in the mid-forties when doing my English homework. We could hardly be called a bookish family.

My mother took a weekly woman's magazine called *Woman's Pictorial* (long since defunct) and for a time we subscribed either by weekly or monthly instalments to some sort of encyclopaedia published by Harmsworth Press, but we never completed the set. During the war we took *Picture Post* and *The War Illustrated*, which again was paperbacked and in instalments. I had my comics. I graduated one at a time from *Tiny Tots, Chicks' Own, Tiger Tim* and the *Rainbow* to *The Beano* and later to *Adventure* and *Hotspur*. The latter three I regularly swopped – John Rands's *Dandy* for my *Beano*, and Derek Smith's *Champion* and *Wizard* for my *Adventure* and *Hotspur*. The comicbook stories were my weekly imaginative fare for years. I wanted to eat cow pies like Desperate Dan and be pals with Lord Snooty. I was amused by the antics of 'Big Ego', the ostrich, and wondered how he always seemed to retain all his tail feathers. Later I flew with Rockfist Rogan and was awed by the feats of Wilson. I could never hope to emulate the scoring achievements of Roy of the Rovers, nor the record-breaking of the ubiquitous Alf Tupper, always triumphing over mountainous obstacles, but I followed their successes avidly.

My father would read about Tiger Tim's adventures to me in bed on a Sunday morning when I was very young. I must also have had another book, because a favourite story was about a cow called Clara. It began: *'Clank! Clank! Clara could hear the milkmaid coming.'* This was such a favourite that I knew it by heart and would quickly correct Dad if he substituted a word or erred from the original text.

I suppose that the accumulator-driven wireless was my principal source of culture. The first one I can remember had no name, but was a squat, rectangular metal box containing valves and the 'works', and from it issued some wires that were connected to the accumulators that had to stand on the back window ledge and another wire that went through the window frame, up the side of the house to the roof aerial. But in the late thirties we bought a spanking new Cossor that was encased in wood and contained within it the rechargeable accumulator. It also had an in-built speaker from which the sound was much more penetrating and audible. Before we had had to strain to catch the words. Now we could sit at ease in the armchairs and hear everything. Only when the accumulator was running out of juice did we have to gather round the instrument and put our ear to the speaker. *Children's Hour* received my rapt attention. I replied *'Good night, Uncle Mac'* when he wished *'Good night, children, everywhere!'* and I listened avidly to stories told by Auntie Vi (Violet Carson in her pre-*Coronation Street* days). But I can't remember ever being exposed on wireless or by book to the magical worlds of Winnie the Pooh, Alice or Beatrix Potter when I was young. I do, however, remember eagerly looking forward on the wireless to SG Hulme Beaman's stories, featuring Larry the Lamb, Dennis the Dachshund (not a favourite post-1939), Ernest the policeman and the irascible Mr Growser. I could do passable imitations of the nervously bleating Larry and something approximating to Mr Growser's *'It's disgraceful!'* Surely he was the prototype for Victor Meldrew.

I was able to read haltingly from infant school days and had a good fluency by seven, so it seems incredible now that I was ten before I was introduced to the County Library. It happened by accident. One Saturday I was with Jack White, whose father owned JW White's 'pop' factory down Elwes Street and who lived in a large, detached house on Wrawby Road. Jack and I were to be form-mates through Brigg Grammar School and contemporaries, reading English, at Oxford. We found ourselves in town and he had to return a library book. *'Coming?'* he said and I followed him to the upper room in the Town Hall building which housed Brigg's County Library collection at that time. I entered a high-ceilinged room with apparently rows and rows of books stacked along the walls and on large, freestanding bookcases. It was all rather gloomy and dimly lit with low-watt electric lights. I had never seen so many books together in my life before. I must have been asked by a librarian if I wanted to join and in a bemused state I was enrolled as a temporary member. My name was written on a small square library ticket in a scratchy pen that had a relief nib and had to be dipped into an ink bottle and the excess shaken off. I was directed to the children's shelves and gazed at hundreds of titles, all arranged in alphabetical order. The books were certainly nothing like present-day children's literature. There were no brightly coloured drawings, varied fonts or technicoloured covers. In the thirties books had to last. Instant eye appeal meant nothing; longevity was everything. Even the books deemed suitable for ten-year-olds were all in a standard library format. The outsides were of stout cardboard covered with hard-wearing, damson grosgrain, which wouldn't show dirty finger marks and early wear. For extra longevity their spines were further protected by a heavy backing material like black Elastoplast. Many parents forbade their children access to the County Library, because you didn't know where the books had been, nor what germs and unmentionable dangers might lurk within the pages.

I opened several volumes, but finally selected the one with the most pages. I can recall the book clearly now. It was entitled *The Rajah's Ruby*, though I have long forgotten the name of the author, if I ever knew it. The book had a coloured frontispiece like a poor reproduction of a late Victorian painting extolling Empire. It showed an eminent person sitting on a throne and wearing a turban to which was attached a dazzling ruby as big as a pigeon's egg. This imposing personage was surrounded by fawning natives, some wafting cooling plumes above his head. Centre stage was a boy about my age in an open-neck white shirt, short grey trousers and sandals, gazing defiantly at the fat Rajah. I was back for another book the following Saturday, when I became a fully enrolled member. And so began my long love affair with the County Library service. *The Rajah's Ruby* was the first of more than a hundred thousand books issued to me over the years. I even persuaded my mother to join. However, her staple diet remained Mills and Boon-like romances to the end. What Zane Grey was to Grandad Rhodes, Ethel M Dell and Ruby Ayres were to my mother. I must have carried home in total hundredweights of books in which the 'nice' nurse overcame her scheming rival and won the hand of the debonair doctor, who for two hundred pages or more had been completely unaware of her charms.

From this time of joining the library I embarked upon a lifelong voyage of discovery in the wonderful world of books. I would read anything that came to hand – even sugar paper, if my mother is to be believed. It is possible that all this new reading affected my vision. In a random check-up at the school clinic (a forbidding Victorian house in Bigby Road where the dreaded school dentist lurked), I was discovered to have a 'lazy' eye. I am never sure what exactly that means, but it was determined that I should wear glasses. I was disquieted, but only by the fact that I should soon be serenaded by catcalls of 'Old Four-eyes'. This was in pre-National Health days and there was a war on: thus, though there were financial constraints, there was little choice of frames anyway. I was equipped with my first pair of cheap, metal-framed spectacles that had springy end-pieces which curled round my ears in a semicircle. I didn't think they did much for my manly appearance. Nor was I aware of improved vision, but I have now worn glasses for more than sixty-five years. At first I stoically put up with the catcalls, but 'Four-eyes' as a nickname never stuck. I wore these first glasses for most of my secondary education, but then the war ended and the National 'Elf offered a brave new future. In the Sixth Form I went to consult a new phenomenon. Charles V Irvine, with impressive but meaningless letters after his name – as impressive as that mysterious and never-divulged 'V' for his second Christian name – opened an optician's shop in Wrawby Street. Unlike the school clinic this had new, upholstered chairs and a formidable array of new eye-testing apparatus. You were taken to a darkened room in which there were illuminated letter-charts and rotating symbols not only in black but also in red and green. My utility metal frames were replaced by more dignified tortoiseshell ones which I fancied gave me a more intellectual appearance. However, they soon posed a problem. I played in goal and was often involved in goalmouth *mêlées* at people's feet. The tortoiseshell spectacles were ill-adapted for such mayhem. A solution was forthcoming: my father still had his 'gas-glasses'. These were a pair of sturdy, close-fitting, steel-framed spectacles designed to be worn under his wartime gas mask if there were a gas attack when he was on Special Constabulary duty. They had never been used in anger and came in very handy. Charles V Irvine changed the lens to my specification and I proudly wore those spectacles for the next fifteen years in keeping goal at football and later hockey. They were to achieve fame in the fifties when a national photographer snapped me diving at someone's feet in soccer trials at Oxford: these frames, with me attached, duly appeared in the sports pages of *The Times*.

7
CHURCH, CUBS AND THE CINEMA

The incidence of set events in the annual cycle of Brigg happenings in my young life was matched by equally fixed events in the weekly cycle. Cubs was on Wednesday evening, church choir practices on Tuesday and Friday, church and Sunday School on Sunday, both morning and night, and the cinema on Saturday afternoon. It was a busy programme, but it left Monday and Thursday evenings free.

Miss Kath Waters, the daughter of the butchering family in Wrawby Street, opposite Staples' fish and chips, was our Arkhela (Cub leader) and our Pack room was in semi-condemned buildings behind the Congregational Chapel (Coney Court?). Here we dibbed-dibbed and chanted the approved doggerel. We promised to serve our Country, God and the King with our fingers clamped to the side of our heads in a two-fingered salute. We learned to recognise flags and discovered the components of the Union Jack, featuring crosses of St George and St Andrew. At eight I was able to tie sheepshanks and roving bowlines and knew that the flat reef knot was best for tying bandages. We played team games and there was keen competition among the various 'sixes'. We made occasional excursions to Wrawby sandpits, where we strenuously strove in 'British Bulldog', which meant securing your opponents' flag from one end of the quarry and returning safely with it to your own base, while at the same time endeavouring to keep your flag protected. It was all rough, knockabout stuff, but it did also call for fox-like cunning, diversionary measures and elementary tactics.

I was inordinately proud of my green, yellow-braided cap with two metal stars affixed, my green jumper, smart sand shoes (specially whitened by my mother each Wednesday) and the green tabs protruding from my stocking tops on an elastic garter. My green jumper eventually became festooned with various embroidered badges, carefully sewn on by Mother. I was even prouder when at the age of nine-plus I became a 'Sixer' with two yellow tapes encircling my upper arm. I took my responsibilities as Sixer seriously, but I cannot recall the names of any of the younger boys in my six. I don't think we went on church parades, nor did we ever go camping for a weekend. But we did go to Cleethorpes as an annual treat. We went on the train in full Cub uniform and Kath supplied wonderful ham sandwiches courtesy of her father. Memory fantasises that the sun always shone on these days, that the sea was blue and warm in July (even in the Humber estuary), that the Shetland ponies ran like Derby winners, that the Big Dipper in

Wonderland was at least ten times its diminutive size, and that I kept my eyes open all the time, shouting in delight as I rode the Ghost Train. Instead, I dreaded the apparitions that appeared from nowhere and screamed as a giant spider's web covered me, while I shuddered and kept my eyes firmly closed. Cubs was enjoyable, but I finished with it in my tenth summer. I never became a Scout, because I couldn't do homework insisted on at the Grammar School and all my other activities.

From an early age I went to church and have continued to attend regularly for almost seventy years. We were C of E and attended the Parish Church, St John's. It was with some suspicion that we regarded those who went to the Catholic Church in Bigby Street, the 'Cons' (Congregationalists) in Wrawby Street and the Primitive Methodists (the 'Prims') over the bridge. My mother was the first regular attender and had become so while she was expecting me. She went along with her friend, Lil Rands, and for nearly fifty years they sat in the same pew, just in front of the pillar by the back crossing to the right of the central aisle. Min and Lil would sit there in their best coats and various hats, noting the attire of the other female members of the congregation and slipping peppermints to one another at the start of the sermon. My father became a regular some years later, being in the choir, serving on the PCC and becoming churchwarden over the next thirty years. Uncle Alf never became a regular worshipper, though he was there occasionally when Brigg Prize Silver Band was present for some special service. Band practice was on a Sunday morning.

John Rands and I started at Sunday School, which was held in what had been a classroom in the old church school, which stood at the junction of Bigby Street and Princes Street. The building was later modernised and became the Public Library after it moved from its cramped premises in the Town Hall building. Sunday School was taken by Mrs Burgess, the wife of the vicar, who in her own right was an excellent raconteur in a strong Lincolnshire accent with its heavy use of diphthongs for simple vowels. She gave talks on dialect to Mothers' Unions and other groups all over North Lincolnshire. She was a large lady still addicted to the dress of the previous reign of Edward VII and the large and imposing hats of that era. She was rather stiff and unmaternal, but with a rigid sense of duty and she stood no nonsense. We received instruction in the church's tenets and festivals with strong emphasis on doing our best and the importance of obedience and respecting the establishment. The story of a child playing on the railway lines against orders still sticks in my mind. The errant child saved his life, when an express train came along, because he obeyed implicitly his mother's instructions to lie still between the lines. I'm afraid my imagination filled itself with vivid pictures of what might have happened if he had moved, but I suppose that really reinforced the point of the story. We also received a stamp each week, which I carefully stuck in the album when I returned home. The album was kept in the top left-hand drawer of the sideboard along with the rent book. These stamps invariably showed pictures of Our Lord in a white robe. He had long, dark hair, He was clean-shaven and had unmistakably Caucasian features. The stamps showed him performing miracles or they indicated some other event in his ministry in a sanitised Holy Land. Sometimes a series of stamps was based on the Old Testament. These were much more interesting, because they showed David cutting off Goliath's head, Joshua trumpeting his way around the walls of Jericho or even Adam and Eve in the Garden of Eden, coyly demure in the presence of the serpent and more than adequately screened by the lush foliage.

I think Mrs Burgess may have had some helpers, probably in the guise of older girls, but I cannot recall them. Mrs B was definitely in charge of the proceedings. She played the piano, as we learned to sing 'All Things Bright and Beautiful' or Mrs CF Alexander's 'There is a Green Hill Faraway'. We learnt to pray in a proper posture – no slouching or peeping. We occasionally cut out sheep and a donkey in coloured gummed paper to stick on a Nativity frieze or crosses if Good Friday was approaching. After some three-quarters of an hour we were crocodiled down Bigby Street to take part in the later stages of Matins – after the sermon was done. When I became a chorister, I would leave Sunday School early in order to get down to church for the beginning of Matins. This lasted for about a year and then I put away childish Sunday School and went directly to church. However, one amusing episode involved both choir and Sunday School. Just before Christmas at Sunday School volunteers were requested to sing a verse of their favourite carol. We had recently learned Christina Rossetti's fine carol (English Hymnal no. 25) and I volunteered. I suppose I also wanted to show off. All bright, alert and shining with pride I rendered *'In the blinking winter'* in a confident treble voice. I had misheard the words and adults were always complaining in the ice, fog and snow about the *'blinking winter'*!

St John's church choir played a prominent part in my young life. Choir practices were held in the now disappeared Church House, a double-fronted Victorian villa (that had once been a pub with family connections, as I found out much later) on the site of the present Church Hall. The boys met for three-quarters of an hour on Tuesday evenings and on Fridays there was a boys' practice for half an hour before the men joined in at 7.30pm for a further hour. I was a probationer for six months: this meant I could not wear a white surplice but only a black cassock and I couldn't process in with the full choir. Probationers had to slip into the choir stalls or onto the extra chairs through the side door of the vestry just before the service began. It was a very proud day when I was deemed fit to receive my surplice from Canon Burgess and become a fully-fledged chorister. The surplice had been specially washed, starched and ironed by my mother and she was to have many more years of doing this. On the Sunday before Christmas, Easter and Harvest Festival, Dad and I would take our surplices home and they were duly given Mother's full treatment. Then as the choir processed on the High Days and festivals in church, she would take quiet pride in the obvious fact that the two Rhodeses were more starchily white than any other member of the choir. Some years later, when I was supposedly a tenor, my younger brother was a leading boy chorister – and then there were three!

I was at first taken to and from Tuesday choir practice by an older choirboy, Hubert Dove, who lived nearby in East Parade – except on Fridays when I usually came home with my father, even though it sometimes meant waiting for another half hour while the men came to terms with a particularly difficult psalm. Church House was ruled over by Miss Grundy, a plump, elderly martinet, who had wispy white hair and who sprouted many facial whiskers that covered her chin and jutted from her various moles. She was the live-in caretaker and didn't like little boys. We were constantly adjured to wipe our feet and not to clump up the stairs, because the gas-lit room where we practised was on the first floor. It was really a meeting room, but it held a Victorian piano that was not always in tune, especially if we choirboys had been striking the keys forcefully in an attempt to make meaningful sounds in the hiatus before the choirmaster or mistress arrived. Miss Grundy would come stomping up the stairs to tell us to leave the piano alone and to stop chasing about. However, by the time I was ten, I could knock out, one-fingered, a recognisable version of the National Anthem.

We would practise the next Sunday's hymns and rehearse new hymns or anthems for three or four weeks before they were needed. I also learnt to read and understand the pointing of the psalms and the canticles. It seemed in those days we sang all the verses of the psalms, usually twenty-five or more. If we hit upon a shorter one, then we had to sing a second one with two full Glorias to make up. We sang *Venite, Te Deum* and *Benedictus* most weeks, but once a month substituted *Benedicite Omnia Opera* for *Te Deum*. We boys were visibly flagging by the time we came to *O Ananais, Azarias* and *Misael*. Through constant familiarity and repetition I came to enjoy the canticles and the psalms. My favourite was no. 114 to the haunting, ancient plainsong chant *Tonus Peregrinus*, supposedly the oldest known tune in the world. I was always mystified that *'Moab* [was] *my washpot'* and intrigued at the idea of The Lord *'going up with the sound of the trump'*, because to me a 'trump' was a fart!

In addition to the weekly Matins we sang the Holy Communion service on the first Sunday of the month – 'Eucharist' was not widely used in the thirties: it smacked too much of popery. And so I came to learn Merbecke and Stanford from large thin booklets with square black notes. Festivals called for extra-long practices as we learnt new carols, or *Hail Thee, Festival Day!* (two different versions for Easter and Whitsun), or *Christ, Our Passover, is sacrificed for us*. Later I was chosen to sing the occasional solo such as Psalm 23 to *Crimond* or a verse of a carol, but I never did manage the one I desired, *O for the Wings of a Dove!* However, one Harvest Festival I sang the treble solo in *Thou visitest the Earth and blessest it* – very difficult to get your tongue round that lot! – while my father sang the tenor solo: a very Rhodesian affair that gave my parents much satisfaction.

In the choir there were usually about twelve boys, though we did not manage a full muster every week. Our ages ranged from seven to fourteen and the two senior boys wore round their necks a red riband with a medallion attached. We did not listen to the sermons, but had various means of whiling away the time: we would count the number of words in the hymns or the day's psalm. There would then be a heated, whispered debate as to what was the correct answer, until a choirman would lean over from the choir stall behind and cuff our ears, if we continued to ignore his *'Shhh-Shhhs!'* We would also look up the Tables of Affinity in the back of the prayer book and write against the first prohibition (*A Man may not marry his Grandmother*) a heartfelt 'O Lord, incline my heart to keep this Thy law!' Or we would carry on furtive conversations behind the backs of our hands. We boys sat in the first choir stalls on either side of the chancel, which was open to the nave. Behind us there were about seven men, three tenors to the left and four basses to the right. In the far back row sat three middle-aged lady altos, uncassocked and unsurpliced but always wearing hats, which retained a fascination for us choirboys as they changed in many minor ways in shape and drab colours according to the season. Canon Burgess, then later Canon Chappell, held sway on the right-hand side and the lay reader, Horace West, on the left. In the very back stall by the organ was the verger, Ron Thompson, whose loud bass voice was usually a beat behind the rest of us: Ron never came to choir practices.

The conduct of the services rarely contained surprises, and the very familiarity of the Anglican liturgy was comforting. We stood, we sang, we sat, we prayed; the vicar droned on and the occasional visiting preacher failed to electrify us. Nevertheless, slowly a love for the Anglican ritual, the

English hymnal, the prayers of Thomas More and the sonorous cadences of King James's 1602 bible took hold and have left me with an abiding passion. But at the time I was not conscious of this.

I was conscious of the more than *petit mal* suffered by a choirboy two years my senior, next to whom I stood for a couple of years. Cyril would suddenly go deathly pale, his eyes would stare unseeingly and he would fall unconscious against me and so onto the pew or the floor. It became an all too familiar process, as two choirmen would come and pick him up to carry him to the vestry, while I would trail behind with his glasses and books. Sometimes his unconscious body would begin the convulsions as he was being carried to the vestry. Then there were undignified efforts to hold onto the threshing limbs, but usually he was laid out on an old cassock on the vestry floor before this stage. I would fetch a tumbler of water and stare as his feet drummed on the ground, his head and body twisted, unearthly moans were uttered and foam flecked his pale lips. One of the men would watch carefully and had fingers ready to ensure he didn't swallow his tongue. After three or four minutes it was all over. Cyril would open and focus his eyes, giving a loud, relieved sigh. He would be helped to a chair and I would offer the glass of water. On the first two occasions I found it frightening, but then it became accepted through familiarity and later new drugs better controlled the attacks, which became more intermittent. Subsequently I was at Grammar School with Cyril and he played a full part in House sporting activities: he could swim well and was particularly strong in the shot put. He was not ostracised or kept under wraps like the unfortunate Prince John in the 2003 television drama.

We were paid for our services as choirboys, at first half a crown a quarter for virtually full attendance at practices and both Matins and Evensong. But inflation took its toll even then and by the time I was head chorister we received seven shillings and sixpence a quarter. We also received a sixpenny bonus on Christmas Day and a further sixpence when we boys went to sing at the Harvest Festival at the nearby Cadney church. Cadney was a secluded hamlet that time seemed to have passed by. There were few houses, no pub and one general store but an ancient church and a vicarage, where lived a lay reader called Pinder, whom I remember chiefly because he had a beautiful blonde daughter named Ruth of about my age. That church had no choir, as there were precious few souls in the village and none of choirboy age. This annual trip was a treat we looked forward to. The neighbouring farmers had brought 'the choicest of their store' and the small church was overwhelmed by sheaves of corn and prize vegetable produce. We were always given an apple and a fresh farm egg as further recognition of our efforts. That apple was the rosiest and the egg was always the most golden yellow, most scrumptious-tasting of the year. We also had an annual boys' choir trip, which in pre-war days invariably took us to Cleethorpes, where I repeated the pattern set by the Cub outing.

◆◆◆

If Sundays were fully occupied with churchgoing – sometimes during the war three times a Sunday when to Matins and Evensong was added serving at 8am Communion on a rota basis – Saturdays were definitely secular. From the age of six I would go to the pictures for the 2pm matinee. In my parents' younger days they would watch flickering silent films with explanatory captions and a piano accompaniment in the old Parish Hall, situated in Elwes Street. This was a drab, corrugated iron building, heated by a couple of covered coke stoves, but the moving shadows on the screen inflamed the passions of the young Briggites and encouraged some daring explorations of an amatory nature. However, I was six and had the resplendent, specially built Grand Cinema in Wrawby Street facing up Cross Street. The Grand lived up to its name with the plushest of plush seats and red Turkey-patterned carpets in the foyer and up the stairs to the balcony. It had a large screen, retractable curtains and a loud sound system together with lights that went from dimmest to dim to full brilliance in about three minutes. When I first went the obligatory playing of the National Anthem at the end was accompanied by black and white footage of a bearded George V and the stately, dignified Queen Mary, waving wanly from a state coach or standing on the balcony of Buckingham Palace. Three years later we had coloured shots of a uniformed George VI with his smiling, floral-hatted Queen and their two young daughters.

The cinema doors would open at 1.30pm on a Saturday afternoon, but I had to be there at least twenty minutes before that. I would hurriedly eat my dinner, usually on a Saturday fish (tuppence each) and chips (one penny a bag) for which I had queued at Hewson's wooden shack in Glebe Road. I would quickly join my friends and we would scurry down to the cinema via Glebe Road and Grammar School Road, picking up other children on the way. We then flung ourselves into a milling mass on the steps outside the closed doors at the front of the cinema. At 1.30pm the proprietor appeared, a small, rotund Mr Webster, who was proud of his dapper appearance, complete with waxed moustache and tiny goatee beard. He also wore light grey spats and could have well been a minor character in one of the Hollywood romances he showed to the adults. He would slip the bolts and vainly try to control the onset of excited children, eager to pay their two pennies' entrance and secure a seat on the front row of the stalls. It was well called 'the tuppenny rush'! Once we had secured our seats, as close to the screen as possible, we would pass the time by yelling greetings to our friends or howling insults at rival groups of children from over the bridge. We would examine the bag of sweets we had brought from home and institute negotiations for swapping one bull's eye for three liquorice allsorts or two of Mrs Stephenson's home-made humbugs for a long string of 'spanish'. The lights would be 'up' during this period and there would be a resounding cheer when they began their long dimming and the curtains covering the screen would gracefully if noisily be withdrawn to reveal the traditional certificate from the censoring British Film Board of Control. Soon we would be thrilling to the exploits of Sexton Blake, who drove long black cars at speed after villains in equally long black cars – there is an extensive history of the car chase in the cinema. We tried to fathom out the identity of the Lone Ranger and eventually succeeded as all the other possibilities were eliminated in various ways over the forty-odd episodes. He and Tonto were the subject of many playtimes at school and I could *'Heigh-ho, Silver!'* with the best of them. Tom Mix and later the more effeminate Roy Rodgers ruled the ranges. They too helped to shape our play, especially when we had cheap silver guns that fired rolls of caps from Woolworths. The early Disney cartoons had us rolling in our seats with amusement and we sang Popeye's song in as gravelly a voice as our squeaking trebles permitted, though spinach never formed part of our diet. We enjoyed the short cartoon films or serial episodes, but the 'big' films are the ones to remain in the mind after sixty-odd years. I remember being visibly affected by certain early Henry Fonda films, one based on circus life and one involving the death of a young boy caught in a cattle stampede down the main street of Dodge City. (I impatiently dashed tears from my eyes and surreptitiously dried my cheeks on a grubby handkerchief before the lights came up.) We cheered on early Robin Hoods, beset by Basil Rathbone, whom we booed as the Sheriff of Nottingham or King John. We also encouraged Errol Flynn to greater deeds of derring-do, whether he was singeing the King of Spain's beard for Good Queen Bess (was that Flora Robson?) or swinging down from the yardarm with a cutlass between his teeth in some piratical adventure. Yet at the time our greatest pleasure was in watching George Formby triumph over the basest machinations of his rivals or laughing at Will Hay, whether he was headmaster, station master or lost in darkest Africa.

At half past four we would stagger out into glaring sunshine or chill fog, according to the season, blissfully happy and content with our lot. I had a further treat in store, because on many Saturdays I would visit with my father Mr Binns's sweet shop in Wrawby Street and select my own soft mushroom-shaped sweets covered with desiccated coconut or hard-boiled fishy shapes in many colours, which were long-lasting and tasted strongly of pear drops.

Grand Cinema, Wrawby Street, Brigg

8
MY WAR 1939–45

When the Second World War broke out I was nearly nine and to my consternation and surprise had a younger brother, who had been born the previous November. I have no memories of the period before September 3rd and no premonition of hostilities, except for a faint recollection of being at no. 31 Central Square when my mother and Auntie Lil were listening to the wireless (as we called it then) with solemn faces to what could have been Chamberlain's return from Germany, bringing his so-called 'Peace with Honour': of course, it may have been to do with Edward VIII's abdication. However, I can remember the Sunday morning when Chamberlain told the nation we were at war with Germany. Playing in the back garden, I listened to the broadcast through the open room window: our wireless was not moveable and was in the room, connected to its aerial and firmly attached to its wet battery or 'accumulator', which was not then a betting term. My father was constructing blackout shutters from empty tea chests. By this time he had been working for the Lindsey Blind Society for nearly two years and tea was one of the items that the society sold and distributed, so there was no shortage of plywood panels. These shutters lasted as long as the blackout. They were stored in the cupboard under the stairs and slotted into position each night and then held there by wooden fasteners screwed to the window frame, which were simply turned round to hold the shutter in position. We had four shutters for the living room and two for the kitchen, but none for the bathroom. I suppose we must have had shutters for my parents' bedroom, because David shared their room then and would need to be tended to and the gaslight lit for illumination. My bedroom was not blacked out and later from my bed I could see searchlights probing and on some occasions was awake and crept to the window to see a distant glow that was supposed to be the results of a night bombing raid on Hull.

✦✦✦

In reality I had a quiet war. Nothing wildly exciting or life-threatening happened and only one of my immediate family was called up. Aunt Ethel joined the WAAF and served for several years as a cook, eventually earning a stripe. She was stationed at Coningsby, which though in the same county could have been at the other end of the country. She was at Coningsby when Guy Gibson and the Dam-busting squadron were there. She did her usual good job and would put herself out to be of service, cooking food for the aircrews at all kinds of unsocial hours. She was proud of being a WAAF and doing her not inconsiderable bit for the war effort. Grandad Rhodes was even prouder: he was in his eighties and followed the progress of the war very closely. He also displayed a framed photograph of Winston Churchill in ebullient mood on his living room wall. When Aunt Ethel received a commendation in dispatches, this was framed and placed proudly next to 'Winnie's' portrait.

Arthur Sedgwick, who had come to live next door at no. 28 with his wife, Nan, just before the war, and who worked at the gasworks down Riverside, was called up to join the army in the middle of the war and served in Burma. Happily he returned safely – unlike many Old Boys of Brigg Grammar School. I well remember many morning assemblies, when 'Duffy' Daughton, the headmaster, sadly but proudly read the names of Old Boys who had been killed or were missing in action. It seemed that those former pupils who became aircrew were particularly vulnerable. After the war I was asked to write up a Roll of Honour in Old English script on vellum. I was about fifteen at the time and did my best, but was not satisfied with the result. I was no good at Art, but enjoyed lettering and was asked by the then new headmaster, Cale 'Stan' Matthews, on the recommendation of the Art master, 'Cabby' Cabourne, to do it.

❖❖❖

During the war Lincolnshire became one vast airfield. Within a twenty-mile radius of Brigg in North Lincolnshire there must have been nearly twenty air stations, ranging from insignificant to major. Fighters were based at Hibaldstow, Kirmington and Kirton Lindsey while Hemswell, Elsham, Binbrook and Scampton housed bombers. The skies overhead were crowded and we soon came to recognise easily Hampdens and Halifaxes and the later Wellingtons and Lancasters among the bombers, and Spitfires, Hurricanes and later the American Mustangs and Lightnings among the fighters. We also in the second half of the war came to know Flying Fortresses.

It was the war in the air that most affected our daily lives. We saw khaki mainly on soldiers guarding the airfields or prisoners of war and the occasional naval uniform when townsfolk serving in the navy were on leave, but the predominating uniform was Royal Air Force blue, to which was later added the smartly cut brown uniform of the American Army Air Force. Among the RAF crews I was vaguely aware that some were Australians, and others in considerable numbers were Poles and Czechs. My father was a Special Constable and came into closer contact with these exotic flyers when he had to arrest airmen who got fighting drunk in Brigg on a Saturday night and were taken to cool off and sober up in the cells of the police station in Wrawby Street between the Grand Cinema and the workhouse-cum-hospital complex. There they were left to the tender mercies of Sergeant Hatton, who stood no nonsense, before being released to return to their respective airfields.

For at least the first two years of the war our sleep was at a premium and regularly disturbed by the air-raid siren, which came to be called with humorous resignation 'Moaning Minnie'. (As my mother's name was Minnie, she didn't think much of that soubriquet.) However, I can well recall the sound that began with a glissading crescendo and continued for several minutes in a wild ululation before subsiding into a long drawn-out metallic sigh. The siren was affixed to the fire station roof opposite the police station and there was a further siren at the sugar factory some two miles away which we could hear quite audibly on calm nights. I don't know how the villages were warned; I can't think that Elsham had its own siren, but it did have its own airfield and presumably one sounded there.

Some families had their own individual shelter: they dug out the foundations and erected the ubiquitous Anderson shelter in the back garden. The Anderson shelter consisted of sunken corrugated iron arcs fixed to a central concrete beam and was protected by earth and sandbags. Others strengthened outhouses with sandbags and used those. Since our house was barely two hundred yards from the air-raid shelters built in the grounds of the Girls' High School in a direct line, we used these shelters. By road these shelters would have been half a mile away, but stepladders were placed at the bottom of the garden to the Leesons' house in Woodbine Avenue and by means of these ladders we mounted the seven-foot-high wire fence that surrounded the northern perimeter of the High School. Since David was only one and a bit at the time of the first air raids, he was transported in a carrying cot made out of the handy tea-chest panels. I helped to carry the cot, but it must have been tricky to pass over the high fence, especially on the very many occasions when Dad was on Special Constabulary duty. Presumably Mother was helped by neighbours also seeking the assumed safety of the High School shelters. These shelters were simply elongated, brick-built boxes with a concrete roof and floor and standing on the tarmacked playground. I can't think they would have been much protection from high explosive bombs dropping nearby, though they could possibly have coped with incendiaries. Inside the shelters there were three or four lines of slatted benches, each about fifty feet long, and we sat on these and waited for the all-clear to sound. The shelters at the Boys' Grammar School into which I had to seek shelter when the siren sounded during lesson time were situated along the Glebe Road side of the school playing field and were darker and smellier but stronger, since they were sunken, earth-covered and grass grew well there. The space between the shelters was to make a suitable stage for a memorable production of *A Midsummer Night's Dream* after the war in 1945 with the now disused shelters providing the wings and 'a marvellous green spot for our rehearsal'. One night I somehow became separated from my mother and brother, probably because there was more panic that night as German bombers were passing overhead on their way to Sheffield or Hull. I was unconcerned when I found myself in a shelter, because I was surrounded by families I knew well as neighbours. My mother, however, must have been frantic and somehow alerted my father who was on constabulary duty as usual that night. We were in the shelters longer than usual and it was some considerable time before my father in tin hat, dark serge uniform and gas mask appeared at the shelter desperately enquiring if *'anyone had seen our John'*. They had and I was soon reunited with my mother in one of the other shelters in the High School grounds.

Because there was no need to suppose that the Luftwaffe would single Brigg out as an important target on which to drop their bombs, by the autumn of 1942 people stopped getting up, dressing and making their way to the shelters. But we were aware that some cities were suffering badly from the bombing. One night when Hull (some 25 miles away across the Humber) was under attack, we could see flashes and an unusual red glow from that direction through our bedroom windows. On other occasions we would lie in bed and listen to the different but unmistakeable sound of the Heinkel or Junkers engine as German planes headed west to Sheffield. Here much damage was done and many lives lost, but we did not have any first-hand knowledge as no pictures of damage were printed in the local papers. The West Riding/South Yorkshire was unknown country.

I suppose I must have seen pictures of damage in Hull, because one of the two local papers was the *Hull and North Lincolnshire Times*, but I can't remember any. The national newspapers carried grainy pictures of successes but more often of reverses in that first part of the war. There was also a magazine that recorded the progress of the war in pictures – possibly Hulton Press's *Picture Post*. I seem to remember some sixteen pages of murky photographs within a yellow and black cover. The sinking of the *Admiral Graf Spee* comes to mind and the rescue of British sailors from a German prison ship, the *Altmark*, by a British destroyer. I also remember pictures of the loss of the *Hood* and the *Ark Royal* with terrible loss of life, but curiously nothing about Dunkirk.

◆◆◆

One of the things that did make an impact upon the local community was the arrival and dispersal of the evacuees. In Brigg the majority of the evacuees came from Hull. I can't remember on what principles the children were allocated, but it seemed that because we lived in council houses children from impoverished backgrounds were billeted on us, whereas the big owner-occupied houses on Wrawby Road were offered more fragrant children. It could not have been an easy relationship for any of those involved. For most of the Hull children to be uprooted from an urban milieu (however unsatisfactory) that they knew well and transplanted to a small market town among new and alien faces must have been traumatic. However, the majority did not stay long and after a few months most had returned to Hull, the danger of frequent air raids notwithstanding. We hosted a boy about a year younger than me called Brian J. The whole family did its best to make him feel at home. With some shifting about he was provided with his own bedroom, he was introduced to our friends and we tried to involve him in our games, activities in which other evacuees joined with alacrity. However, Brian was very withdrawn and not at all self-confident. His nervousness made him prone to bedwetting, which did not help, although I can't ever remember him being reprimanded for this and my mother did the extra washing without complaint. His mother came to visit him on one occasion, travelling on the ferry to New Holland and thence by train, changing at Barnetby. It can't have been much later that Brian returned to Hull, he much relieved and unlamented by me. Peter D, who was the Rands's evacuee two doors away, was a much more positive character, though some three years younger than John Rands and myself. He revelled in the new experience and was much more content with his lot in Brigg, for it seemed he came from a very underprivileged background in Hull. These are the only two I can remember with any clarity, though there must have been scores of evacuees in the estates surrounding Central Square. One or two evacuees later in the war came from further afield, especially at the time of the London blitz and subsequently when 'doodlebugs' (as the V1s and V2s were called) started dropping on the capital. I remember two girls, one a skinny, dishevelled and belligerent lass, whom we disparagingly called 'Cockney' and avoided, and the other a small, pert, blonde beauty called, exotically, Zena (Walker?), on whom we thirteen-year-olds gazed with admiring passion.

When Coventry was in danger, probably at the time of the blitz on the city, Bablake School, either in part or in whole, was evacuated to Brigg and accommodated in the boarding house at Brigg Grammar School. By this time, in 1942/43, I was a 'Grammar-gog' myself, but the senior boys of Bablake were public school with more impressive blazers and an innate sense of their God-given superiority. They can't have been with us long, but they were certainly there one summer term, taught separately by their own staff, and have remained in the memory. On one memorable Wednesday half-day, in which the afternoons were given over to inter-school matches, the First XIs of Bablake and Brigg Grammar School did battle. I was probably in UIVA, aged thirteen and fiercely supportive of Brigg. We desperately wanted to see the 'snooty, toffee-nosed types' from Bablake get their comeuppance. Since we had compulsory Saturday morning school, attendance on a Wednesday afternoon was not expected, but there was a large gathering to see this match. One or two tradesmen from the town came up, as it was half-day closing on a Wednesday. Bablake batted first and we were impressed by their immaculate flannelled appearance – not all our team had 'whites'. Their star batsman found his form and soon stroked a comfortable and chanceless forty-odd runs. This was worrying because on our wicket few batsmen managed to score twenty and total team scores were usually in the fifties or sixties. We were particularly irritated by the polished accents of the Bablakians acclaiming *'Well played, Peter!'* as their star drove yet another boundary. We were much relieved to hear *'Hard luck, Peter!'* when he was finally caught.

Bablake scored well over a hundred and twenty runs and we did not think we could possibly approach that score. However, cometh the hour, cometh the man: in the shape of Bob Atkinson. 'Akky' was in the fifth form, some three years older than me, but he seemed to be of another generation. Living nearly opposite us in Woodbine Avenue, he was always man to my boy. 'Akky' scored sixty-nine not out, an unheard-of achievement in my experience at that time and Brigg gained a notable victory. We juniors took immense pleasure in greeting each of his runs with loud shouts in affected, cut-glass accents of *'Well played, Robert!'* No-one ever called 'Akky' Robert, not even his parents. Bob Atkinson later played a good club class of cricket locally and was an outstanding centre-half for Brigg Town after the war. He died in his late thirties, much lamented.

◆◆◆

In the early part of the war my daily routine changed relatively little. I still went along to school some three hundred yards away in Glebe Road, where was the elementary school that catered for all ages up to fourteen. It was here I participated in May Queen celebrations and took the Eleven-Plus. Our teachers were either elderly males or middle-aged women, but this had been the pattern at Glebe Road pre-war. When I went to the Grammar School in September 1941 a similar pattern was repeated, but with significant differences. The males were largely over fifty, but supplemented by twin novelties – one or two ladies were brought on the staff for probably the first time and we had one young teacher (Mr Cobbold – Chemistry) who held a great fascination for us, as it was rumoured he had been invalided out of the Commandoes. He made a great impression on me when at the first lesson he took he surveyed the class and saying not a word took an iron clamp stand and bent it in two before straightening it out again. We gazed in silent awe and, unlike some other staff, he never had any difficulty with discipline in our class. We went to school with our gas masks in their squat, cardboard boxes, slung over our shoulders, and we had gas-mask drills. Fortunately we never had to don them in earnest, but initially we were interested in their novelty and in the different types. Mine and my mother's were common or garden gas masks, but my young brother originally had a large incubator-like contraption into which he fitted completely. He then graduated to a Mickey-Mouse type for toddlers. My father was issued with a much more grandiose affair that had a large gorilla-like headpiece that incorporated two large, goggle eyepieces and a thick tube ran from the jaw to a canister at his belt that held special filtering chemicals. The carrying of gas masks at first obligatory and involuntary eventually gave way to a sporadic carrying until finally our gas masks were stored under the stairs where they remained from the spring of 1942 to the end of the war. I can't remember the government ever collecting the things, but at the outset everybody, bearing in mind what had happened in the First World War trenches, expected gas attacks at any time.

The blackout caused most disruption. No longer were the gas standards lit each night, and the few cars and lorries were fitted with slotted covers over their headlights while sidelights were made smaller with the use of black insulating tape. Hand-held torches were also masked to decrease their beams. But we still went out at night to our regular activities. Cubs was on a Wednesday night and our 'den' or clubhouse was in an upstairs room of semi-derelict buildings behind and between the shop and the Congregational Chapel. Friday nights and usually Tuesday nights were choir practice nights: Tuesdays were boys only and Fridays were boys at 6.30pm and the men joined us at 7.30pm. These practices were held in Church House, a Victorian dwelling on the site of the present Church Hall, and took place in an upstairs room with hard chairs, a chenille-covered table and an ancient piano that was rarely in tune, especially after we choirboys had been banging on the keys before the practice. The organist/choir-trainers who tried to wring hymn tunes from this failing instrument were successively John Bradley, Eva Turner, Harold Chesher and Miss Bly.

✦✦✦

During the war I never went hungry and somehow my mother managed to prepare at least one hot, cooked meal a day. We ate at lunchtime and my father used to have his meal reheated when he came in from work. He was travelling extensively around much of Lincolnshire and particularly in the winter months he was often late because of the blackout, Humber fogs or pressure of business. He sometimes would come in at gone 8pm, hurry his meal and dash off to perform his night duties as a Special Constable starting at 9pm. We had our ration books and our identity cards. My number was TMCB 119/3: some things you never forget. The ration book had multi-hued coupons stamped with the names of various foodstuffs and weekly dates. Mother went to Rowbottom's in Bigby Street for most things, but a few were with Varlow's in the Market Place. I think Mother must have continued with her pre-war routine and continued to make her weekly visit to the grocers on a Thursday afternoon, calling first at Rowbottom's, where Mr Rowbottom would ceremoniously cut out the appropriate coupons in the ration books for 'sugar' or for 'marge', and then on to Varlow's, where the scissors would excise the coupons for 'bacon' and for 'cheese'. You didn't put all your eggs in one basket – except there were very few fresh eggs and we had to make do with dried egg powder. Fresh eggs were a luxury and if one of his 'country cousins' gave Dad on his Lindsey Blind round three eggs, that was indeed a red-letter day. It was also the reason we choirboys liked to go to sing at the Harvest Festival at Cadney Church, because in addition to the sixpence we got, we received a fresh egg from the donated produce.

There were no coupons for sweets and Mrs Stephenson at no. 24 Central Square could no longer buy or obtain the sugar to make her famous peppermints or coconut ice. Whenever news reached us of a consignment of sweets or confectionery at some little shop in the town, we would hare off and queue for a long time for whatever was available – perhaps a small Cadbury's chocolate bar, a liquorice stick or even dolly mixture. Mrs East in Woodbine Avenue and Mr Binns in Wrawby Street were where we were most successful. The sweet-shop owners had unimaginable power in those days, but we rarely heard any complaints about favouritism or other abuse of power.

I have said that my father was a Special Constable, but other middle-aged neighbours also had their particular roles. Our close friend Mr Alf Rands was on duty at the nerve centre of our local defence administration to co-ordinate the efforts of all the services. It was somewhere near the police station, but I never knew exactly where, nor 'Uncle' Alf's precise duties. Mr Bill Denton from further round the Square was an air-raid warden and he could have been the model for the warden in *Dad's Army*. 'Cabby' Cabourne, the Art master at the Grammar School, was something important in the Home Guard and very Mainwaring-esque, though he had only three stripes. Other neighbours were ambulance men, fire-fighters and Red Cross nurses. Those neighbours who worked shifts at the Scunthorpe steelworks were excused these extra responsibilities. I was greatly envious of those near contemporaries who were old enough to be recruited with their bicycles to act as messenger boys. Even my mother was recruited in mid-war to be a fire-watcher. She and Auntie Lil were put on a rota and their duty was to circumnavigate Central Square and report any incendiary bombs that were dropped. I think they must have been given some rudimentary instruction in how to use a stirrup pump in case of an emergency. Fortunately such an emergency never occurred. I can't remember where the stirrup pump was stored, but somehow after the war it surfaced in our shed and was much used over the years to spray the cabbages with soapy water from wash day as a deterrent to greenfly. Mum and her friend certainly had tin hats and possibly armbands, but no other equipment. Since they were just patrolling the Square, I'm sure my brother and I were left at home and in bed to sleep; babysitters were unheard of in those days, for the word is of post-war coinage. One night Min and Lil had the fright of their lives and nearly saturated their voluminous pink knickers. There was some air traffic and the Pingley Camp searchlights and others were probing the skies. Min and Lil were gazing skywards and revolving to catch sight of any enemy aircraft. Suddenly there was an almighty bang and half-suppressed screams. However, there was no danger. The two ladies, eyes heavenwards, had come back to back in their rotation and their tin helmets had crashed together with the sound of a thunderclap.

◆◆◆

The wireless played a vital part in informing us of the progress of the war and in sustaining our morale. I am told that I did hear some of Winston Churchill's stirring speeches to the nation verbatim, but they made no inspiring impression on this twelve-year-old at the time. However, I can remember having to be still and listen to the speeches of King George VI on Christmas Day. News bulletins were turned on at one o'clock, six o'clock and nine o'clock. More important than all these was the programme that was a 'must' on Thursday nights at 8.30pm: *ITMA*. It was essential listening with Tommy Handley, Jack Train (the multi-voiced favourite), Derek Guyler and the inimitable Mrs Mopp. The catchphrases from this programme littered our daily conversation – and still do: *'Can I do you now, sir?'*, *'I don't mind if I do'*, *'After you, Claude'* – *'No, after you, Cecil'*, and of course we never did forget the diver. I was amused by Rob Wilton and his 'The day war broke out' soliloquy and Harry Korris, Lovejoy and their ubiquitous friend, Enoch. Everything stopped at our house on a Saturday night when it was *In Town Tonight* and for Henry Hall's *Guest Night* and *Much Binding in the Marsh* with Dicky Murdoch and Kenneth Horne. Frank Randle, 'Gillie' Potter, Arthur Askey, Eric Barker and Billy Cotton all gave pleasure and added to our vocabulary other watchwords that enlivened our conversation. In the memory they all coalesce – I'm sure some of these entertainers were post-war too.

It would have been an unmitigated disaster if the wireless battery had run out between half past eight and nine o'clock on a Thursday night and I did my best to ensure we had a freshly charged battery at that time. We had two sulphuric-acid batteries that were interchanged and charged at Proctors, who had a house, shop and garage at the Grammar School Road end of Glebe Road. Many surrounding families had their batteries charged there; others went to Sass's near the Monument. All the batteries for charging were connected up and an electric charge passed through their plates. It was fascinating to watch the bubbles attached to the plates winking and then detaching themselves, moving slowly to the top of the acid. Sometimes the battery wasn't fully charged when it was tested and we had to come back later. I was never scientifically inclined, but I can well remember the huge pipette with a monstrous, bulbous rubber head that was inserted into the battery and squeezed to see if the float would come up to the required level. A Mr Bains was in charge of this area and he practised the testing with all the flourishes of a celebrity chef, while we waited breathlessly to see if he would pronounce himself satisfied with the state of our battery. I would exchange the used battery for the recharged one and pay my threepence, then return home, gaily swinging the battery alongside my bare, short-trousered knees. Most weeks I would make the journey down Glebe Road with the old sulphuric-acid-filled battery and return with a charged one. I can't remember having any accidents, but there must have been a real danger of acid burns. In those days the Health and Safety agency was unheard of and its nannying would have been derided. Care and common sense were enough and not legislateable.

The Grand Cinema in Wrawby Street, next to the White Horse and facing up Cross Street, was also important to our morale-boosting leisure activities. It was owned and run by a Mr Webster (who had a fine house on Wrawby Road) and had been a place of enchantment for Brigg's townsfolk since the early thirties. I was a regular at the Saturday afternoon 'rush', which was the matinee for which we invariably queued up with ill-concealed impatience, then pushed and shoved our way forward when the doors were finally opened, paying our tuppence before dashing to grab a seat as near the front as possible. I was rarely able to go upstairs to the balcony, for those seats cost as much as a shilling, but sometimes I made my way furtively and urgently upstairs to the more resplendent and scented toilets during the interval if there were a long queue for the cramped and usually malodorous facilities downstairs. Such visits were frowned upon and the way was usually barred by a burly assistant. However, I remember I was on one occasion able to elude the guard and answer the insistent call of nature, but my relief was curtailed by being unable to return downstairs because of a newly stationed guard. I hastily concealed myself in a dark corner of the more opulent dress circle and watched the second half of the programme from there with a guilty conscience and much nervous glancing around.

At the Grand we were regaled with the various gripping and comic adventures of Will Hay and his two amusing sidekicks, Moore Marriot and Graham Moffat, in places ranging from darkest Africa to gun-running Ireland. George Formby also brightened our Saturday afternoons and we added his catchphrase – *'Turned out nice again'* – to our repertoire. With him we twanged imaginary ukuleles and waited at the lamppost on the corner of the street, until a certain little lady came by. It was at the Grand that I saw Noel Coward performing his heroics in *In Which We Serve*, Eric Portman in *49th Parallel* and the more relevant to our daily lives, *One of Our Aircraft is Missing*. American films gave us some sort of a foretaste of the Yanks who were to be stationed amongst us in the second half of the war and who wrought such havoc upon the local post-pubescent girls with their exotic charms, their nylons and their tall stories. They were also to attract our interest and invoked daring cadging by some of my more adventurous contemporaries – *'Got any gum, chum?'* However, it was Abbott and Costello, the Bowery Boys and the Three Stooges who were our regular celluloid fare together with Pathé News.

◆◆◆

From about twelve or so I played an insignificant part in the war effort. I was adept at scouring and scavenging around the Square for items that could provide scrap metal and was especially adept at persuading Mother and our neighbours to part with unusable aluminium saucepans. Mind you, they were only unusable after they had been repaired at least twice by circular discs (about an inch in diameter), which were screw-bolted in the bottom to cover holes that regularly appeared in the thin metal. However, we collected assiduously aluminium pots and pans that could be melted down to be made into frames for more Spitfires and Hurricanes. 'Wings for Victory Week' was a time to remember. There were many fundraising events and efforts to collect reusable scrap and it culminated in a big parade through the town one Saturday afternoon. There were marching airmen, an RAF band and a number of lorries festooned with patriotic flags and carrying parts of aeroplanes, working guns and other fascinating memorabilia. By this time I was at the Grammar School and to my dismay was put in Saturday afternoon detention on that particular weekend for some forgotten misdemeanour. 'Tiger' Richards, the Latin master, was taking the detention and his nature belied his nickname, devolved from his initials, 'TGR'. He was a soft touch and he obviously wanted to see the procession himself. So it was agreed that he would escort us down to Wrawby Street to witness the procession on condition we were 'good'. We went – and we were. The navy and the army had their special fundraising weeks and I must have taken part, possibly appearing on concerts organised among schoolchildren. I seem to remember being in a choir and Purcell's 'Fairest Isle' sticks in my mind, but with no great clarity.

Memories of my agricultural assistance in feeding the nation are much clearer. Obviously it was important that as far as possible the country should be self-supporting in all the food we could grow in England. Gardens and allotments had always supplemented or provided much of the produce that we consumed, but more areas were given over to food production. I remember that several acres of the Brigg Grammar School playing fields were ploughed up on a borrowed tractor by 'Chips' Morris, the French master. Potatoes were planted and later harvested by members of the school, who probably consumed most of the harvest in school dinners, either at the canteen or in the Boarding House.

School holidays were rearranged to fit in with the crop cycle. The summer holidays were shortened and there were three-week breaks at Easter and in October. The first was to plant or 'set' the potatoes and the October one to collect them – 'spud-yacking' as we called it. 'Chips' Morris was friendly with Mr Herring, who farmed some hundreds of acres at Wrawby. He arranged for volunteers from Brigg Grammar School to pick potatoes on his farm and some twenty of us duly cycled over to Wrawby in the holidays for this. I was one of the youngest ones, just over twelve when I first went, and we were paid by age and by the length of the 'stint' we picked. I received three shillings and sixpence a day (which equates with sixpence – or 2.5p – an hour), with extra on Saturday mornings; those aged fourteen to fifteen were paid five shillings a day and the most senior boys seven shillings and sixpence. Spud-yacking was a formative experience, deserving of a later chapter to itself. It was in this way I did my bit and was introduced to a side of life I had never encountered before. The labour force at spud-yacking time included, as well as schoolboys, women from the area who were earning some extra pin money and, more colourfully, prisoners of war from the Pingley POW camp on the road out of Brigg towards Bigby. Here an area had been securely fenced off and huts erected on land belonging to Pingley Farm. It can't have been a strong security prison like Stalag Luft 17 or Colditz and it housed both German and Italian prisoners, more of the latter. We rarely held conversations with these 'Jerries' and 'Eyties' and we never got to know much about them, but we did admire their facility in carving rings out of pieces of perspex and in making cigarette lighters out of bullet cases. They did add colour to our potato-picking lives and we even learned a few foreign swearwords, now long forgotten. However, the POWs were more interested in the ladies than in us schoolboys, though 'ladies' may have been a misnomer. My mother and her friends with their stiff lower middle-class morality would have looked askance at their dress and behaviour, for there were strict class divisions in Brigg society in the 1940s. We were nowhere near the top, indeed well in the bottom half, but my mother's friends would have considered themselves 'better' than these cheerful women in cast-off clothes, mud-stained wellington boots and usually uncorsetted with their toothy grins and ribald remarks.

One Wednesday afternoon my friends and I volunteered for another duty which enabled us to do our bit. A plane had crashed in a field just outside Brigg, somewhere at the end of Westrum Lane, which contained a few imposing houses on the town's outskirts over the level crossing on Bigby Road. The larger pieces had all been cleared away by RAF lorries, but there still remained innumerable pieces of glass, perspex and metal scattered around the field. We were invited to clear the field so that the spring sowing could be done. We formed up in lines and proceeded with buckets or baskets along the length of the field, picking up the debris as we went. It was rather like harrowing a potato field. I have indistinct memories of this and cannot say whether the plane was a bomber or a fighter, a Jerry or one of ours that had been trying to find its way back to its Lincolnshire base but failed. However, in the deep recesses of my mind I recollect someone finding an item of pilot's clothing with body parts attached. It is probably apocryphal, but folklore soon recalled a flying helmet with a bloody pulp of squashed brains inside and many of us later cast ourselves in the role of the intrepid discoverer of the helmet.

◆◆◆

Thus the war proceeded. The news became more and more encouraging and I suppose our hearts were lighter, but nothing memorable affected my daily routine of lessons, homework, school sport on both Wednesday and Saturday afternoons and church for both Matins and Evensong on Sundays. D-Day caused a ripple of excitement, but it was all far-removed and none of the foregathering had taken place in our part of Lincolnshire. Eventually came VE Day and sometime later VJ Day.

There were parties and knees-ups and the gaslights were lit again after five years. The long-silent bells of St John's pealed out again and a brave new world was about to be created. Well, at least it was to be different. There were street parties, though I can't remember one taking place on the road between Woodbine Avenue and Central Square. Our celebrations took place in Farmer Hill's field bordering on Wrawby Road and East Parade. I seem to remember keenly contested races, a tug-of-war, a surprising array of food and a fancy dress competition. The latter sticks in my mind, because my brother (by then aged about six) won a prize. He was a Bevin Boy: at least that is what it said on a placard round his neck, for I had carefully constructed and filled in the large letters. He had on an old flat cap of Dad's and somewhat ragged clothes liberally spattered with coal dust. His face was also smeared with coal as he commemorated the many young men specially recruited for the mines by Ernest Bevin, the wartime Minister of Labour. David's success caused much resentment and indignation in the breast of his contemporary, Herbert Collingham, who in his inimitable, gruff and adenoidal voice said in disgust, *'Have you seen David Rhodes? They've given him five shillings for having a dirty face and mucky clothes.'*

I, of course, was fourteen at the VE celebrations, far above fancy dress and too unathletic to have any chance of racing success, not even in the sack race or the slow bicycle race. I was at the awkward age – too old to go to bed before the evening events and not old enough to go on celebrating after midnight. However, I do remember parading along Wrawby Street and into the Market Place, linked to older boys and girls in conga shuffles and tagged on the ends of impromptu Palais-Glide lines, fiercely attempting to remain attached and to perform the right kicks and knee-bendings at the appropriate time. I also remember we surrounded policemen and serenaded them, which caused much good-humoured embarrassment. Even Sergeant Hatton was ringed under one lamppost while we raucously and repeatedly assured him that Lloyd George loved my father and that the former prime minister reciprocated his affections with equal fervour. I felt I had reached adulthood at last.

Similar festivities were staged on VJ Day, but they did not have the same mint-fresh novelty and are muted in the memory. They certainly didn't have the exhilarating effect of the activities surrounding VE Day. This was probably due to two main reasons. Hitler was a much more realistic and immediate enemy, for he had occupied our minds for years, and he was dead and his forces that might have been an occupying power had been overcome; Japan and the Japanese were a much more intangible concept, far removed from our understanding both geographically and culturally. Moreover, we were slowly coming to terms with the awesome power of the nuclear bombs that had brought about the Japanese surrender. We were at peace at last, but a most uncertain future lay ahead.

For me School Certificate was a year away, but I can't say it had entered my consciousness in the summer of 1945 and the results of the October General Election did not make much impact on me either. However, the war was over, having proved a not unsatisfactory experience for me and having left no adverse effects. A new, post-war period was about to start, but we still had rationing and we had to scavenge around all the likely sources for any sweets. I felt a sense of achievement when I tracked down and purchased some humbugs from two elderly ladies who kept a small sweet shop in the front room of their terraced house in Bridge Street. However, as 1945 turned into 1946 the challenge of School Certificate did impinge upon my consciousness and somewhat belatedly I realised that this year was to be the beginning of a new and crucial chapter of my life.

Lancaster at Elsham getting ready

9
BRIGG GRAMMAR SCHOOL 1941–48

Somehow in the late spring of 1941 I had nearly passed the scholarship examination and been put on the 'interview' list. I paid my first official visit to Brigg Grammar School some few weeks later and, having been interviewed by three people and having read certain passages and answered questions on them, I was awarded a Lindsey Junior Scholarship. I still have the certificate, signed by 'FJ Birkbeck', which confirms it was tenable at 'Brigg Grammar'. My parents were pleased, especially my father, who dreamed I might have opportunities he had never had. He had never taken an examination in his life: he was an experienced driver when driving tests were introduced and I'm not counting any tests he took as a Special Constable during the war to see if he were competent to deal with gas contamination. I was the first in our immediate family to have a full secondary education, since my father had left school at fourteen and five years later he was in France, wounded at Ypres. Nor did I have any close family members who had been to Grammar School to give me some hints of what I might expect.

✦✦✦

As a pupil at Glebe Road School I had derided and despised most 'Grammar-gogs' – or 'Grammer-gogs', with our pronunciation. I was familiar with the badged blazer and cap, grey trousers, grey or white shirt and school tie that comprised the uniform. Safe in a group of contemporaries, I shouted scornful epithets at the Grammar-gogs I passed on our respective ways to school. Occasionally we would try to snatch the cap of some small, inoffensive junior and then play football with it in the dusty street. From the vantage point of the choir stalls at St John's Parish Church I surveyed the assembled ranks of the boarders who had to attend Matins each Sunday in term time. They were usually accompanied by the slight, tonsured figure of JT Daughton, the headmaster. He in turn was often accompanied by the imposingly large and behatted Mrs Daughton, who could have been cast as Violet Elizabeth's mother in the *Just William* stories. Rarely did their daughter Betty come, since I think she went away to school, and Mr Gaze, the master in the boarding house, came only in the absence of the headmaster. I smirked in disdain as the boarders were crocodiled back to School House after the service with the senior boys as prefects chivvying and snapping at the younger ones to keep in line and keep up, just as if they were a flock of sheep being coerced by sheepdogs.

I had also had closer and potentially more dangerous connections before I became a member of Brigg Grammar School. As a nine and ten-year-old I often played in the area of rough ground behind Woodbine Avenue that adjoined the Grammar School playing field. Because there were venerable, climbable trees from which we had hung swinging ropes just on the other side of the dividing hedge, we often strayed through the hedge to play on the school field. The boarders naturally strongly resented these incursions onto their land and tried to take retaliatory action. But we had a clear view of the approach of any vengeful group from the boarding house across the field and could easily slip away and take refuge in the back garden of one of our number who lived in Woodbine Avenue: here we were untouchable. However, on one occasion, using a clever strategy, the party of boarders thirsting for revenge went the long way round by Glebe Road and planned to come at us from the rear. Fortunately we were warned in time and managed to reach the haven of the back garden. The boarders were livid in their frustration, as from a safe twenty-feet distance we hurled abuse at each other: they were 'snooty Grammar-gogs' and we were 'snotty council house oiks'. It was a stand-off and at last they departed. As they made their way over the rough ground to the school field, they spotted a den we had made. Their enraged leader (whom I later learned was Johnny Duerdin – I kept out of his way at Brigg Grammar School) took great pleasure in trashing it before being the last to make his way back to the boarding house.

❖❖❖

And so it was in the summer of 1941 I was still a 'council house oik' but also an incipient 'Grammar-gog'. I had visited Walter Shaw's shop in the Market Place and been fitted out with blazer, new short grey trousers, grey socks topped with two rings of dark and light blue and a school tie of the same colours. There was also a navy blue cap, bearing the escutcheon of the Nelthorpe family with a gold crescent on the left and in the middle an upright, jewelled sword on which was superimposed a small shield, featuring what I later discovered was 'the bloody hand of Ulster'. I also had a quartered football shirt that was a hand-me-down from Billy McKaill, who lived in Central Square and who had outgrown it. Cash's nametapes had been purchased ready for my mother to sew on everything I was to take to school. Secretly I was impressed to see my name 'JOHN A RHODES' in bold red capitals and repeated some forty times on the narrow white tape.

Brigg Grammar School was the making of me, even if it took some years.

Yet it was literally very nearly the death of me, before my first term started. My friend, John Rands, was already at Brigg Grammar in the prep department and so was able to use the swimming bath during the summer holidays. The bath was open on occasions in the morning, though there was never any adult supervision. Dad, who sang in the Brigg Choral Society of which Daughton was a member, had been granted permission for me to use the bath too. One August morning John Rands and I went along. There were some eight much bigger boys there already; all were Brigg lads and therefore 'Anchors', members of the House I was destined to join. Some were in the pool, which was surrounded by a large wooden fence, while others were standing around the sides. The deep end (six feet) was nearer the rudimentary wooden changing room and the shallow end (three and a half feet) was some fifteen yards down the bath. We changed and I emerged in a woollen, knitted costume somewhat apprehensively. I had never been in water deeper than the eighteen inches of the Scarborough boating/paddling lake. It wasn't a particularly sunny morning and, nervously hugging my towel, I stared at the dark, unwelcoming water. Suddenly my towel was snatched away from me and I was given a sharp push. I was taken completely by surprise and with an almighty splash I found myself totally immersed in water. I had been standing near the deep end and was well out of my depth. I rose to the surface once, spluttering, frantically beating my arms and gasping for breath. I was sinking for the third time when someone had the presence of mind to grab me and haul me up and I was helped to scramble out of the bath, breathless, shaken and water in every orifice. I lay by the side of the pool, coughing, panting to get my breath back and ashen-faced. It is well over sixty years since that episode, but I have never gained any confidence or pleasure in being immersed in water: I remain the only one in my family who can't swim and have no real desire to do so. It could so easily have ended in tragedy, but I had survived.

Thus early in September, kitted out in my new school uniform and running a gauntlet of taunts from my erstwhile classmates at Glebe Road School, I made my way up the drive from Grammar School Road, round the Physics lab corner and into the main quadrangle. I stood in a group of equally nervous newcomers and looked around me in dazed awe. The bigger boys were really young men, nearly eighteen years old. I had never seen so many older boys together before and was both impressed and perturbed, for we had been fed pernicious rumours of how new boys were ceremoniously initiated into the school by having their heads ducked in the sinks of the cloakrooms or plunged down a basin in the toilets and the chain pulled. A gowned master appeared and with the help of prefects we new boys were shepherded into the School Hall. This was in reality two classrooms with a dividing partition concertinaed back against the wall. There was a small dais, a grand piano under a green-baized cover and on the wall a large painting of Sir John Nelthorpe in mid-seventeenth-century armour. A local knight and supporter of the Stuarts, Nelthorpe had caused the school to be founded in 1669. In 1941 the school numbered three hundred and twenty-four pupils, of whom just over sixty were new boys like myself. The catchment area was from Scunthorpe in the west to near Grimsby in the east, from Ferriby in the north to Hemswell and Grayingham in the south, with the boarders from even further afield.

We had already been graded into forms and when the names were read out I found myself allocated to 3A along with thirty-three other boys. Our form room was an old wooden army hut away from main school, beyond the swimming bath and adjoining the back gardens of the houses in Glebe Road. Tradition held that all the huts (1A and 2A in the prep department were housed in the other double hut) had been condemned after the end of the First World War. Our form teacher was Mr Pratt. The hut was raised up on a brick stand and we ascended by three steps. There was a blackboard affixed to the end wall and this was supplemented by a freestanding board and easel. Thirty-odd heavy wooden desks with seats attached were arranged in pairs. There was a large, locked cupboard containing fresh exercise books and other items. On top of this cupboard were half a dozen or so solid geometrical shapes in wood and painted battleship grey – square, cylinder, cone and two strange beasts we were told were tetrahedron and octahedron. I can't remember if a rare dodecahedron lurked in the background. The master's desk stood at the front not far from the main feature of the room – a cast-iron, enclosed coke stove with its attendant coke-scuttle and small shovel and surrounded by a large mesh guard. We had electric light, but this was our sole source of heat. There was a small detachable piece in the top of the stove, whose metal flue went up and through the roof, and the monster was fed by means of this hole. Near the base was a hinged flap through which it could be riddled. On winter mornings grey/black smoke billowed into the air. We couldn't control the temperature – we shivered or overheated – and the atmosphere was often flavoured with gaseous fumes. Sometimes the stove became overheated if the flue was left open and the cast-iron casing would glow red-hot. This was useful at morning break (for we could remain in the form room unsupervised) because Jack Clark's sold penny buns, fresh every morning from Lyon's bakery. Jack Clark's was recognised as the unofficial school tuck shop and was situated opposite the school on the other side of Grammar School Road. When the bell rang for morning break there was a rush pell-mell, a mad dash heedlessly across the road to wait our turn in a disorderly queue for our bun – usually singular, because there was a war on. Members of 3A could take their bun back to their form room and having broken it in half and impaled the half on a fully opened compass point could toast it against the stove, once the guard had been temporarily removed and the bottom aperture opened. The old-fashioned brass compasses made ideal toasting forks and the lesson after break was conducted in an atmosphere redolent of fresh toast from October to Easter.

Many things about Brigg Grammar School were new and sometimes inconvenient, but we bore them all with a true Lincolnshire stoicism. The schoolday was from 9am to 12.45pm with a short morning break and from 2pm to 3.30pm, but the school week was different: we attended on Saturday mornings (12.30pm finish) and had Wednesday afternoons free. This was largely to make life more tolerable for the boarders, but it made possible two afternoons for school sporting events. It also enabled two school detentions to be held each week. A few words about the Brigg Grammar system of punishment might not be out of place here. There was corporal punishment in the form of a cane, administered usually by the headmaster and just occasionally by the senior master, 'Bumper Knight'. I was caned only once at school, when I inadvertently hit the headmaster himself with a snowball as he emerged round the Physics lab corner, after he had specifically banned such activities near buildings. I was told to report forthwith to his study, where I bent down and received three of the best. Some staff would at times clip ears or hurl a board rubber. There were also lines, given quite freely by staff and prefects – 'I must not be impertinent to my betters', a hundred times and for the next day. Then there was detention on Wednesday and Saturday afternoons. Names of miscreants were read out in assembly and you had to report to Room 2 at 2pm for either an hour or two hours, depending upon the nature of the crime. You could be put in detention for fighting with other boys, for fancied impertinence, poor or copied work, lateness to school or lessons and any behaviour staff deemed un-Briggensian. In my first four years I must have done detention some ten times. Sometimes you had to sit quietly, hands on head, sometimes you were set to copy passages from a book or tables were to be written out or earlier poor work redone. Sometimes litter around the school or on the school field had to be cleared up. Staff took detention on a rota basis and you knew those staff who were so stern you dare not breathe audibly and those who were more lax and you could hold a whispered conversation with other detainees. 'Tiger' Richards was one of the more amenable and, as previously mentioned, once when I was in detention on the Saturday and there was to be a big parade through the town on the occasion of 'Wings for Victory Week', we persuaded him to escort us down town so we could all see the parade.

Another thing that I had to get used to was that most masters wore academic gowns and had to be addressed as 'Sir'. It was also strange that I was now in a 'form' and not a 'class'. Different subjects were taught by different staff, though in the first year our form teacher took us for English grammar and two-thirds of the Maths curriculum. In all, 3A had six male teachers and in 1941 a real novelty: Mrs Chapman had that term been appointed the first lady teacher in main school and taught us Geography. I had to cope with three completely new subjects – Physics, Chemistry and French. English featured Grammar and Composition as well as Literature, and 'Sums' were now called Maths and we wrestled with new, fearsome Algebra and Geometry. Scripture was called Divinity, but History and Geography were recognisable old friends. And we had Drawing.

Often our lessons were punctuated by prolonged, piercing squeals. Our form room adjoined the back gardens of houses in Glebe Road and at the bottom of the gardens more than one householder kept a pig during the war years. The pig-killer was a frequent visitor with his long barrow on which the pig was slaughtered. We couldn't see what was happening, but once the pig's throat was cut, we heard its squeals. They grew to a resounding crescendo and then became fainter as the last lifeblood was pumped out by raising and lowering its hind leg. In the ensuing silence we could hear the carcass being scrubbed in boiling water. Later Orsino's lines in *Twelfth Night* ('It had a dying fall; O, it came o'er my ear like a sweet sound') recalled these events and seemed inappropriate.

Reports were single sheets and issued each term. Parents were informed of the number of pupils in the form and the position in the form of the particular child. Positions in every subject were written down and the member of staff made brief – very brief and not very meaningful by modern criteria – comments, such as 'Fair', 'Very sound', or in my case 'Could do better'. There was an entry for conduct ('Satisfactory') and room for a form teacher's remarks and, over a cyclostyled signature, those of the headmaster: 'Generally satisfactory' on my first report. The report indicated the beginning and end of the following term and boarders were reminded on each report that they had to return the previous evening. Finally at the bottom of the report printed in bold was the stern admonition that 'No boy will be admitted at the beginning of term unless he is in the possession of a Health Certificate'. However, I can't remember ever producing such a document.

On my first report I was placed twentieth out of thirty-four and at Easter fifteenth. However, this was as good as it got and for terms I struggled. In the summer term we had more formal examinations and I was thirtieth out of thirty-three. There had already been some small adjustments between 3A and 3B. I forget who had been relegated, but we had been joined by my former classmate at Glebe Road, Don France, who had mistakenly been cast into 3B at the initial selection. I knew he was bright and consistently over the next four years he was awarded the form prize presented at the Annual Speech Day. I must have been considered for relegation from the 'A' form, but somehow I managed to hang in there, scraping along near the bottom of the form throughout my years in the Lower IVth and the Upper IVth. My father even prevailed upon Headmaster Daughton to give me a private, 'pull your socks up' pep talk one morning in the summer holidays of 1943. I was overawed and tearful, but it failed to have the desired effect.

◆◆◆

The change in my academic fortunes was as sudden as it was unexpected. In September 1944 a new headmaster arrived and Cale 'Stan' Matthews decided Brigg Grammar School needed a kick-start to dispel any torpor that had established itself in Daughton's twilight years. The three termly reports and major examinations at the end of the school year were deemed insufficient and the new head instituted a system of half-termly marks in each of the subjects, which were then totalled to give a form position. These positions were read out one morning assembly before the whole school: it was a clarion call to wake up and work harder or be publicly shamed. In October the first set of results was read out and when Lower VA positions were announced, I couldn't believe my ears. Instead of being three from the bottom, I was third (equal) from the top! This was earth-shattering and even the staff were incredulous. I cannot account for it. I thought it might be a result of some crass arithmetical error by our form teacher, Malcolm Gaze, who was no mathematician. But the entire results were tabulated and placed on the school noticeboard for all to see and check. The new wake-up call seemed to have worked for me and though I could not maintain those heady heights, for the rest of my time I never sank below halfway in the form and in the Upper Fifth was always in the top six. I went on to gain a thoroughly commendable School Certificate (with exemption from matriculation) and finally a Lindsey Senior Scholarship on my results at Higher School Certificate. All the painful plodding and hesitant efforts brought about a fine late flowering of my academic abilities. My reports changed from 'Rather weak' through 'Has made progress' to 'Has worked with much keenness'. From termly subject positions that rarely ventured into the teens, I received the occasional top position in History or Latin when I was in the Fifth Form.

I was never a self-confident student with an eager, incisive mind, asking pertinent questions and offering original ideas. My young mind was indeed a *tabula rasa* – indeed more *rasa* than most – but it received things like an overused piece of blotting paper, which soaked up a disparate mass, became over full and left messy blotches. However, I persevered through a tunnel of ignorance and eventually emerged into the light, understanding much (but by no means all) of what I was taught. I accepted that my teachers knew best and tried to assimilate their offerings. Winston Churchill questioned his teacher at Harrow about the use of the vocative case in Latin on the grounds that *tabla* as vocative singular was meaningless, as he never addressed a table. At Brigg Grammar School I was much more accepting: if 'Tiger' Richards said a table had to be addressed, then that table had to be addressed!

Latin was a subject I enjoyed, probably because when we started it in Lower IVA it was new to us all and there was a level playing field. 'LATIN FOR TODAY BOOK I' is still firmly embedded in my mind and the delights of *Discipuli, picturam spectate* (students, look at the map) remain. It was comforting to have confirmed that *Britannia est insula* and that *Germania non est insula*. It was enlightening to discover that *Italia est paeninsula* – i.e. almost an island – and from such beginnings stems a lifelong interest in derivations, word structures and etymology generally. Not all of us liked Latin and I rattled off with the others doggerel about Latin killing off all the Romans and now killing me, but in reality I found it fascinating. I revelled in the classical tales that were new to me about winged horses, three-headed dogs and women with snakes in their hair. I was particularly impressed by the myth of Ceres and Proserpina and the vivid engraving in the textbook that showed Pluto, the God of the Underworld, lashing the three dark, fiery steeds that pulled his chariot and heading back to Hades, having abducted Proserpina. As twelve and thirteen-year-olds we noted the innuendo when Atalanta was described as a 'fast maiden' and we sniggered when we translated that Murcius Scaevola thrust his hand into a brazier, which we pronounced 'brassiere'. I let the names roll around my tongue – 'Quintus Fabius Maximus, Cunctator' – and built up a large vocabulary, whose strong similarities to contemporary English words staggered me. I learnt my declensions and my tenses, being initiated in the mysteries of pluperfects and jussive subjunctives, which were fascinating new concepts for consideration. I memorised Tiger's long list of Latin Rules that he dictated to us and even took to translating small Latin textbooks that I picked up for sixpence in the second-hand bookshops on the Steep Hill in Lincoln. My efforts were rewarded by a 'Credit' at School Certificate, good marks at Higher and a lifelong delight in trying to decipher Latin epitaphs in churches. 'Tiger' Richards was a dedicated teacher, not too strong on disciplining refractory pupils, but caring and encouraging to those who wanted to learn. He gave Jack White and I, his two candidates in Latin for Higher, extra coaching in his garden at home while his lately married wife served us with home-made lemonade. He contributed splendidly to any success I may have had at Brigg Grammar School.

Another new subject, and one that impressed my erstwhile friends at Glebe Road and my father, who had spent some time in France during the First World War without picking up much of a vocabulary, was French. This was the language of our supposed allies and I could now make sense of the short italicised fragments that appeared in my *Hotspur* or *Wizard* as spoken by the brave *Maquis* – '*Mon Dieu, une bombe!*' 'Sam Prague' (our name either separately or together for Mr Gregory) started us off and then 'Chips' Morris took over. We toiled over irregular verbs and learning vocabulary, including that mysterious new element 'gender'. Why was a table feminine and a cupboard masculine – simply because it started with a vowel? I slowly came to terms with future perfects and subjunctives in French and I developed skills in making good guesses at words I didn't know in French 'unseens'. The one thing I didn't get much practice in was speaking the stuff and, of course, we never had the chance to try it out on the other side of the Channel. In the forties little attention was paid to the oral side – it wasn't tested at School Certificate. I still think in English, try to remember the French equivalents for the individual words and then try to string them together in some halting sequence. I continued to take French at a subsidiary level in the Sixth Form and could dash off translations of French verse as well as prose. I remember we even made up a version in French of the then current favourite 'Don't Fence Me In'. The Sixth Form room would ring for weeks with the sounds of *Ne m'enferme pas*, delivered out of tune and in execrable accents.

I found Maths difficult and never shone at this subject. I found it strange to hypothesise – let x be the number of boys and y the number of girls in the class: I knew there were thirty-one boys in our class – and no girls. I was baffled by the fact that the square on the hypotenuse should equal the squares of the other two sides, even when I had painstakingly blocked it out on graph paper. I could never put my finger on the right line of figures in working out logarithms and the complexity of cosines and tangents was unnerving. I had set off on my mathematical journey in Form 3A complete with new pencil case, containing protractor, set squares and compasses, but by the time I had reached Upper VA my mind was cluttered with uncomprehended theorems and formulae. In my first year Messrs Pratt and Watts tried to instruct me in the basics and then in Lower IVA I was taught by 'Slunk' Illingworth, whose temper was always on a short fuse and who gloated at my inadequacies. He marked in green ink, which ought to signify something Freudian. Then for three years I had 'Bumper' Knight, second master and an institution at Brigg Grammar School. I remember that in his first Speech Day address 'Stan' Matthews paid a handsome tribute to the debt he owed Knight in settling in to the school and spoke of leaning 'on Abraham's bosom', which parents thought a risky allusion and which passed over our heads. 'Bumper' never faltered in trying to enlighten my ignorance. He forgave me when my next-door neighbour, who studied Algebra at night school, completed a particularly difficult assignment and I presented it as my own: I was one of only two who could do it. Even when in Algebra at mock School Certificate I realised a risible 13% he didn't quail. It was entirely due to his patient efforts that I gained a 'Credit' in the real School Certificate, which was an essential ingredient of a 'matric', without which education at degree level was impossible. I owe him a great deal and I think my result shows his supreme ability to accomplish the impossible.

Science also was difficult. The subject in my time was divided into Physics and Chemistry, taught in two adjacent labs near where the change of lesson bell was rung. Biology was only for girls and was not taught in my time at Brigg Grammar, so I never had any lessons in the birds and the bees, nor in sex education, an area as taboo for Grammar School masters as it was for my parents. My introduction to Chemistry came from a young master called Cobbold, who as previously mentioned was rumoured to have been invalided out of the Commandoes and who had ensured good discipline in class with his silent but awe-inspiring bending in two and subsequent straightening out of an iron clamp stand. Once when I was near the back of the class and my attention had manifestly strayed in the middle of his demonstration and explanation of some chemical reaction, he hurled a wooden blackboard rubber in my direction. Sensing it just in time, I ducked. The board rubber continued on its way and crashed into a large demijohn of distilled water. The glass shattered and the liquid contents flooded the floor. It seemed most unfair that I had to clear up the mess. He gained his revenge a little later. I was now permanently seated at the front and we were to learn about sulphur dioxide, of which I was in blissful ignorance. Did we know what it smelt like? No? Would we like to find out? I showed some interest in this and leaned forward, whereupon he opened the clamp as I inhaled deeply. As I recoiled violently, gasping, choking and with tears in my eyes, he said, *'Well, now you know it smells of rotten eggs!'* – and I also knew why the subject was called in our schoolboy slang of the period 'Stinks'. Cobbold departed after his convalescence, whether back to the Commandoes I know not, and he was replaced by 'Jock' Ketterick, a gnarled Scots seafarer, who had been torpedoed in the Atlantic and then released on health grounds from the merchant navy. He stayed years at Brigg Grammar and died in harness. Judging by Sixth Form Chemistry results he was an able teacher, but to me his subject was uncongenial. When at the onset of School Certificate we had a simple choice between Chemistry and Geography, there was no contest. I dropped the subject with alacrity and have remained ignorant; while I do recognise the meaning of H_2O and H_2SO_4, the principles of the periodic table and valency escape me.

'Blood' Thumwood took me for Physics right up to School Certificate. Again it had been a straight choice – Physics or Woodwork – and my liking and aptitude for Woodwork were even less than those for Physics. ('Timber' Watts was relieved and could see improved results in Woodwork at School Certificate.) I still have Physics exercise books in which my lack of urgency and interest is plainly visible. The time-hallowed three-part structure of Object of Experiment, Method and Conclusion was invariably incomplete. The heading is underlined and the purpose carefully written down; so is the Conclusion, where I have written down at dictation what we were supposed to have discovered from our observations. However, in the section devoted to Method there is usually a hotchpotch of uncompleted drawings and half-completed, meaningless data. I could draw a fine bunsen burner with the aid of my celluloid stencil, but that was as far as it went. Nevertheless, by the time I had been exposed to five years of half-understood Physics I was deemed to have merited a weak pass at School Certificate.

A pass was also the result of my artistic efforts. Cabourne, a precursor of Arthur Lowe's Captain Mainwaring in *Dad's Army*, was a main stay of Brigg Grammar School. He had overseen the Preparatory Department and when that closed about 1942, he became the senior (and sole) Art master. The subject was called 'Drawing' on the report and I couldn't draw. My efforts were pitiable and out of perspective, no matter how much I held up my pencil and squinted along its line into the distance. However, under 'Cabby' my lifelong delight in lettering was nurtured and the words on my 'Wings for Victory' poster were impeccably presented; it was unfortunate that my supposed Lancaster looked like a pregnant, flying pig, dropping 'sausage' bombs. I enjoyed the half-year that was devoted to Heraldry. I copied the armorial bearings of cities and noble families in considerable numbers. I even designed a shield for Ancholme House - *pike proper on field d'or over wavy bands azure*. I loved the archaic language and revelled in *bar sinister*, *chevron gules* and *lion passant gardant*. But I was not able to use these skills in School Certificate and my attempts to present Pierrots at an end-of-pier show are best consigned to utter oblivion. Nevertheless, I rose to the dizzy heights of Chairman of the School Art Society, as the magazine bears witness, and I did the lettering in a Memorial Book, dedicated to those Old Boys who died for their country 1941–45.

History and Geography were both subjects I studied for seven years. My first Geography teacher was Brigg Grammar's first female teacher. 'Ma' Chapman, otherwise known as 'Fanny', was a small, well-rounded figure with whom we took no liberties. She was followed by the wife of 'Jimmy' Jarvis, on active service fighting fires. 'Ma' Jarvis, alternatively known as 'Fanny' – originality was not our strong suit, we stuck with the familiar – was equally strict and we had to listen carefully to decipher her high-pitched, Welsh warblings. However, in Upper IVA we were taught by 'Sid' Walker, a Leeds graduate and a desperate choice, since there had been no other candidate. His classes played up, partly in retaliation for his unutterably boring methods of teaching: we wrote down questions and answers on a particular topic at his dictation in wearisome detail. *'What are the climatic conditions of Outer Mongolia?'* – *'The climatic conditions of Outer Mongolia are...'* We didn't learn much under him and he never seemed to learn. At least four times a term he would push open the door to our classroom to have a wastepaper basket and its contents fall on his head and during the lesson half of us would request permission to leave the room for urgent relief – and permission was never refused. 'Sid' didn't last the year at Brigg Grammar and suffered a breakdown, from which he recuperated by taking a manual job at the sugar factory. The onset of the School Certificate course brought 'Ma' Haigh, at first known as 'Fanny' but subsequently universally known as 'Whisky'. She was a youngish maiden lady, but not all that attractive and of an uncertain temper. She would at times slap us hard around the head for inattention or indifferent work. Most of us accepted this as the natural order of things, especially from an ageing spinster – she must have been nearly thirty. So we sat in stunned silence when one day Hugh Avery, who had been soundly cuffed around the ears, stood up and out of his desk and, towering over the lady, told her firmly that she was not allowed to do that and he would report her to the headmaster, whereupon Hugh marched out of the room. Presumably he knew what he was talking about, because his father was head of an elementary school in Scunthorpe, but I don't think anything very much came of this startling event. 'Whisky' did, however, revise her approach. She began to wear more make-up and fresh aromas began to circulate – it wasn't Pond's Lily of the Valley that Mother favoured and which I presented on her birthday. Moreover she took to sitting on the teacher's desk and swinging her crossed legs. This was to draw our attention to the fact that she was wearing those new, priceless objects of American origin – nylons. We preferred the earlier, combative model and were uncertain of her intentions. We put our heads down and gave more attention to our books. As a whole the class did well in Geography at School Certificate. In the Sixth Form I took only the Physical paper in Geography and the newly 'demobbed' Ernie Urry was the teacher. I learned about millibars, contour levels and cumulonimbus with him.

I was lucky enough to have 'Toddy' Henthorn to teach me History for most of my time at Brigg Grammar. I filled innumerable exercise books with maps, drawings and notes from representations of an Ancient Briton and his lifestyle to the intricacies of Italian Reunification. I also must have written over a hundred essays on such riveting topics as Gladstone and Home Rule and Bismarck's Foreign Policy. Henthorn had an encyclopaedic knowledge of his subject, but his teaching style was idiosyncratic. In the Sixth Form (which in History meant five of us) he would settle himself comfortably in the chair behind the teacher's table. He would then reach out for copies of the *Illustrated London News* and *The Spectator* that were usually there and would open his file of notes, though he never seemed to consult them. As he flicked through the pages of these magazines and gave careful attention to anything that caught his interest, he would be dilating in a conversational tone on the Schleswig-Holstein question or the relationship between Queen Victoria and her prime minister, Disraeli. We would be furiously scribbling notes down in rough. We had earlier been trained in Toddy's way of writing notes with underlined main headings, subheadings and salient points in Roman-numerical order. We then had to make sense of our notes and write them up cogently and coherently in our exercise books. The method would today be castigated, but it was most successful and History results were always exceptional. Mind you, it helped that he was also an excellent tipster, spotting questions and topics that could well appear on the paper. At Higher School Certificate he gave us eight suggestions for both English and European History. In European all eight were on the final paper; in English he was less successful, spotting only five, but then we had to attempt only four questions in the three-hour paper. 'Toddy' was also my housemaster and a person I revered.

An ES Thompson took our form for two terms in History and the designated topic was the Civil War. I remember I enjoyed drawing rectangles and crayoning them in different colours to distinguish Cromwell's New Model Army from the ranks of the Royalists and the cavalry from the infantry. I used to put a rectangle on the adjoining page to signify Prince Rupert, who had gone haring off into the next county in pursuit of a few disordered Roundheads. Then for one term there was a Mr Burridge (I think), who was a young ex-serviceman waiting to go up to Oxford to read History – or the other way round. He failed to hold my interest and had some difficulty in controlling the class. I met him some ten years later when he was a temporary lecturer at the Oxford University Education Department and he ineffectually tried to demonstrate how to use a Gestetner machine to a group of us.

When Cale Matthews arrived, he decided to do some limited teaching to get to know the feel of the school and he took Lower VA for History. He was an extrovert in the classroom and gave graphic descriptions of Wellington's Peninsular campaigns and Napoleon's tactics at Waterloo. Corn Laws and the Reform Bills were also part of Stan's brief. However, he was keen to widen our interests and would read extracts from historical novels to us: he introduced me to the incomparable CS Forester. Not all the extracts were historical, for it was from his lips that I first heard of the events at the cricket match in AG Macdonell's *England, Their England*. It was a relaxed and entertaining time in his History classes, but it also meant that 'Toddy' Henthorn had to do much catching up the next year and drive us hard to ensure we were ready for School Certificate.

At that time five periods of English per week were the norm and I jumped through all the hoops that comprised the English secondary curriculum. I learned to do Clause Analysis, to compile lists of irregular plurals (like 'appendices', 'criteria' and 'formulae'), and I unfailingly knew where to place the apostrophe. I did uninteresting comprehensions about cathedrals with 'Rupert' Pratt and learned rudimentary skills in making Preces. In Literature I struggled through *A Tale of Two Cities* with 'Tiger' Richards and met not only the witches in *Macbeth* but also the conspirators in *Julius Caesar*.

One afternoon our form, and Don France in particular, was convulsed when someone suggested Shakespeare's name could easily have been 'Willie Wagajavelin'. We made our hilarity last – and managed to escape having to memorise the 'Tomorrow and tomorrow and tomorrow' speech. I also have a vivid recollection of a Shakespeare lesson outside in the open air, actually on the pavilion steps, where we were to enact the murder of Caesar and its consequences. I had been detailed to be Mark Antony. Flourishing a ruler for my sword and jabbing it into the supposed wounds that had treacherously killed Jack White, I besought members of Upper IVA to lend me their ears with eloquent effect. Malcolm Gaze took us for School Certificate and his selections from the Cambridge Board's set books now seem less than inspired: *Eothen* by AW Kinglake, *Strife* by Galsworthy, a book of narrative verse (I can't remember the poems, but it had a light brown cover) and *As You Like It*. This was not a collection to set the blood racing. However, I persevered and found favour with the examiners.

In addition to the academic subjects our curriculum also included 'Manual Instruction', which curiously metamorphosed itself into

'Handicraft' on the report form of 1942. Of course, it was universally referred to as 'Woodwork' and was taught by 'Willie' Watts (otherwise known as 'Timber'), who had had joined the school as a permanent member of staff with me in September 1941.

My grandfather had been a master wheelwright and still retained his manual skills in the 1940s when he was well over eighty. Unfortunately his prowess was entirely absent in the next two generations. My three years of labouring in the subject were littered with a variety of joints that would never join, even with a liberal application of the foul-smelling glue that bubbled in a crusted pot at one end of the ill-adapted Woodwork room on the other side of Grammar School Road. My attempt at the frame of a small stool, which was to have a seagrass bottom, was never remotely finished: indeed it never stood squarely on four sound legs. My version of a watch stand did have two pieces of wood at what purported to be right angles but were nearer seventy degrees and there was a hook screwed into place more or less in the right position. The trouble was that no-one in my immediate circle possessed a pocket watch.

However, at home I still have a very useful relic of my woodworking days at Brigg Grammar. It started off to be a candlestick and is stained and retains a sheen of beeswax. Alas, the upright is out of all proportion to the badly bevelled base, since I had to have three or four goes at the crucial mortise and tenon joint, sawing off the early poor efforts and starting afresh to produce a reasonable mortise, or was it tenon? When I came to bore a hole in the top to hold the candle, I broke the 'bit' of the brace and bit and was forbidden to try again or gouge a more rounded hole. For over sixty years it has served my various homes as a doorstop. My one limited success was to make in the autumn term of 1944 a tommy gun as a Christmas present for my younger brother. The body was recognisably gun-shaped if you used a vivid imagination and a piece of dowelling projected almost horizontally at the front. On the side you turned a ratcheted wheel of my own design with a handle like my mother's old-fashioned whisk. When rotated, this produced a fine 'rat-a-tat-tat' against a piece of springy plywood screwed above the wheel. It is no wonder I did not pursue my study of the subject.

◆◆◆

So in the summer of 1946 I took my School Certificate and was pleasantly surprised at the results that gave me exemption from matriculation. I think the staff were dumbfounded by my comparative success. Don France, of course, gained the best School Certificate of our year and probably Alan Riggott the second best, but Jack White and I gained equal third. I had

Distinction grades in English Literature and History, Credits in English Language, Latin, French, Geography and – *mirabile dictu* – Maths, together with passes in Art and Physics. In those days you had to gain passes in at least five given subjects to gain a School Certificate and had to reach Credit standard in some five or six subjects (which had to include English Language, a foreign language and Maths, but fortunately not a Science) to be awarded a 'matric'. The pass standard required a mark in excess of 33%, a Credit was over 50% and a Distinction reputedly over 75%. Brigg Grammar School had a good reputation throughout Lincolnshire for its academic success. It was a 'good' school and it certainly served me very well indeed. Yet when I consider the results overall they were not as good as they should have been. The school took about the top 20% over a wide catchment area and streamed the boys into A or B forms. Not even all the boys in the A form managed to impress the Cambridge examiners sufficiently well in at least five subjects to be awarded a School Certificate, notwithstanding a low 'pass' mark. In the B form it was considered a good year if five or six gained their School Certificate. And this with the top 20%. When I was a comprehensive school head, governors and parents expected well over 50% to gain five A–C passes at GCE, which meant over 45% in each subject.

My parents had been most supportive in their attitude while I was in main school at Brigg Grammar, even if what I was doing was completely outside their experience. They – or rather Dad – decided that I should stay on into the Sixth Form, although at considerable cost to their standard of living: it was some years before that little Standard 8 was purchased. So in September 1946, in a bigger blazer and new long trousers, white shirt and school tie, I entered the Sixth Form and 'our' room that was in the corner by the Chemistry lab and was also the School Library. The cap was not now obligatory and had not been for two years: I had mixed feelings about this, because in my comics the seniors at public schools wore splendid, tasselled versions. The Lower Sixth (divided into Modern and Science according to which subjects were to be studied for Higher School Certificate) totalled less than a dozen and there were far fewer in the Upper Sixth. We were a select band, vaguely conscious of our special status. JC White ('Jack'), RJH Sumpter ('Sally'), AG West ('Aggie' or 'Barrow') and myself ('Effie' – the nickname is explained later) formed the Modern group and in the second year we were joined by RHM Markarian ('Mac'), who had stayed on a further year to gain improved grades and entrance to Oxford University. The Science group comprised DW France ('Don'), a newcomer, JCM Lyon ('Leo'), AN Jones ('Jonah') and BS Organ ('Brin') and maybe one or two more who didn't last the course. They were hardly economic groups, but we received some almost individualised teaching and thrived under the attention.

At Higher School Certificate you took subjects at one of three levels: Subsidiary (one paper, one point and long discontinued), Ordinary (two papers, two points and equivalent to modern 'A' level) and Advanced (three papers, three points and equivalent to the old 'S' level). You could take a maximum of nine points and I, for want of more cautious advice, took the lot. I chose to take English at Advanced level, and History and Latin at Ordinary level. As the Physical Geography paper was supposedly more compact than that for Regional Geography and the French-to-English paper easier than the English-to-French paper, it was decided for me that I should take those papers and thus those subjects at Subsidiary level.

❖❖❖

I blossomed in the Sixth Form. I was encouraged to have and defend my own views, but I was only too content to accept the views and opinions put forward by my teachers. I found the subjects interesting and, since there was no television and my social activities were severely circumscribed by lack of opportunity and on financial grounds – half a crown a week did not go very far – I worked hard. I relished the greater intimacy of Sixth Form teaching and a new relationship with staff, who had been aloof and Olympian before. All this was encouraged by the head. It was as though Zeus, a new Apollo, Poseidon and Mars had come down from the Greek mountain and walked among us.

'Nero' Romans had been appointed senior English master from September 1946. He was unlike any other English teacher I had had. He had pitted features, smoked a pungent briar pipe and wore a sports coat and corduroys, not a well-worn suit. It was rumoured that he had been in 'intelligence' during the war. He hailed from Gloucestershire and was a keen adherent of the county's cricket team. I supported Yorkshire equally strongly and many were the spirited conversations we had during the summer term over the fortunes of our respective teams as the season progressed. I remember gloating when Yorkshire built up a seemingly unassailable lead over Gloucestershire and was chagrined when Tom Goddard went to work on a sticky Bristol wicket in the final innings, gaining a notable though narrow victory. Nero obviously loved the canon of English Literature and he revealed unsuspected glories to me, from the majesty of *King Lear* to the inventiveness of the 'tun of lard', Falstaff, from the wonder of Dickens to the stern morality of George Eliot. I read Romantic poetry for the first time and immersed myself in the soaring spirit of Shelley, in Wordsworthian mysticism and in the sensuousness of Keats. How I delighted in visualising the 'pillow of my love's fair, ripening breast' and the panting of Porphyro in

Madeline's chamber – it had to be all in the mind in the forties! Then there was Thomas Hardy: not having a major author from his own county, Nero's favourite was from neighbouring Dorset. We admired Gabriel Oak, were in awe of Henchard and fancied Tess together. He read extracts from *Under the Greenwood Tree* at a Christmas concert in wonderfully warm, cidery tones. He contrasted the hesitant Hamlet with that action-man favourite of his, Wally Hammond, the cricketer. He also liked his beer and, after I left school, we would walk over to the White Horse at Wrawby for a pint and a discussion of books I was studying at university and life at Oxford. Nero had a distinct formative influence on the course of my life. He, with some help from 'Rupert' Pratt (who took two of the set books in the Lower Sixth), was responsible for my main subject. The well known and incomparable 'Toddy' Henthorn and 'Tiger' Richards took us for all the History and Latin papers. 'Chips' Morris with a little help from the new language teacher, 'Steady' Barker, looked after the French and 'Ernie' Urry took us for Physical Geography. I was very lucky in my teachers.

I gained status and became a prefect. I and my contemporaries were the first to wear the new prefects' tie, instituted by 'Stan' Matthews. This was to add another subtle touch towards making Brigg Grammar more like the public school from which he had come. Gowns for prefects would have been too much for town and pupils, but we wore our ties (which were school ties with a third stripe of red introduced between the alternating bands of light and dark blue) with pride. We had marshalling duties principally at assemblies and at school dinners. We patrolled the cloakrooms at morning break, clearing them on fine days and maintaining some semblance of order among the milling crowds on wet ones. We also read biblical passages at assembly. I think we may have had a prefects' detention, but I can't be certain. We certainly clipped the ears of cheeky juniors and helped them on their way with a well-directed foot. Our one 'perk' was a free school dinner on the day we were on dinner duty. For me this was Wednesday. I normally went home for dinner – I had always lived within four hundred yards of whatever school I attended – so school dinner was a novelty. The prefects supervised the queues and wandered around while the boys were eating and saw to it that they left in an orderly manner, leaving little mess. Then the prefect had his own dinner: this was usually the pick of what was left, but just occasionally there was so little left that a special fry-up had to be quickly concocted. The school cook (as opposed to the boarding house cook) was the redoubtable Mrs Fairbanks, who was a member of the Ladies' section of Brigg Bowling Club like my mother. Thus I received favourable treatment, especially as it was harder to quantify numbers staying on the Wednesday half-day. Any dried-up remnants of the cottage pie were scraped into the capacious pig-bin and I had bacon, egg and liver with probably some freshly opened fruit salad that was destined for the dinner ladies' own lunch.

◆◆◆

One day early in the summer term of 1947, 'Stan' Matthews called all ten members of the Lower Sixth into his room. We hastily reviewed our sins and omissions, but could make no guess at the purpose of these summons. We were thus thoroughly bemused when he said, *'Well, I suppose you're all thinking about going up to university now.'* We gazed at each other dumbfounded. The thought had never entered my head – nobody in our family had been to university or even considered it – nor, I think, had it crossed the mind of any of the others. We were lined up before him in his study and I was at one end. He beamed at me – and his beam always had the hint of a leer, like Tommy Cooper's – and said, *'Where were you thinking of applying, then?'* At that time I doubt if I could have named more than five universities. I knew there was one in London, but I'd never been there and thought it too large and dangerous a place for a sheltered Brigg lad. There was one across the Humber in Hull, but no self-respecting 'Yeller-belly' ever wanted to go to Hull. I thought there was also one in Sheffield, but I wasn't sure. There were, of course, Oxford and Cambridge, because they rowed in a boat race. I remembered that recently the Oxford crew had been successful on the Tideway and without more thought blurted out, *'Oxford, sir.'* I think a look of incredulity flitted across his face, but he made no comment and passed on to the next in line. However, he must have taken me at my word, for that autumn I filled in application forms for Oxford Entrance. I knew nothing of Oxford colleges and 'Stan' decided on Wadham. He entered Raif Markarian and Jack White at his own old college of Exeter, but three would have been stretching it. The two Hunt brothers, who were four and five years ahead of me at school, were at Wadham, one reading Physics and one Theology, after starting in Law. So Wadham it was. I think I might have seen the odd past paper, but I had no special coaching or preparation. The English texts we were studying for Higher School Certificate and what I had done at School Certificate would have to furnish my answers on the specialist papers. The General Paper we had to take at Higher School Certificate would suffice for the Oxford General Paper and for the Essay. The Latin and French unseens were covered by what we were doing in these subjects for Higher.

Thus in early March 1948 my father saw me off at Brigg station and I embarked on my journey to unknown academe, passing through (to me) uncharted waters. First I had to change at Retford and then, more scarily, make my way from Kings Cross to Paddington. I had never been to London before and the Underground was cavernously daunting. At Paddington I somehow managed to find the right platform and boarded the train for Oxford, along with a considerable number of mature young men, seemingly far older than my seventeen years and six months. Three sat in the same compartment as myself and proceeded to talk loudly, confidently and in refined tones of their public schools, their old students who were gaining plaudits at the colleges for which they too were destined and about their headmasters' friendships with the masters of the various colleges. My self-confidence ebbed further. At Oxford I walked up to the city, carrying my shabby suitcase, and trudged along The Broad under the critical if battered gaze of the Roman Emperors, whose heads were held high on pillars outside the Sheldonian Theatre. I saw the King's Arms that I had been told was my landmark and turned into South Parks Road to catch my first glimpse of 'Wadh. Coll. In Acad. Oxon.'

I spent three days and three nights there, my mind a mixture of dazed bewilderment and delight in my handsome surroundings that fused into a fervent wish that this might be mine. A porter gave me directions to my rooms (an impressive plural) on a staircase in the main quad. I staggered up the staircase and surveyed the faded grandeur of a sizeable room with two adjoining bedrooms, though on this occasion I was to be the sole occupant. There was, of course, no en-suite – in fact no water on tap at all – and this was worrying. I explored the grounds (being stunned by the magnificent, overarching copper beech in the garden), visited the Chapel (where I invoked help from the Almighty in a silent prayer) and located the Hall, where I ate on my first night and was waited upon by white-coated 'scouts' – with not a woggle between them. Another scout awakened me the next morning, bearing hot water in an ewer for washing and shaving. The latter was not at all necessary, but I lathered and scraped my chin and cheeks. I had breakfast in Hall and after things had been cleared away sat down with some sixty or so others to face whatever the fates had in store. Various 'dons' in academic dress gave out papers to those who were hoping to read their particular subject. I remember some fifteen papers in English being handed out by a relaxed young don, who had a cigarette hanging out of the corner of his mouth, his eyes squinting against the curling smoke, and whose gown had slipped halfway off his shoulders. The college clock struck half past nine, the dons departed and I toiled away for the next three hours on the Shakespeare paper. I had a reasonable knowledge (as I thought) of *King Lear*, *Henry IV* (part i) and *The Tempest*, my set books for Higher School Certificate, of *As You Like It* (which I had done for School Certificate) and was desperately trying to remember something about *Julius Caesar* and *Macbeth* we had read in class during the Upper IVth. One question I could not even attempt: it asked me to comment upon the difficulties in staging Shakespeare, when I had never seen any Shakespearian presentation. To my amazement at noon when the buttery in the crypt opened some dozen candidates left the Hall and returned with pints of beer to lubricate their final thoughts. I could never have done this and anyway I found myself scribbling to the end.

There were six papers altogether. I could just about cope with the French and Latin unseens and can remember that on the General Paper I was invited to comment upon Lord Acton's axiom that 'All power corrupts and absolute power corrupts absolutely'. Hitler, Mussolini, King Lear, Macbeth, Henry VIII and George III all played some significant part in my response. I can't remember now the one word that appeared as the subject of the Essay, but it was during this final paper that it was my turn to be interviewed. I left my half-written paper and the Hall to mount the spiral staircase leading to what I later learned was the Senior Common Room. I knocked on the door and entered to be confronted by a horseshoe arrangement of some twelve dons in full academic regalia. I was overawed by the black, scarlet and gold-fringed gowns and the multi-hued hoods and hastily tried to unscramble my wits, as I took the vacant seat at the foot of the horseshoe. They were understanding and my questioners concentrated chiefly on what I was doing for Higher School Certificate. I did my best to make cogent replies. One questioned the rationale behind lumping Chaucer, Milton, Goldsmith and Lamb on one paper. I answered in all seriousness, *'But that's the Cambridge Board, sir'*, and received a superior chortle from the assembled dons. I had my ten minutes and then made my way back to the Hall to finish the Essay.

That was the end of the College Entrance Examination and I somehow made my way back to Brigg. My mind was still befogged and I could give only sketchy answers to questions about my experiences both at home and at school. I had had a glimpse of a whole new world of learning and gracious surroundings. I could not dare believe that I had done enough to be accepted, but dared to hope and prayed that a miracle might happen.

I was still in bed at the beginning of the Easter holidays and it was my mother's birthday (March 31st) when Dad came into the bedroom bearing a small white envelope, postmarked 'Oxford' and addressed to 'JA Rhodes Esq'. I only ever received envelopes on my birthday. I couldn't bring myself to open it, so Dad did. *'You're in,'* he said! I took the small sheet of notepaper, headed 'Wadham College', and it informed me that the warden, CM Bowra, was 'happy to say that we shall be pleased to take you in October 1950 and I shall keep a place for you accordingly'. To me a warden was someone who supervised a youth hostel: I had no idea then of the eminence of that small rotund figure, Sir Maurice Bowra, warden of Wadham, familiar of the cognoscenti and baiter of Hitler, who was to gain my admiration and warm veneration in the early fifties. My father was pleased, but audibly concerned – *'How are we going to pay for this?'* he said. I hastily dressed and went over to school to tell 'Stan'. He beamed at me, but his first words were *'Jack White is going to be even more disappointed'*, for Jack had already received news that whereas Raif Markarian had gained a place at Exeter, he had not. However, Jack was later offered a place at Pembroke College and we were English freshmen together.

Brigg Grammar School did a fine job on that small Upper Sixth of 1948. Don France went to Cambridge, Jones and Lyon went to Nottingham, West to Sheffield and Markarian, White and myself to Oxford. Robin Sumpter became an articled solicitor and Bob Hadow a vet. The previous two years had seen 'Ollie' Kingdon gaining a place at Cambridge and Ken Horton at Nottingham and 'Cec' (pronounced as in pit) Taylor winning a scholarship at Imperial College, London, a tremendous achievement.

By taking the Oxford Entrance I had had to start what was also my Higher School Certificate revision early and so in June I was as well prepared as I could have hoped to be. However, I was as usual nervous in approaching the exams, more especially as in those days you could fail Higher School Certificate completely if you failed to satisfy the examiners on the General Paper. We had been told the cautionary tale several times of the farmer's son who, failing to read the question carefully, had written a fascinating essay on 'Dairies': unfortunately the examiners had set the question on 'Diaries' and refused to grant him a Higher School Certificate. It was a long wait till the results came out in late August. When they were released, I was on a family holiday at Scarborough for the Cricket Festival and witnessing Don Bradman's final innings in England – he didn't score many, I regret. I had not had the wit to leave a postcard at school, so I returned home unaware and indeed somewhat forgetful of what was being weighed in the balance. We reached Brigg and Aunt Lil had arranged tea for us all. We were eating this when 'Stan' surprisingly and unexpectedly appeared on his old, large and sturdy bicycle. He had heard we were home and had located us to give me the good tidings that I had been successful at Higher School Certificate and had in fact been awarded a Lindsey Senior Scholarship. This entitled me to have my fees at Wadham paid and provided £205 per annum – the maximum because of the family's low income – for me to enjoy the delights of academic life at Oxford. And I owed all this to 'Stan' Matthews and the staff at Brigg Grammar; it was a complete vindication of the system whereby Junior and Senior County Scholarships and the Grammar Schools gave undreamed-of opportunities to children from less affluent backgrounds.

◆◆◆

114

For most of my time at Brigg Grammar School there was a war on. I have written elsewhere in more detail about 'My War 1939–45'. We took the wartime conditions in our stride. We coped with broken nights when in the first year or so at the school the siren had summoned us from our beds to go to the shelters: I think we may even have had an hour's dispensation and told to arrive at school for ten o'clock on some few occasions. I collected old saucepans and other aluminium objects in the run-up to 'Wings for Victory Week', which in reality was a savings campaign to raise extra funds for the war effort. I also designed an indifferent poster advertising the event: it was displayed – well at the back – in Lacey and Clark's window. I also sang in a special 'Wings for Victory' concert as a member of the school choir. We sang Purcell's 'Fairest Isle' and 'Where the bee sucks there suck I', largely for the words 'And merrily do I fly now'.

The previous year we had had a Warships Week when posters had such patriotic slogans as 'Keep the Lion Afloat' and 'Save for the Brave'. The school raised £1,008–13s–8d that week. A Physics exercise book I have of the period where I had inadvertently left half a page unused bears the terse and tart comment 'Wasting paper lengthens the War'.

School assemblies were clouded by the announcement of names of Old Boys who had been killed or were missing in action. Occasionally we saw Old Boys visiting the school in their smart uniforms, mainly RAF.

The school formed its own branch of the Air Training Corps, Flight no. 1542 – but I was never a member. The Scouts continued to meet regularly and undertook various activities to aid the war effort, like collecting wastepaper and clearing and chopping wood from Colonel Nelthorpe's Scawby *desmesne* to present a sack of logs to the old and needy at Christmas. The school magazine, though still published each term, was printed on wartime paper and limited in size. In March 1944 it had a skimpy sixteen pages: it was, the editor apologised, that or nothing.

The magazine contained black-edged boxes, denoting those Old Boys who had died for their country. It also contained jingoistic poems, such as 'Hitler's Nightmare', 'Siren Song' and 'A War Alphabet'. Ironically the latter has the line 'S for our strong base in Singapore'! There was welcome news that JB Bell, whose ship had been sunk in the eastern Atlantic and who had been missing for six anxious weeks, had been reported safe 'in a British possession'. Mind you, Old Boys could be injured on the home front too. GR Wraith was seriously injured working in a quarry, when he was trapped under a Lancaster that failed to rise. The Debating Society continued and in 1941 there was a 'discussion': *That this House considers America should pursue a more vigorous war policy*, which motion was carried by a large majority. (As I write this in March 2003 it has a topical if plangent ring!) At the Old Boys'

Dinner a special collection raised £9–10s–9d for Red Cross food parcels to be sent to Old Briggensians who were languishing in POW camps in Germany. Old Boys met all over the world in various theatres of war and others recounted how in training in America, Canada or South Africa they found time to explore the prairies, climb Kilimanjaro or visit New York. There was, however, a sad and serious side: the magazine of 1943 contains the names of twenty-one Old Boys killed in action and several who were missing.

But Old Briggensians were doing their bit for King and Country and one wrote in the magazine, describing a skirmish in graphic detail and yet in a curiously dated, Rockfist Rogan, gung-ho frame of mind. He tells of being on a troopship in early 1943 in the Atlantic, harried by submarines and dogged by a Focke-Wulf fighter-bomber. They 'were plodding along nicely when two torpedoes flashed past us' and they played a cat-and-mouse game in the mist. Then the Focke-Wulf appeared. 'We bade him good morning with a wicked burst of guns. He replied with cannon fire and the swine closed in and let go his torpedo. Then ensued a few terrible seconds, but he missed us. He came back and dropped a couple of bombs and only the expert handling of the ship by the Captain saved us.' The writer concludes on a most sexist, politically incorrect note: 'I must also pay tribute to the women on board. I never heard one frightened scream – I wish they were as good when there is no apparent danger.'

Many of our out-of-school activities were directed at helping the war effort. Holidays were reorganised so we could set potatoes at Easter and pick them in early October. Headmaster Daughton reported at Speech Day in December 1941 that over two hundred members of the school had assisted in the potato harvest. Others singled (or weeded) beet in spring and toiled from morning to dusk to bring in the cereal harvest in the summer holidays. I also went on a couple of farm camps, where we stayed for a week in spartan conditions in a decaying country house near Barrow and helped with work on local farms.

As far as extracurricular activities went they were extremely limited in wartime because staff were under all sorts of pressure, from serving in the Home Guard to being ARP wardens, from acting as fire-watchers on the school premises to being auxiliary firemen. However, 'Rupert' Pratt managed to keep a school orchestra going and I sawed away as a second violin on Speech Days and at various patriotic concerts. The big event was just after the war when the magazine was pleased to note a 'recrudescence' of dramatic activity. The school celebrated Hitler's overthrow by an open-air production of *A Midsummer Night's Dream*, which was presented between two grass-covered air-raid shelters on the edge of the school field. It was a co-production. Gaze directed the scenes involving the lovers, Miss Wright (who taught French) those involving the fairies and 'Chips' Morris the 'rude mechanicals'. I was one of the latter, being selected to play Flute, the bellows-mender, and so the unfortunate Thisbe too. Most of the players came from the Lower Fifth and Upper Fourth, since those taking public examinations were not considered. Oliver Baudert, our refugee from Holland, was a regal Theseus, so chosen because his modulated English vowels were far superior to the diphthongs of the native 'Yeller-bellies'. Robin Sumpter was a most becoming Hippolyta and everyone in memory seems to have been born to play their particular part. I remember best our group of Athenian artisans – 'Jonah' was an interferingly bossy Bottom, Jack White was a long-suffering Peter Quince, 'Enoch' Eccles played Snug and John Cheeseman Starveling. 'Aggie' West was Snout and revelled in portraying the divisive Wall in a cumbersome frame that made him seem Humpty Dumpty and Wall in one. With blacked-out front teeth, he gave the audience a cavernous grin and delighted in holding up his two fingers in insulting gestures, as he provided the chink in the wall for the lovers to whisper through. As Flute I (eventually) grabbed my big scene in both hands and died with the most operatic flamboyance.

For weeks afterwards I was accosted with the swooping inflexions of my rendering of *'Asleep, my love? What – dead, my dove!'* by members of the school wherever I went and the magazine comments upon my 'unlovely appearance'. At first Chips could not get us in the right frame of mind to play this 'lamentable comedy' and we failed to relax. After one stiff rehearsal he took Jonah and myself across to the boarding house and into Stan's drawing room. Stan urged us both to be more relaxed and to 'ham it up'. He seemed to know the parts involving Pyramus and Thisbe by heart and he scrambled about his drawing room carpet, intoning and acting out both our parts. We were invited to try again and this time all inhibitions left us, as we began to enjoy ourselves.

At the subsequent public performances we happily went OTT, rivalling the excesses of Miss Hermione Gringold. I now seemed to be typecast, for the other school production I was in was AA Milne's *The Boy Comes Home* in the spring of 1947, when I suppose the play's theme of a soldier returning from the First World War seemed topical. Romans and Morris co-produced it and I was Mrs Higgins, a bad-tempered and busty cook. I remember flourishing a rolling pin and having rolled bath towels strapped across my chest. I raised a laugh and left the serious stuff to Raif Markarian, Jack White, Robin Sumpter and Oliver Baudert.

Also in the post-war period, when I was in the newly formed Geographical Society, we had a school trip. You must remember that petrol rationing and the presence of German troops all over Europe had completely curtailed the sort of school trips and foreign jaunts which modern schoolchildren take for granted. This trip was to Nottingham, where we visited both the Raleigh cycle factory and Player's cigarette factory. We toured Raleigh and witnessed the various processes in action and the overalled workers: when I later saw Albert Finney in *Saturday Night and Sunday Morning* it was with a distinct feeling of *déjà vu*. At Raleigh we were given a curved metal badge that was affixed to the cycles and represented the 'heron's head' trademark of the company – and remains so today. At Player's we received some cigarette cards. The accompanying staff were offered cigarettes, but they didn't smoke. We pupils felt strongly that they could have passed the fags on to us, because most of us had tried out the habit as a rite of passage and one or two were already addicted. I had already given up smoking, but had experimented briefly. This meant I shared five Woodbines with two friends in the warm anonymity of one of the Scunthorpe cinemas, where we occasionally went to enjoy the adventures of Jon Hall or Sabu and to ogle lasciviously the incomparable Maria Montez.

✦✦✦

Brigg Grammar School was, of course, in my time a monastic institution and for years girls played no part in my life. School and church occupied some 95% of my wakened moments. Eventually the hormones stirred and the testosterone tingled. Instead of ignoring the High School girls, we took notice and our eyes dropped appraisingly below the skirt to assess their legs and ankles: green blazers and gingham dresses were designed to disguise any feminine contours higher up. As for the relatively few older Convent girls, they rarely excited our attention because they were usually escorted by black and white starched nuns. At morning break we congregated at the Rubicon, which was the small stream that divided the adjoining fields of Brigg Grammar School and the Girls' High School, but prefects were on hand to send us away and when we were prefects this was part of our duty. Fraternising with girls in High School uniform was not only frowned upon, it was expressly forbidden.

The boarders and the Brigg lads were the most likely offenders and I well remember 'Toddy' Henthorn giving a fresh, stern warning on the subject at a House assembly when I was a school prefect. Unfortunately, that afternoon after school I had been into WH Smith's for something and met his elder daughter, Caroline, who was at the High School and a year my junior. I knew Caroline well from church and the newly founded Church Youth Group, held on a Sunday evening. We were chatting about matters of mutual interest outside the shop when suddenly Toddy came along on his cycle. We were peremptorily ordered on our respective ways. It seems incredible nowadays that such could have been the mindset at that time. It was as though the reputations of the two schools could be seriously tarnished in the eyes of the general Brigg population if members of the opposite sex in their full school uniforms were seen together.

However, there was one occasion when fraternisation was officially encouraged. There was a new headmistress at the High School: in contrast to most of her staff Miss Burt dressed stylishly, had her hair permed and presented an attractive feminine image. For some reason she and 'Stan' decided it would be a good thing for the Lower Sixths of both schools to hold a 'Social Afternoon' – the capitals are fully merited. It was fixed for a Wednesday afternoon in July 1947. This was normally a half-day for the boys, but not the girls, who had no Saturday morning school. A programme of tennis (of which few of us boys knew anything about), rounders and a treasure hunt together with tea, arranged by the girls and my Aunt Ethel (High School cook), was set up. The spinsterish staff of the High School looked upon this social experiment with ill-concealed distaste and at the prospect of young males disporting themselves within their hallowed precincts. On the day itself one Sixth Form young lady ('MC') at the sight of so many in trousers locked herself in a store cupboard and had hysterics. After some two hours she was finally persuaded out with difficulty and taken home.

'Nero' Romans was our Sixth Form pastoral head and he and Stan made the best of what must have been for them an uncomfortable afternoon. However, for the vast majority of the Sixth Formers it was an overwhelming success; indeed so successful that it was never repeated to my knowledge. We boys graciously bowed to the girls' superior expertise in tennis and displayed our greater strength by belting the ball for miles at rounders. We did full justice to the delicious tea and had a seemingly unending number of young ladies to engage in the mildest of flirting. A friend and I became acquainted with two maidens from distant parts, Redbourne and Kirton Lindsey. For a time vague amorous thoughts blossomed. I waved to her on the Vessey's bus as it trundled past from the High School on its way to pick up the members of Nelthorpe House who lived at Scawby and beyond at Brigg Grammar. That summer holiday I cycled miles to Messingham and Scunthorpe to attend gymkhanas where Rachel, resplendent in riding mac and hard hat and mounted on a mighty chestnut, was taking part. But it was a relationship doomed to failure and very temporary heartache.

It is consequently true that sex (of whatever variety) had a minimal role to play in my career at Brigg Grammar. Biology was not taught then and my sexual knowledge was negligible. I can't remember any rude words scrawled in the toilets. I had heard the words, but had only the sketchiest sense of their meaning. I used them occasionally, as when repeating the mantra about one of my form mates who had an unfortunate surname: 'Alcock – no balls!'

✦✦✦

Sport was far more important. Not that I was much good at sport, and a willing keenness could not disguise a distinct lack of real talent. As a junior I supported school teams in cricket and football with a zeal verging on fanaticism. Most Wednesday and Saturday afternoons when a match was on I was back at school, cheering on my heroes. Those good at sport were idolised as demigods when I was in 3A or the Lower Fourth – oh, my Girdhams, Westobys, Baggotts and Atkinsons of long ago! And as previously mentioned when in the summer of 1942 Brigg Grammar School played and beat a public school, Bablake (billeted in the boarding house after the Coventry blitz), I was there! I rejoiced greatly as Bob Atkinson ('Akky') scored an immaculate and unheard-of sixty-nine not out. At school sporting heroes tended to do well at both football and cricket. Atkinson was a very good cricketer and a firm centre-half at both School and House level. His mantle was taken over by 'Cec' Taylor, who was an accomplished centre-half, and both opened the batting for the First XI and kept wicket. Such skills and expertise were quite beyond me, but because of my willingness to attend nets and have a go, I later found a place in School Second XIs at both cricket and football. In my last year I captained each.

In football I kept goal and was reasonably successful in keeping scores down. Three soccer memories stand out. One was going away to play Winteringham Grammar School at Grimsby one cold winter Saturday afternoon. We travelled by train and I had an extra sweater and a flask of Camp coffee to keep the very obvious signs of flu at bay. I think I only went because Winteringham was one of the rare co-educational Grammar Schools and the girls volunteered to serve the teas afterwards. As captain I had to give a vote of thanks to the ladies. The second memory is of a home match against Barton Grammar School. Barton then, like De Aston, was thought to be of inferior sporting prowess and fit only to compete with Brigg Second XIs. Our younger players had played well and we had a comfortable 4-0 lead when near the end we were awarded a penalty. As captain I elected to take it myself and duly 'toggy-ended' it past the opposing keeper. That was the only goal I ever scored at Brigg Grammar – and it was most satisfying. My other happy memory is of the Monday night matches when I was a Sixth Former. They were played between the School First XI and a team mainly of staff, but containing some four members of the Second XI in those positions that the staff couldn't fill. They had no-one wishing to keep goal, so I played. These matches were very keenly contested and challenges were not shirked – especially not by 'Hacker' Hadow of the Sixth Form and 'Paddy' Paisley, the first and freshly appointed Biology teacher, who confronted each other in midfield.

I was very keen on cricket and could tell you in minute detail of Yorkshire's progress and success in the County Championship. I read a number of books on cricket and 'Plum' Warner's *Book of Cricket* was the best authority. I purported to be an off-spin bowler and a number seven batsman. One season I experimented with a new bowling action that necessitated wreathing my arms in serpentine motions as I trotted up to bowl. It failed to impress the opposing batsmen and was greeted by derision from my peers and elders.

An older Brigg boy, called Batchelor, mimicked my action and referred to me as 'Glamour', meaning all show and no use. For a few weeks the name stuck, but was discarded when I became 'Effie' to my form mates and later to the whole school, staff and pupils alike. I had taken to school a bible that bore the name of an aunt on the inside cover. A so-called friend spotted 'Effie Rhodes' and started calling me 'Effie' derisively. At first I didn't care for the name, but eventually accepted it as a badge of distinction. It could have been much worse. The boy Batchelor I mentioned earlier was, I think, called Hugh, but we all knew him by his nickname and used it constantly. He was 'Fart' as his name was the same as that of a notable firm that canned peas. But back to the cricket…

'Bumper' Knight watched me several times at the nets, but I never did enough to impress him or merit a place in the First XI. I played for and then captained the Second XI and we usually did well, since there were many promising players who had to wait their turn to get into the top team. I rarely troubled the scorers much, but on a favourable wicket I could turn the ball and was good for one or two wickets. My greatest feat was in my last season when we had played six matches, winning four, tying one and losing the first against Barton.

Our last match was the return fixture against Barton. We made a disastrous start and when I went in at number seven we were nine for five. Derek Sumpter was at the other end and had begun to see the ball clearly. I blocked away and scampered the occasional single when the ball snicked off the edge of my bat, while Derek scored many cleanly driven boundaries and we ran threes when he lofted the ball into the outfield. After he was out for thirty-one the other batsmen failed and I was left at five not out. However, we had amassed a surprising total of forty-eight runs. When they went in to bat, our opening bowlers could make no impression. They had reached twenty-seven for one wicket and were coasting to victory, when a thunderstorm intervened. It was short but quite violent and halted play, leaving pools on the pitch. It looked as though the match could not be finished. We took an early tea and the sun came out. Miraculously most of the water had drained away and we were able to continue. The hitherto docile pitch had changed its nature completely. My slow off-breaks became possessed of demons and popped like a jack-in-the-box. I found myself turning the ball two feet or more and having LBW appeals turned down because, having pitched well outside the off stump and having beaten the bat, the ball was heading off in the direction of square leg. Nevertheless several balls popped off the bat and offered 'dolly' catches – I even took one myself. The final wicket was taken, fittingly enough, by Derek Sumpter – with some help from me. Their number eleven batsman decided to swipe and go for glory, although we had not realised his intentions. I was fielding in a true captain's position, silly mid-off – with emphasis on the first word. The batsman heaved and connected. The ball came flashing at my head. Involuntarily I put up my hands to protect my face and the ball stuck. They were all out for thirty-six. A famous victory had been achieved and the magazine has in brackets after their score '(*Rhodes 5 for 5*)'.

Not only was I a member of Brigg Grammar School and played sport at inter-school level, I was also a member of Ancholme House. In fact I was a rabid green Anchor. The House system was firmly embedded in the ethos of Brigg Grammar and there was strong rivalry among the various Houses. There was School House (whose housemaster was by tradition the headmaster himself), which comprised the boarders. They were probably fewer in number, but had the advantage of being able to practise more at the various sporting events. Yarborough House, under Mr Knight, covered all the boys to the east of Brigg. Sheffield House (under first Mr Cabourne and then Ernie Urry) consisted of those who came from Broughton and those many who made the journey from Scunthorpe every day. The Daisy bus service travelled especially from Broughton and the Enterprise and Silver Dawn from Scunthorpe. Nelthorpe House (Mr Morris) was the base for those who lived in Scawby Brook and in all the many villages to the south and west of Brigg.

The last three Houses all had aristocratic pedigrees, having been named after the noble, landed families in the locality. Ancholme House was a newcomer, an upstart carved out of Nelthorpe House when numbers became disproportionate. It had been in existence barely five years when I started in 1941 and the founding housemaster was 'Toddy' Henthorn. This House harboured all the Brigg lads and was beyond question the best House. Each

House had its own colour: School – orangey yellow; Yarborough – black; Sheffield – red; Nelthorpe – blue; and Ancholme – green. We all competed in the school's five major sports (football, cricket, cross-country, swimming and athletics) and vied strongly and passionately to win the Cock House Cup. To do well on Sports Day merited a whip-round and a donation from the housemaster to fetch a crate of Laws' or JW White's 'pop' from Jack Clark's tuck shop; to have become Cock House demanded three crates.

As I mentioned at the beginning, I can't swim and so never took part in any of the swimming competitions, but I cheered on our heroes with passion – John Dunham, Don France, Mike Silverwood, Bob Stringer, Roy O'Neill, to name a few. At cross-country I had no such excuse and an innate aversion for long-distance running did not count. My one relative at the school, Cyril Stokes, who was four years my senior, had excelled at the sport for Sheffield House, but such expertise had missed our side of the family and I was out of breath and labouring before we reached Sass's and the Monument. Brigg Grammar School was noted for its cross-country running and the *Hull Times* regularly sent a photographer to take pictures of the white-singleted horde coming down the school drive and into Grammar School Road. Exhibitionists (like FD Bowskill) used to start off at a sprint and would appear in the next week's paper comfortably leading the field at that stage. They had faded before they reached the Grand Cinema. I would walk up St Helen's Lane and stumble slowly round the Bull Field. On the downhill section by Wrawby sandpits I usually managed to break into a trot, but I walked most of Brickyard Lane before breaking into another laboured trot when we re-approached civilisation in Grammar School Road. I felt a sense of achievement if, in a field of fractionally over a hundred, I scraped into the late nineties. One-eyed Ralph Girdham was usually the winner, having tussled with the plucky, pigeon-toed, short-striding Roger Cobb all the way. Ralph Girdham was to win the Lincolnshire Open Mile several times in his twenties.

Although my brother was to become *Victor Ludorum* some years later, such was my athletic prowess that I never once appeared on Sports Day, when the finals were held. I was built for comfort not speed and had no staying power. In my first year I was compulsorily retired in the heats of the high jump (Div E), having landed on and broken three precious wooden lathes that were placed across the uprights, in trying to reach the standard height of 3' 6", worth one point to my House. 'Standard' points were awarded for reaching given times, heights and distances at varying age-levels and all these counted towards House points in athletics. When I was a senior, an extra incentive was introduced and points were also awarded for entering and completing the course. I felt I had to encourage the juniors and put myself down for my full quota of events. This meant that I approached every high hurdle from the side and executed my best scissors-jump and that I was lapped by all the other competitors as I puffed and panted my way around the five laps that constituted the mile circuit. That year Ancholme won the Athletics Cup by a mere handful of points from School House. I had done my bit.

I played regularly for the House at cricket and football. In my early years at Brigg Grammar each House fielded a First XI and a Second XI. The First XI contained all the useful senior players and the Second XI contained a mixture of large, strong and clumsily inept older boys with a few willing juniors. This was subsequently changed to a First XI and a Junior XI. I can remember the pride when my name first appeared on the noticeboard to represent Ancholme. The usual goalkeeper in the Upper Vth couldn't play and Rhodes from the Lower IVth was drafted in to play against the 'Nellies' (Nelthorpe House). We played in the waterlogged section of the field not far from the stream. There were no nets and rain had almost obliterated the pitch markings. There was also a strong wind. I had made some routine saves and rolled the ball out to the full-backs to whack upfield. Twice the ball had gone in well over the top of my head and out of reach, but we had equalised on each occasion.

Near the end, when we were playing into the teeth of the wind, Jack Wright (son of the fish and chip man) attempted a clearance from the penalty area. He launched an almighty 'toggy-ender' at the ball, which flew precipitously high into the air. After it reached the top of its steep parabola, the wind caught it and it turned back on itself. To my horror it began to descend towards our goal and an own goal seemed certain. At that time we played with heavy leather balls and this one was also liberally coated in mud. I was transfixed as it continued on its inexorable course. Suddenly it started to home in on me with all the menace of a Scud missile. It struck me amidships, but I grasped it firmly as I was knocked to the ground and all the breath exploded out of me. Still it was a save and we managed a point for the draw.

In my last year I was House football captain, since we had no-one in the First XI and I captained the Second XI. Our senior team was soundly beaten by School House, who had most members in the school team, but our juniors showed much promise and won all their matches. If we seniors could beat Yarborough in our final match, we could share the House Football Cup. And we did.

◆◆◆

I have mentioned those who started at Brigg Grammar School with me and continued in the various forms up to the Upper Sixth, but after more than sixty years it is amazing how many names of that original 3A I can remember. A substantial number may now be dead, yet I recall them with smiling morning face coming not too unwillingly to Brigg Grammar. Their nicknames are still mint-fresh in my mind, as are the Houses to which they belonged. In Ancholme there was Don France, Jack White, Derek Smith ('Smiffie') and Ron Howlett, whom 'Chips' Morris tried to call 'Hibou', from some obscure Franglais pun on Shakespeare's 'howlet's wing', but it never stuck. School House mustered Alan Riggott ('Riggy'), Alan West ('Aggie'), Robin Sumpter ('Sally'), Bob Hadow ('Hacker' – from his tendency to hack your shins on the soccer field) and Charles Eccles ('Enoch'). From Sheffield House there was 'Bunty' Doran, 'Bill' Bradbury, Geoff Beard ('Whiskers') and Gordon Maw ('Wogga'), and from Yarborough 'Bob' Chapman, 'Tinker' Bell, 'Ben' Holah and John Skipworth, whom 'Tiger' Richards christened 'Scipio' after the Roman general: this stuck only in its shortened form, 'Scip'. There were more Nelthorpes in our form than from any other House. At least three of them had the advantage of having elder brothers either at the school or recently left. There was 'Brin' Creasey, Brian Organ (confusingly also called 'Brin' – we never showed much invention) and George Lawrence, called like his brother 'Punch', who was the no. 1 goalkeeper to my no. 2. In addition there was Neville Jones ('Jonah'), Hugh Avery ('Birdie'), RA Kitchen ('Fritz' – I can't think why), Alan Smeeth ('Smeethy'), Alan McDermott ('Mac'), John Fillingham ('Fill') and Johnny Alcock, with his unfortunate name. Finally there was George Woodhead, who had the distinction of gaining his School Certificate as a married man and a father.

Most of our attention was focused on our own form, but in the B form I recall John Sennett ('Pod' – from the laxative, senna pods), Peter Robinson ('Pee-Jay' – after his initials), a stylish opening bat, 'Fairy' Clark, Gordon Fisher ('Gordie') and Brian Lockwood (another 'Brin'). There were others, but my memory is fitful.

Brigg Grammar School had a most formative influence on all our lives and I recall the staff with respectful admiration and my contemporaries with genuine affection. The school gave me a good basic knowledge and, more importantly, opened up unimagined prospects. It nurtured me through any difficulties and finally enabled me to reach what potential I had. To use a modern idiom, it 'empowered' me. The staff presented me with models I kept in mind during my own teaching career, for which they must take much responsibility. For over forty years I tried to inculcate the principles and best practices of Brigg Grammar in the various schools in which I served and aimed to foster the abilities of my students.

On Speech Day we used lustily to proclaim our thanks to the Founder in the words of the School Song:

'Twas in the days of Charles / The second of the name
On his desmesne at Scawby / A man of fairer fame
There dwelt a good Sir John / A Nelthorpe true was he.
His motto ours shall be – **Forti – 2, 3, 4, 5, 6 – dine!** (As we audibly counted out the beats in the last line.)

Floreat Schol. Grammat. Glan. Briggens 1669, now in its new incarnation as the Sir John Nelthorpe School!

Brigg Grammar School's production of A Midsummer Night's Dream, *1945*

10
INITIALS AND NICKNAMES

From the length of the last chapter it is obvious that Brigg Grammar School, or 'BEE GEE ESS' as we called it, played a crucial part in my young life and its teachers had a most important formative influence. Their initials, which were appended with comments to the termly reports, were both familiar and menacing. But however much business executives address each other by initials in television series, we schoolboys never referred to our teachers by their initials and in the staffroom they were hardly ever used either: staff almost always referred to their colleagues in our hearing by their surnames and 'Mr', although in private the 'Mr' was dropped. In the forties nicknames were widely used both for our teachers and for our form mates. It seems to me a pity that today's schoolchildren do not use nicknames for their teachers as commonly as my generation did. These names were usually a mark of affection and respect, although they could be used to indicate dislike and disdain.

By the time I reached Brigg Grammar School in 1941 most staff were long-serving and already had nicknames hallowed by generations of use, but those few who came new to the school were labelled within a very short time. There might at first be more than one contender, yet we quickly by common assent decided upon one and it stuck irremovably and irrevocably. I say 'we' but in reality the names were invented for us by the fashion-leaders in the upper school and we gladly accepted them as they were leached down to us juniors or as we heard the seniors using a newly minted soubriquet. Not until we were in the top end of the school did we do the baptising.

❖❖❖

My reports were signed at the bottom with exhortations to work harder first by 'JT Daughton' and then later by 'NC Matthews', two widely contrasting headmasters. We never knew what the 'J' or the 'T' stood for in Daughton's name, though it was rudely rumoured it was 'John Thomas'. (You may have to ask grandparents to explain that one!) To us he was 'Duffy', but for no reason we could tell. Daughton was a small, bespectacled figure with a monk-like fringe of white hair to his bald head. His were the first dark glasses I ever saw and because of his weak eyesight he usually wore, in addition, a dark green, semi-circular eye-shade, attached to his head by elastic. We knew from our visits to the Grand Cinema that American newspaper editors and French women tennis stars wore such things, but not headmasters. Nevertheless, despite his unrobust appearance 'Duffy' wielded a strong right arm, as he proved on several occasions when I bent over before him in his study, especially on one occasion when I had inadvertently hit him with a badly aimed snowball.

We knew Mr Matthews' names from the beginning: Nigel Cale. He came to Brigg Grammar from a minor public school, Denstone, and was large and imposing, in strong contrast to Mr Daughton. In the Lincolnshire of the forties Nigel was an exotic name, unusual and faintly aristocratic: certainly there were no Nigels among my contemporaries. But neither Nigel nor Cale gave rise to inspiration; possibly because of his commanding presence, we felt it unwise to attempt liberties. All we could get from Cale was an association with turnips – and we certainly dare not use 'Turnip', even behind his back and at a safe distance. So Matthews became 'Stan', named after the diminutive footballer that in those days played on the right wing for England and for Stoke City in the old First Division (then the top one). The footballer was also called the 'Wizard of Dribble', which again made 'Stan' ironical, for our headmaster with his imposing bulk would have found intricate twists and turns impossible. But 'Stan' he became and remained long after the other Matthews had won a Cup Final for Blackpool and hung up his boots. 'Stan' is a name revered and held in great affection by me.

AE Knight, the senior master, had been at Brigg Grammar for years (seemingly since 'the days of Charles, the second of the name', as the School Song proclaimed) and had been known to generations of Briggensians as 'Bumper'. We happily followed the tradition, but it wasn't until you reached the Fifth Form that you came under his mathematical instruction and had closer contact with 'Bumper', not unless you were in Yarborough House or happened to be a particularly good prospect at cricket, when 'Bumper' would keep a close eye on you in the nets.

I was in Ancholme House, being a Brigg lad, and my housemaster was Mr Henthorn; he had yet to write his historical thesis which earned him a deserved doctorate. His initials appeared regularly on my reports from the Upper Fourth to the Upper Sixth – FH. I don't think there was a third initial, but it is difficult to tell. We knew it was 'F' for Fred or Frederick, but neither found favour and he was universally and affectionately called 'Toddy', though how this came about I never knew.

At Brigg Grammar initials did give rise to a couple of nicknames for teachers. Before I entered the school I already knew one nickname used by my parents, who like him were members of Brigg Choral Society. Thomas Glynn Richards, a Welshman who had been at Brigg since long before the war, taught Latin principally but also Music, English and RE if occasion demanded. He was widely known from his initials as 'Tiger', but orally it had two versions – one with a long 'i' and the other with a short 'i' and a double 'g'. I assume someone must have been fond of AA Milne to have started the second version, but the Pooh stories were utterly unknown to me then and I used both as whim dictated. Again irony was in the use of the name, for 'Tiger' was a most mild-mannered, courteous, gentle chap.

The other initials were RWP – those of Mr Pratt who in 1941 took his form, 3A, for Maths and English, but he was also the main Music master. He trained the school orchestra and under his baton we scraped away painfully at Handel's 'Largo' on Speech Day and lustily sang the School Song with its immortal last word to each verse – '*Forti – 2, 3, 4, 5, 6 – dine!*' I never knew what the 'R' and the 'W' really stood for: 'Reginald William' is my best guess and I shudder to think what later schoolboys might have made of Reg Pratt, but his surname did not then have the connotation of 'fool' that it was to have twenty years later. By some mysterious process we transmogrified his initials into 'Rupert' and so he became, with no known association to the comicbook character, 'Rupert Bear'.

An exception to my earlier claim that rarely did a nickname emanate from a real surname was Mr Cabourne, who was in charge of the Preparatory Department at Brigg Grammar when it had one. This was phased out in my first two years at the school along with fee-paying and Cabourne became the Art teacher. To all he was known as 'Cabby', though not to his face. As mentioned in previous chapters he could easily have been the model for Captain Mainwaring of *Dad's Army* fame: he did hold either commissioned rank or that of sergeant in the Brigg Home Guard and strutted proudly ahead of his men in parades to mark Armistice Day or 'Wings for Victory Week'. 'Cabby' did not much approve of the educational changes in the early forties: his mission was to make the fee-paying sons of the Brigg middle class into gentlemen. He thought that we scholarship boys (as we were known from having passed the scholarship exam that later became the Eleven-Plus) were unfit for membership of Brigg Grammar School. I remember he complained bitterly about the standards of 'council house guttersnipes' in one Art class. I didn't take it personally, though I was brought up at no. 29 Central Square: even at the age of twelve I realised that this was 'Cabby' having a bad day and wildly letting off steam.

The teacher who took Senior French was another whose nickname was universally used around the town. AI Morris was known as 'Chips'. Although he had been at the school for years, it had nothing to do with the Mr Chips whom Robert Donat brought to life on film. The premier fish and chip shop in the town was Morris's: it was in Wrawby Street and not far from its rival, Staples, on the other side. Staples, like Central Fisheries off the Market Place and Hewson's (later Wright's) in Glebe Road, was generally regarded as being of rather less quality. AI Morris was 'A1' as a teacher and he was 'Chips' Morris to everybody, even to my maternal grandparents, for he lodged next door down Riverside in very primitive conditions. 'Chips' was almost completely bald and had been from an unusually early age. At one Old Boys' Dinner he was the victim of the imported comedian: *'Mr Morris went to the barber's. "Shall I take my jacket off?" he said. "No need," said the barber. "You can leave your hat on too, if you like."'*

Junior French was taken by Mr Gregory, who also taught RE because he was a non-conformist lay-preacher. He had a particularly nasal intonation and so none of us had a standard French pronunciation. He also suffered from indifferent health, having been gassed in the First World War. At my time, in the middle of the Second World War, he was called 'Prague', but for reasons lost in the dust of ages. Sometimes we added a first name, 'Sam', possibly because his own Christian name was Samuel.

Other long-serving teachers who remain in the memory are Malcolm Gaze (resident in the boarding house) and WE Thumwood. Long before the former England footballer, Gaze was known as 'Gaza' – with a single 'z'. He taught English and sometimes, reluctantly, RE. 'Gaza' succeeded in getting me through both Englishes with good marks at School Certificate in 1946, even though the set texts were *As You Like It*, the justly long-forgotten *Eothen* by AW Kinglake and the equally forgotten play *Strife* by Galsworthy. 'Gaza' obviously didn't kill off my interest in English, for I spent over forty years teaching the stuff. Thumwood – I don't think there was a middle 'b' – taught Physics, a subject that was my worst yet my brother's best and which eventually resulted in an Oxford First for him. Each term Thumwood's initials appeared on my report after a brief comment upon my incompetence in the subject. You might have expected that 'WET' would have given rise to a particularly derogatory nickname, but Thumwood was 'Blood', a singularly inappropriate name, for he was a most gentlemanly, soft-spoken person, who played the cello in the school orchestra and in local quartets with such local luminaries as Mrs Major Piggott and Miss Bradley (sister of 'Bert' Bradley, one-time Chemistry teacher), sometimes with 'Toddy' Henthorn on his double-bass. No, I think 'Blood' came from his facial appearance, for he was of a very sanguine complexion.

My time at Brigg Grammar School coincided with the end of the Second World War and we had staff returning from active service and a few young newcomers. Messrs Pimlott and Urry were demobbed from the RAF and returned to teach Science and Geography respectively. Both stayed several more years before departing to posts of greater responsibility. Pimlott was

'Pimmy' and was detailed by 'Stan' to widen the mathematical understanding of the fledgling Arts Sixth (or as it was then Sixth Modern – all twelve of us in two years). He attempted in a double period a week over one term to teach us the mysterious delights of calculus: I remember a capital 'N' had some significance, but whatever it was I never got the hang of it. Urry taught the Physical side of Geography in the Sixth and, having been a boy at the school, retained the contraction of his name, 'Ernie'. Jarvis (who returned from active duty as a fire-fighter) also taught Geography, the Regional variety, and his initials were 'JG', but he was called by the diminutive of his first name, 'Jimmy'.

During the war Brigg Grammar had women teachers for the first time. We were unused to female instruction and were at a loss to know how to christen them. The ones I can remember all taught Geography at various times up to School Certificate stage. The first was Mrs Chapman, with whom no-one took liberties; likewise with the wife of 'Jimmy' Jarvis who held the fort for some time while he was fighting fires. Mrs Jarvis was a fierce Welshwoman with a sometimes indecipherable accent. We contented ourselves with bestowing upon these ladies the epithet 'Ma' or 'Fanny' and we behaved most circumspectly in the presence of 'Fanny' Chapman and 'Ma' Jarvis. At first the other lady Geographer was similarly christened despite her unmarried status, but 'Ma' Haig (or was it Hague?) eventually became known for obvious reasons as 'Whisky'.

The ladies had been brought in after a rather disastrous Geography appointment: filling staff vacancies in mid-war was desperately difficult. The school magazine, *The Briggensian,* of March 1943 informs us that 'Mr FW Walker, BSc (Hons Geography, Leeds)' had been appointed to a temporary post at the school. He was a walking disaster and an easy prey for malevolent Fourth Formers. As previously mentioned he forever failed to spot the full wastepaper basket we balanced precariously on the half-open classroom door, awaiting his arrival. We played him up mercilessly, partly in reply to his unpardonably dreary way of imparting Geography to us. He became contemptuously referred to as 'Sid' after Sid Walker, a rag-and-bone man in a wartime radio programme.

Radio – remember there was no television then – provided us with the nickname of RA Barker, who came to introduce German to Brigg Grammar School after the end of the war. He was quickly dubbed 'Steady' after the catchphrase from Eric Barker's programme *Merry-Go-Round,* in which the hero was frequently advised *'Steady, Barker!'* when in some parlous predicament. About this time a young Science teacher was appointed to start Biology in the school. His surname was Paisley and he was Irish; very quickly he became with no subtlety whatsoever 'Paddy'. 'Paddy' was also an effective wing-back in hockey, which he was instrumental in introducing into the Brigg Grammar sporting calendar. Nationality was the key to the name rather unimaginatively given to Mr Ketterick, who came to teach Chemistry. He was from Glasgow with an almost impenetrable Scottish accent. He quickly became 'Jock' – as he had been in the wartime navy before being released on health grounds.

Most nicknames soon became endowed with a warm affection for its appellant, but this was not invariably so. Mr Illingsworth came to teach Maths and he is remembered for marking in green ink and for his snide remarks. He had difficulty in keeping discipline, even in the Sixth Form. On one famous occasion he put the whole of the Maths Sixth in detention for some fancied, collective misdemeanour. In those days detentions were held on both Wednesday and Saturday afternoons and those to be detained had their names read out by the headmaster at Tuesday and Friday morning assemblies. 'Stan' Matthews scrupulously avoided reading out the Sixth Formers' names in the detention book and this brought a loud and angry interjection into the silence of the assembly from Illingsworth: *'Mr Headmaster, I put the members of the Maths Sixth into detention and I must insist…'* Somehow 'Stan' managed to stem the outburst and I don't know how the matter was resolved. But Illingsworth was popular neither with his colleagues nor with us boys. He would quietly creep around when on duty, prowling to find offenders committing trivial misdemeanours and then gleefully inscribe their names in the detention book. There was no doubt he did slink about to try to catch people. He thus became 'Slunk' Illingsworth, with an audible distaste when his name was mentioned.

Among those who came to teach at Brigg after the war was Geoffrey Romans, who became the senior English teacher when 'Gaza' retired. He was one of the most important formative influences on my life. It was not long before his English Sixth had christened him 'Nero' and this stuck for the many years he was at the school.

We also had a Maths and Science teacher called Earp. His parents had sadistically given him the names 'Thomas William'; at least his initials were 'TW'. He must have gone through agonies when he was a pupil, but we rarely used the inevitable combination of initials and surname and he was usually 'Earpy'.

Mr Watts taught Woodwork and later Technical Drawing. He was responsible for writing out the athletics heats in his immaculate script and at the bottom of each sheet was neatly written 'WB Watts'. He had two widely used nicknames, but both were rather obvious. 'Willie' and 'Timber' became over the years terms of genuine affection.

I can recall no really subtle names being bestowed, but I suppose to catch on readily nicknames have to be fairly obvious. Certainly at Brigg Grammar School we had no 'Thrombie' or 'Isaiah'. The first was the name given to an awkward colleague, disliked by both staff and pupils for his unpleasantness and lack of co-operation. He could never understand his name until he was advised to look up 'Thrombosis' in the dictionary: 'a bloody clot that obstructs the system'! The latter was a rather cruel reference to the lopsidedness of a colleague's face: one eye definitely was higher than the other!

BRIGG GRAMMAR SCHOOL.

AUTUMN TERM 1943.

The Autumn Term will commence on Tuesday, 31st August and end on Tuesday, 21st December. There will be a break from 1st October to 1st November so that members of the School may help in the lifting of potatoes and sugar beet.

I regret this interruption with the normal work of the School, but the increased demand for assistance on the farm calls us to offer all the help possible. During the last three years masters and boys of the School have rendered great service in helping to harvest valuable food stuffs.

J. T. DAUGHTON

11
POTATO-PICKING SIXTY YEARS AGO

I was a schoolboy just past my twelfth birthday in North Lincolnshire and there was a war on. Food supplies were vital and it was important to grow as much food on British soil as possible and to gather in all the harvests. Labour was in short supply and all sources had to be explored. To this end the school holidays in July and August were curtailed and we schoolboys had three-week breaks at Easter and in October. The Easter break was to 'set' the potatoes and in October we gathered them in. 'Tattie-setting' and 'spud-yacking' provided me with a temporary but very welcome addition of funds, yet they were also significant rites of passage.

Lincolnshire was one large food-growing county, though liberally clotted with scores of airfields, from where Wellingtons and later Lancasters flew off to blast Germany and Spitfires and Hurricanes were scrambled to fly south to do battle with marauding Heinkels, Junkers and Messerschmitts. The potato harvest was ready for picking from early October and the varieties have a nostalgic ring to them – King Edwards, Majestics, Arran Pilots and Limestone Edwards, the latter a variety specially developed by a Lincolnshire farmer to grow prolifically in the chalk uplands of the Wolds. It was so successful that he later called one of his racehorses after it, but the horse did not enjoy similar success in the Grand National.

We lads at Brigg Grammar School were encouraged to do our patriotic bit and help bring in the potato harvest. The school's French master was a particular friend of a local farmer, who had several hundred acres outside nearby Wrawby in the Ancholme valley. The soil was good and the fields bountiful. Thus one October in the early forties I and a dozen or so other boys from school found ourselves performing our first serious work and receiving our first pay packets. I was one of the youngest as others from the school were sixteen. We were not the only labourers. We supplemented a curious mixture of other workers, comprising a few German and Italian POWs from the Pingley Farm Camp and a handful of 'ladies' from Brigg, largely in their thirties and forties. The 'ladies' in inverted commas is deliberate, but more of them later.

We worked an eight-hour day from eight in the morning to half past four in the afternoon with a half hour for lunch and an odd quarter of an hour squeezed in at about half past nine for breakfast. This meant we had to be up by seven and out into the moist October morning just after half past. Our transport was our trusty bicycles. Some had relatively new pre-war Hoppers and Elswicks, but mine was a large, cumbersome machine totally unsuited to my twelve-year-old frame. I would join a few friends and we pedalled sluggishly to Wrawby with a canvas bag containing our provisions hanging from our handlebars. It was always a relief when the field we were seeking was not up Wrawby Hill, but in the lower-lying Vale of Ancholme on the Barton Road.

Dress was not really a problem and there was then no sense of rivalry in being fashionably *chic* with designer labels. We wore old clothes that had become too shabby for school. The thin woollen vests and pants might have faded 'Chilprufe' labels and the old grey shirt with tattered collar might have 'Banner' inside the neck, but so did everyone else's. Well-darned school socks were slipped into the ubiquitous wellies. We had an equally well-darned pullover in case of chill morning winds and old, patched school trousers, short if you were under thirteen, long if you were older. These were of solid worsted, for denim was as yet unknown except in the far reaches of Midwest America. Anoraks may have clothed Eskimos at that time, but we recognised neither the clothing nor the name. In case it should rain we had an old navy blue gaberdine raincoat rolled up and attached to the carrier on the back of our bikes. It didn't take long to dress or to wash in cold water. We hastily ate a first breakfast of home-made jam sandwich or occasionally porridge. It was at this moment that sometimes the prospect of another day's drudgery seemed too appalling and sickening butterflies would flutter insistently in the stomach. A second and unnecessary visit to the lavatory was made in order to delay the cycle journey. Thoughts of feigning illness were attractive, but all silent pleas and reproachful looks were counteracted with stern injunctions not to be a 'cissy' and to show some 'pluck', then considered a highly admirable quality. My parents did not pander in the slightest to my desire for an easy way out. There was a war on and we all had to show our mettle. Looking back, I am pleased they were firm and so I would, however reluctantly, get on my bike and cycle off to Wrawby.

At eight o'clock our toil would begin. We worked in pairs and were paid according to the length of our 'stint'. This varied in relation to the length of the field, the number and ages of the pickers and according to some arcane mathematical formula devised by the farm foreman and his abstruse calculations. He was an imposing figure and was reputed to be so ferocious that he could overcome all others from miles around in a bare-knuckle fight. I never saw him in action, but all the permanent labourers were in awe of him and none of the POWs ever crossed him. He was of a swarthy complexion – probably some Romany blood in his veins – and he had strong features and piercing eyes. In my imagination I could picture him as a hard taskmaster in charge of slaves rowing an Egyptian or Moorish galley. He wore a soiled trilby, moleskin trousers stuffed into formidable boots, together with a jacket and a coloured 'weskit'. His shirt was open at the neck, around which was knotted a red handkerchief with white polka dots. He had a large Wellingtonian nose and prominent teeth, which seemed always to be set in a sardonic, not to say sadistic, grin.

It was his task to set out the 'stints'. He did this by pacing out the length of the field and then, considering the number and ages of the pickers, he would arrive at the length of each individual stint. You picked with a friend of a similar age. Those under fourteen were paid three shillings and sixpence a day, those between fourteen and sixteen five shillings and those over sixteen and adults seven shillings and sixpence. Thus in theory the adults were picking a stint just over twice the size of the smallest stint and those earning five shillings a day were picking half as much again as we did. The foreman did all these complicated calculations in his head and there was no appeal against his decision. But the stints were not fixed irremovably. If some pickers failed to turn up for the day, all the remaining stints were lengthened arbitrarily by the foreman to make up for the shortfall – and, of course, there was no extra pay. We were not unionised labour.

He would cut some twenty elder switches for markers from the hedges and shave off the lower leaves, and then he would pace out the field again. Having determined the appropriate length for the stint, he would stick a marker into a furrow some twelve yards in from where we were to pick. My friend and I were convinced the foreman had a particular antipathy towards us and we were positive he lengthened his stride perceptibly as he strode out our stint.

When I first started potato-picking, the potatoes were spun out by a horse-drawn spinner with two horses, I think, working side by side. They would be guided by one of the regular farm workers and go up one side of the field, cross over some forty or so furrows at the top end and return down the other side. This area would then be progressively reduced until all the furrows within this span had given up their potatoes. Then the process would be repeated with the next forty or so furrows in the remainder of the large field. After a year the horse-drawn spinner was superseded by machines. A new, more powerful and efficient spinner was hauled by a John Deere tractor in smart yellow and green livery and sometimes by a smaller Ferguson, painted a dull grey. We preferred the horses because they kept up a predictable, steady pace and they could be patted and given apple cores. The speed of the tractors seemed to be determined by the mood of the tractor driver, but it always seemed faster than the patient plod of the horses. The only respite was that sometimes the tractors, especially the John Deere, took some persuading to fire up on a cold morning and just occasionally they would conk out temporarily in mid-furrow because of a blocked fuel pipe. We then had a blessed five minutes' respite and would lie spread-eagled on the warm soil, drawing in large, restorative breaths and easing our stiffened spines. If the problem were more serious and would take longer to fix, we were set to harrowing on the part of the field we had already picked.

The potatoes were spun out from each furrow in a swathe some five feet wide. We younger ones picked side by side, but the bigger boys and the women would pick one ten yards ahead of their partner and overtake as necessary. The POWs did not do the actual picking, but the collecting and pie-construction. Potato-picking was like politics – full of dirty tricks. Even if the stint allocation by the foreman had to be accepted, there were many heated exchanges with our adjacent stint-pickers at their inability to start picking in direct alignment with the stint post. They would be accused of being cockeyed and starting at least two yards out of alignment, so that we had to pick the extra two yards. Another trick was that when the stint post had to be moved further into the field to allow the next section to be picked, you seized the stick and contrived to walk apparently straight but veering inwards to your stint, thus enlarging your neighbours'. It was also amazing how often the stint post would be found to have fallen down at a meal break and need re-erecting with the opportunity for a minor readjustment in your favour. Such fancied readjustments would sometimes lead to blows as you struggled to reassert the status quo. This was not, however, why another colloquialism for what we were doing was 'spud-bashing'. This came about by analogy with what the new entrants to the armed forces were doing – 'square-bashing'.

We picked into baskets. At first they were made from osiers and were rather cumbersome, as clods of damp, muddy soil adhered to the bottom. They could, however, withstand being run over by the tractor or a cart and remain serviceable, unlike the wire mesh baskets that were introduced. These were lighter and presumably cheaper, but any contact with cart or tractor rendered them useless. They had a further disadvantage. Whereas the fixed osier-handled basket could be used as a support to lever the picker along the stint, a wire basket handle, like the modern supermarket basket, afforded no such support and backs ached the more.

Each stint would have between a dozen and twenty baskets, half on one side of the area to be picked, half on the other, and left at staggered intervals. You filled one basket and went on to the next until your stint had been picked clean. Then you hastened across the furrows to the other side, where seemingly thousands of pale yellow spuds, sometimes red-smeared, of all shapes and sizes had already been unearthed by the spinner. Rarely were you able to have a breather and await the arrival of the horse- or tractor-drawn spinner. For Grammar School boys unused to unremitting manual labour it was all something of a shock.

We struggled to keep up. The spinner made its circuits at an alarming rate and the stream of pale, moon-faced potatoes seemed unending. We picked, we sweated and we cursed silently the sadistically grinning foreman, the unfeeling automaton of a spinner, the miserly, low-paying farmer and the weather be it too hot, too cold or drizzling rain. We implored celestial powers to give the horses colic or the tractor a mechanical breakdown. We attempted occasional sabotage by deliberately leaving a basket in the direct line of the spinner, hoping it would have to be stopped in order to remove the obstruction. We also ground potatoes into the earth with our heels as we picked in an attempt to complete our stint more quickly. At such times we felt that had our daily pay been increased tenfold it would still be hard, sweated labour, as we straightened our aching backs and then stooped swiftly to the picking again.

Gradually, however, we grew accustomed to our toil: the aches and pains became less or less noticeable, our skill in picking using two hands and grabbing two 'tates' in each hand improved and towards the end of the week the prospect of a pay packet offered dreams of lavish pleasure. Even the weather improved. There was a strange comfort, even exhilaration, in being close to Nature. We breathed in fresh, reinvigorating air. We savoured the primitive pungency of newly turned earth. We felt warm contact with the clay from which Adam sprang and experienced what I later came to realise were Wordsworthian longings. What was more we could see the results of our efforts as the area of furrowed haulms grew smaller.

Once we had filled the baskets they were collected in a horse-drawn cart accompanied usually by a farm worker and a couple of POWs. These were occasionally supplemented by our Grammar School master, 'Chips' Morris, who would pay us a visit from time to time. They would pick up the full baskets, hoist them shoulder high and then tip the contents into the cart, as the horse continued to plod patiently around the circuit, some four yards outside the course pursued by the spinner. When the cart was full, it would proceed to the spot where the potato pie was to be formed. The potatoes were tipped and as load after load followed, a shape like a Toblerone bar arose. It was usually about five feet high and up to thirty yards long, depending upon the acreage of the field. The pie was then covered with straw and clods of earth were dug from around the pie to cover and weigh down the straw. The pies were then opened early in the following year as the farmer sold off the contents, so many tons at a time. Sometimes the farm workers bagged the potatoes in hundredweight sacks by the side of the newly opened pie, weighing them out on a substantial but mobile set of scales. At other times they were taken directly to the farmyard to be weighed there and sold on to the potato merchant.

When we had picked the last furrow, we had to go 'harrowing' before we could vacate the field. It had already been raked over with harrows and a surprisingly large number of palely glinting spuds that had somehow been missed was now revealed. We would line up on the edge of the field, three yards apart, and walk up and down in lines, gathering up the unearthed potatoes. The collecting cart would follow us and sometimes we should recover a further two cartloads of 'tates'. That last word has to be rolled around the tongue lovingly with a delicious Lincolnshire diphthong to be fully appreciated: 'tay-uts'!

Meal breaks were eagerly anticipated, though any brief respite from the mechanical slog of picking was welcome. We snatched a short quarter of an hour between nine and half past nine for breakfast and then came a half-hour lunch break at one o'clock. Our mothers had packed us up with food, which even under wartime conditions was sufficient and surprisingly varied. The bread was either from Lyon's bakery or was in sliced loaves from Mrs East's wooden shack, our corner shop. The waxed paper wrapping bore the names of long-forgotten bakery firms such as Dytes. The bread was lightly smeared with margarine, though some brought bread covered in dripping. Dripping, the congealed fat from the Sunday roast, was not highly regarded in our family and Mother would never consider packing either my father or myself up with bread and dripping. The contents of my sandwiches were usually home-made jam, either strawberry or plum, made during the summer. A special treat was thin slices of 'hacelet', purchased with meat coupons from the ration book, and the occasional sausage, one of the herbally spiced Lincolnshire ones for which Turner's in Cross Street were justly famous. Sometimes the filling would be sliced tomatoes (also home-grown) and once or twice potted meat, again from the celebrated Turner's. A couple of plain biscuits were usually in the sweet package together with a piece of home-made Victoria sponge or a fairy cake, made from powdered or reconstituted egg. There were, of course, no oranges or bananas in wartime, but there was an apple or a pear, fallen from neighbours' trees. Drink was more of a problem. Some took cold tea in old 'pop' bottles and others had a hot drink in a thermos. I had a thermos for a short time before the silver interior shattered: it contained a milky, sugared mixture of Camp coffee, which was largely chicory. After the breakage I had to be satisfied with a large bottle of water and the occasional bottle of 'pop' from JW White's or from Laws. The 'pop' was usually a saccharined lemonade, but sometimes it had a synthetic orange or grapefruit flavour. Only rarely was it possible to obtain the coveted dandelion and burdock.

We schoolboys chewed our lunch, chattered in small groups and then stretched out luxuriously on the good earth or grass by the hedgerow. Later we might approach the horses, pat them and feed them apple cores off our outstretched palms. We had relatively little contact with the few German or Italian POWs or with the women pickers. There were probably three 'Eyties' or a couple of 'Jerries' from the Pingley Farm Camp on Bigby High Road; they must have been 'trusties' because I cannot remember any British soldier accompanying them. We would occasionally watch with interest as an Italian skilfully crafted a ring out of a piece of perspex by careful filing or produced an empty cartridge case, which he had fashioned into a cigarette lighter. Sometimes an older picker would express a special interest and haggle in a mixture of pigeon English and sign language to make a purchase. Neither rings nor fag-lighters had any appeal to me at that age.

The 'ladies' were a curious lot, mainly concerned to earn some 'pin money' for what little luxuries were available in wartime. To us they seemed quite elderly, mothers of young families or single women not yet swept off to work in factories and not considered suitable for the armed forces. They came largely from the poorer council estates and others came from the less salubrious dwellings of private landlords. They were dressed in old blouses, skirts and dresses, some with ill-repaired tears, and well-worn cardigans. Few if any wore trousers, for these were fashionable only for the bright young things of a higher social class. These women were a lively group and regaled each other with earthy stories and coarse comments upon their surroundings and companions. They went largely uncorsetted and often without bras. They relished being unconfined and sweated comfortably as they bent to their picking. I had never before come across such a coarsely cheerful group of women: they were completely different from my mother and her friends, firmly established in the lowest reaches of middle-class morality. They had much more interest in the POWs than us schoolboys and despite the language barriers they initiated dialogues and established relationships. The POWs would also engage in sexual banter in odd phrases and in gestures. It was the first time that I had heard the phrase 'jig-jig', even though I didn't then grasp the significance.

There were, of course, no latrines or conveniences in the fields. You sought the far side of a suitable hedge to relieve yourself and tried to avoid defecating (or in our terminology of that time, 'doing a number two') until you got home, because there was the problem of toilet paper. The women too would disappear behind the bushes. I thought it odd that occasionally a POW and one of the women would disappear behind the hedge together and were greeted with raucous comments on their return, but I gave it no further consideration. My naivety and sexual innocence were complete at twelve.

The lunch break would end all too soon, the horses were re-harnessed to their carts and the afternoon toil would begin. After another two hours or so of unremitting bending, picking and sweating, the time approached half past four and the welcome news of 'last stint' would be passed down the line. We gathered our bags and our bicycles and set off back to Brigg. It was rarely more than a twenty-minute pedal, but we were exhausted and my heavy cycle took all my efforts to persuade home. Here no hot shower or relaxing bath awaited. We had no hot water on tap and baths were a Friday night ritual for which the gas copper had to be brought in from the garden shed and filled with water from the rainwater barrel outside. Then we had to wait seemingly hours for it to reach the required temperature. When I returned from potato-picking, a kettle would be boiled and I sluiced myself down at the kitchen sink, standing precariously on one leg to wash my knees and feet. I would put on comfortable clothes and probably listen to *Children's Hour* before having my tea, which would be a plate of whatever had been cooked for lunch and heated up. It would become dark and I was often in bed before half past eight – unless it was Thursday evening and the unmissable *ITMA*. Sleep came easily, but all too soon my mother would be waking me, saying, *'Come on. It's gone seven.'* After three weeks it was almost a pleasure to get back into the customary school routine. I could face 'Tiger' Richards' Latin lessons with equanimity and even Maths with 'Slunk' Illingsworth was preferable to the daily grind of 'spud-yacking'.

Time has passed and the world has changed unimaginably from the 1940s. Most potato-picking is now completely mechanical and completed earlier. However, I remember with a mixture of nostalgia and backache those 'spud-bashing' days. It was a novel and formative experience and it assured with a sense of satisfaction that we were doing our bit to feed the country. In addition, those potato-picking days marked a rite of passage in my early adolescence and the hard-earned pay packet was welcome too. It meant we could afford the bus fare into Scunthorpe (nine old pence return for schoolboys) to sample the heady delights of the big town. We went to the old Jubilee cinema and watched Laurence Olivier doing his bit to save England, this time from the might of Spain in the days of the first Elizabeth. The film was *Fire Over England* and with all the incendiaries being dropped by the Germans it was an appropriate title. However, in both instances we came through undaunted, if not completely unscathed.

12
LEISURE AND PLEASURE

For practically the whole of my early life up to the later teenage years there were three centres of my existence – home, school and church. They overlapped to some extent, but these were the foci of all my activities. Until I reached double figures home was the main focus and most of my leisure activities were there. I went through the usual phases of collecting mania – cigarette cards, comics, farm animals, matchboxes and stamps. I even had a phase of making model aircraft from balsa-wood kits, but my manual dexterity and modelling skills were limited. I never made one to fly unlike several of my friends and few were deemed successful enough to suspend from my bedroom ceiling. Stamps and matchboxes were the longer-lasting fads. I had the word 'philatelist' in my vocabulary from about nine, because I read it frequently in my Stanley Gibbons catalogue and in my stamp-collecting magazine, but the word 'cartophilist' did not feature until many years later and unknowingly I had long been one.

I was given a second-hand stamp album containing a starter collection for my ninth birthday: it came from the shop of Mr Bagguley in Louth. Even during the war it was possible to amass stamps at low prices with pocket money and birthday money, though I soon learned to dismiss the siren offers of 'five hundred *different* stamps for a shilling'. You could swop with friends and collect stamps from letters and parcels that arrived for the Lindsey Blind. There were also neighbours who had sons learning to fly in Rhodesia or Canada who could be wheedled into parting with the envelopes or stamps torn off their letters home. Most of all there were books of stamps sent by the ubiquitous Mr Bagguley 'on approval' each month when my father had been to Louth. John Rands and I spent hours coming to anguished decisions on how to spend the half-crown from the latest choir money: was a dull Edward VII shilling stamp better value than a pretty, brightly coloured airmail from Argentina? Thus the collection was enlarged and occasionally a special theme would be decided upon – such as stamps with palaces on them. The impetus for this came from *Children's Hour*, to which I was an ardent listener. At one time the programme offered prizes for a page of stamps on a particular theme with explanatory notes. I put in an entry which featured some large, recently acquired stamps bearing the legend 'España' in varying denominations of pesetas and on which were depicted Spanish galleons in full sail in attractive pastel shades. I arranged them in what I considered an artistic combination on a page of graph paper and wrote some learned notes about galleons, watermarks and perforations, cribbed from Stanley Gibbons. I sent it off and sat back awaiting the arrival of my prize. Some weeks later I listened eagerly to *Children's Hour* as the philately expert commented upon the thousands of entries. I remember particularly the scorn he poured on those entrants who had been so foolish and inept as to lick the backs of unused stamps and stick them directly onto the page. I coloured furiously, did not say a word and reconciled myself to the fact that I should not, as I had fully expected, be among the prize-winners.

Nor did any success come our way when John Rands and I entered a joint effort in another competition, this time to create words and music for a new Christmas carol. I wrote the words, he composed the tune. Mine were a pastiche from existing carols with shepherds 'hieing' to Bethlehem and I think Handel's 'Largo' was the inspiration for his slow and somewhat lugubrious tune. He wrote the final version upon music manuscript and his father, 'Uncle Alf', played it on his viola, while we in quavering trebles tried to fix words to music. Our parents were congratulatory and enthusiastic, but I realised we were not on to a winner, which eventually turned out to be a neat little carol with a sprightly tune about a robin that nested in an old discarded teapot, but came to pipe a lullaby to the dozing Jesus.

For several years I kept my matchboxes in a small, cardboard-like attaché case under my bed. I nagged my mother to vary the kind of matches she bought: this she was loath to do, as she preferred to stick to Bryant and May's Bluebell matches. I did have more success by using my initiative when Grandad Rhodes asked me to buy matches as well as his favourite shag from Jack Clark's in Grammar School Road, but he really preferred Swan Vestas or Old Glory, a box with a dreadnought on one side and a joke on the other. These jokes were a cut above the normal Christmas cracker efforts and I sometimes had to have them explained to me. A favourite was a green, yellow and brown striped box with a snarling tiger in an ellipse on the front: these matches had, I think, come from Malaya. I was also on the lookout for boxes thrown away by smokers in the street. On one occasion I collected discarded tab ends for some unspecified reason – I can't really have been going to make a fag out of the dog-ends, though I knew several impoverished adult smokers who did. Anyway, my mother came across my cache and ensured it was deposited in the dustbin. Again I increased my collection by swopping and my father would sometimes bring home a fine and unusual specimen from the ubiquitous Mr Bagguley, whose main business was that of a tobacconist. Serving soldiers sometimes had boxes bought in foreign fields – these were highly prized. I can't remember what happened in the end to my collection, which probably numbered over a hundred, but likely it was just spring-cleaned away.

I had enjoyed playing with my model farm and building up a small collection of farm animals, implements and agricultural personae. I then went on to create Meccano models, from simple two-dimensional items to carts and lorries that moved on rubber-tyred wheels. Eventually I was able to make working models with a Meccano wind-up engine that could power things through cogs, chains and gears. My favourite and *chef d'oeuvre* was a working windmill some three feet high. Later I spent hours improving my calligraphic skills and creating some illuminated manuscripts. These were of various lengths and themes: sometimes a hackneyed poetic statement – Keats's 'A thing of beauty is a joy for ever'; sometimes biblical texts, especially Isaiah – 'How beautiful upon the mountain are the feet of him that bringeth good tidings, that publisheth peace', and bits about swords and plough shares and spears and pruning hooks, for remember this was in the darkish days of war. One piece still in existence is a framed extract from a Victorian moral maxim, suggested by 'Cabby' Cabourne from Brigg Grammar School – 'For when the One Great Scorer comes / To write against your name / He writes not that you lost or won / But how you played the game'. Nowadays children could produce better, more colourful efforts on their computer in a hundredth of the time it took me, but would they bother? Moral exhortation is not in vogue.

I have already written of the way churchgoing affected my young life. In my teenage years a Church Youth Group was started. We had about a dozen or so regular members and met in either the Church House (where once my maternal great-grandfather had run a pub) or the vicarage. It was not highly organised and it was more secular than religious. We held discussions and sometimes more formal debates on moral and social issues; we held what would now be called quizzes or played paper-and-pencil games such as 'Fish, Flower, Fruit', in which in small teams we would endeavour to find the name of something that would fit some fifteen categories, each beginning with the same initial letter – Pike, Pansy, Pomegranate. We organised Beetle Drives and had play readings: we even prepared a few one-act plays or sketches for presentation at Parish Socials. In summer we played badminton on the vicarage lawn. Although it was a mixed social group there was a completely asexual atmosphere and a particularly chaste air to our proceedings: church and sex did not go together.

In the school holidays we had to make our own entertainment. One year, either 1942 or 1943, when the war news was slightly better and when we could see pictures in the papers and hear on the wireless of the success of the 'Thousand Bomber Raids' over Germany, a group of us had a craze for all things RAF. The group was basically Maurice Proctor ('Proc'), Edwin ('Tich') Bell, John Rands ('Rana') and myself with sometimes Roy Firmedow and

Gordon Kitchen taking part. We were a bomber crew. Our trusty Lancaster was the sizeable loft in the roof space of the Proctors' garage at their home on the corner of Glebe Road and Grammar School Road. The ceiling was boarded over and we climbed into our plane by a stepladder and scrambled aboard. It was, of course, dark and even when we left the garage door open (which was not often) we could see only dimly. However, we strung wires through the rafters and rigged up electric lights by screwing bakelite holders into the rafters and inserting torch bulbs: these were powered by a high-tension battery that was in common use in wirelesses. I write 'we', but sorting out the electrics really devolved upon 'Tich' and 'Rana', who were more scientifically minded. To add verisimilitude we fashioned the cockpit with an instrument panel contrived out of gauges stripped from the dashboards of old Proctor lorries, for their main business was haulage contractors. There was space for a wireless operator, a navigator and a rear gunner. 'Tich' fixed up a communications system. We all bought Bakelite microphones from Curry's – at a cost of two shillings and elevenpence or three and sixpence, I recall – and bought or 'found' yards of two-strand cable. This came from Woolworths because it was cheaper than Curry's, even if of inferior quality. Earphones were no problem as each family had some left over from earlier wirelesses.

'Proc' was the pilot and crew captain, as he was the eldest and we were on his family's premises, but more importantly he had a genuine RAF leather fleeced jacket so beloved of the real aircrew. 'Tich' was the 'Sparks', or wireless operator, constantly sending and receiving messages, and 'Rana' was the navigator with a small board, maps, dividers (from his school geometry set), ruler and pencil. I filled in as the most expendable or insignificant. I was sometimes the co-pilot, who rarely got the chance to fly the plane, even though 'Skipper' Proc was gravely wounded by flak on numerous occasions, or 'Tail-end Charlie' in the rear gun pit. We spent hours doing our own aircraft maintenance, deciding upon our targets in Germany, plotting courses and being briefed by the Skipper, before we actually took off. We modelled ourselves on real heroes, such as Douglas Bader or 'Sailor Malan', and on those who dominated our comics, such as 'Rockfist Rogan'. We had all the jargon – enjoying 'wizard prangs', sadly seeing other crews shot down 'in the drink' and lamenting friends 'gone for a burton'. We invariably found our target and dropped our load successfully. We fought off marauding Messerschmitts. I was in my element in the rear gunner's position, receiving messages from the pilot on our improvised intercom: *'Aye, aye, Skipper, bandits at twelve o'clock; I see them.'* I would point my brush handles at the approaching Huns and loose off orally a convincing staccato rattle of machine-gun fire. We flew many intrepid missions and always managed to limp home after releasing our bomb load over Cologne, Hamburg or usually Berlin. These exploits fully occupied one Easter holiday and continued into the summer vacation, but then the RAF phase or craze passed.

I joined the Young Conservatives for a time in my later schooldays: I suppose it was in the hope of meeting girls and becoming not intimately but certainly tactilely connected, a hope that was never realised. You didn't join through political fervour, but for social reasons. The Brigg constituency pre-war had returned a Tory candidate, probably Berkeley Sheffield. I remember the aristocratic sounding name, but he made no impression upon me and I knew the election result was announced from the balcony of the Angel Hotel in the Market Place. In 1948 a Labour candidate called Mallalieu was returned: several of his posters were defaced by obliterating the initial 'M' and the final 'U', thus suggesting his promises and policies were 'all a lie'. I think there was a young Socialist organisation, but the Tories had more girl members and more attractive ones too.

There may have been some few political discussions, but it was the social side that dominated. The highlight was the annual pantomime trip. The one I remember was to the Alhambra Theatre in Bradford to see Norman Evans in 'Mother Goose'. This was an adventure – going to far-off Yorkshire not with parents but youthful peers of both sexes. It was to a Saturday night performance and we shouldn't be back till the early hours. I can't remember the bus company (Vesseys, Daisy, Enterprise and Silver Dawn?), but expectations of enjoyment were high. We had time for fish and chips before the show and this was, by my standards then, highly polished, richly humorous and technically amazing. The goose did surprising things and Norman Evans in many resplendent Dame outfits cracked hilarious jokes, ground his toothless gums and kept pushing his bountiful bosom in and out of position. The principal boy slapped her thighs as the hero and sang with gusto – as we did when we got the chance in the choruses displayed on a sheet hauled down from the flies. It was undiluted joy and escapism.

On the journey to Bradford the sexes had been entirely segregated, but on the way back those who were more forward or already in embryonic relationships had somehow managed to change seats and cuddled up in the dark. I had no such social skills, neither the requisite forwardness nor could I think of a girl likely to respond to any advances. The frustrated males seated in twos dozed disconsolately – and there were perhaps some equally disappointed girls.

✦✦✦

Some of my leisure activities were based on sport, either as a participant or spectator. During the later stages of the war Games Centres were established nationally to improve the athleticism of young people and boost the feelgood factor. The one in Brigg was centred on the playing field of the Girls' High School and held on a Wednesday evening in summer. There were various adult helpers as coaches and supervisors, all under the direction of the Chief Organiser, who appeared from time to time resplendent in white flannels and a dark blue blazer with a crest of Loughborough College's discus-thrower. We did some physical exercises and practised various athletic events for the first part of the evening and engaged in team events for the second part. Though it was stimulating to see pubescent girls in short, short skirts and Aertex blouses, the sexes were usually rigorously segregated. The boys played touch-rugby, cricket and volleyball and the girls netball and rounders. However, on occasions if there were fewer than normal participants we would play mixed rounders or basketball. We boys tried to impress the girls with our superior throwing and catching skills and greater hitting power in rounders, but preferred basketball with its opportunities for closer contact and brief glimpses of bra straps. If play became too boisterous and a boy thought it were touch-rugby rather than basketball, the whistle shrilled and he was consigned to the sidelines and some early sin-bin, where he languished in shame for ten minutes. Generally the Games Centres were a pleasant if spasmodic diversion in our teenage existence. There was even a competition among centres and this was held in Scunthorpe when representatives from Ashby, Scunthorpe and Brigg competed in various sports. I hazily recall one occasion when some of us ventured further afield and represented Lindsey in a tri-cornered affair against a combined Holland/Kesteven team and one from Nottinghamshire. I was in the touch-rugby group: we managed to beat Holland/Kesteven, but were trounced by Nottinghamshire. However, outside school sport I was more of a spectator in my early teen years. I supported Brigg Town FC and went regularly to the old ground that was behind the Brocklesby Ox public house. I cheered our local heroes on against the likes of Lysaghts, Ashby Institute, Appleby Frodingham and Winterton as well as teams from Gainsborough and Lincoln. I would also cheer ironically when Tom Daubney, our next-door neighbour, ran onto the field with his magic sponge towards an injured player, who always seemed to make a miraculous recovery before Tom's ministrations. I would even watch reserve matches – well, there wasn't much else to do on a Saturday afternoon when I was twelve or so.

As I grew older and the war finished, my father would sometimes take me to Blundell Park to see Grimsby Town – oh, my Tweedy, Betmead, Buck of long ago! – or to Scunthorpe United, who then played in the Midland

League at the Old Show Ground. When I was sixteen or so I was allowed to go to matches at Grimsby either by myself or with friends. I would travel by train and alight near the ground: curiously Grimsby played in Cleethorpes. I would make my way to the small ground and the old tiered wooden stand, where I would jostle with elbows and wriggle towards the front until I had secured a good vantage point. Here I would heckle the opposing players (old 'Baldy' Gorman of Brentford) and the referee and urge on 'Ginger' Hall and Tommy Briggs to further efforts. Grimsby were difficult to beat at home and would regularly trounce such teams as Manchester City and Blackburn Rovers in the old Division Two, often 5-0 if Tommy Briggs were on form. I could just afford five bob (25p today) three or four times a season to cover train fare, ground entrance – and a programme! Rio Ferdinand's current weekly salary would have paid the whole Grimsby Town team for five seasons.

In my mid-teens, particularly in the summer holidays, I would cycle over the bridges to the sugar factory cricket ground, which was sited on land now occupied by the Brigg Leisure Centre. Occasionally there was a chance of playing if either the sugar factory or their opponents were a man short. There was no need to wear whites and in summer I was usually wearing 'daps' as the then equivalent to trainers were called: all you had to do was run after the ball in the outfield and catch it if it ever came at you head high. If there were a real emergency, such as the non-appearance of an umpire, I could be asked to do that job in so-called friendly matches, putting on the appropriate, floor-reaching white coat. Usually I was relegated perpetually to be the square-leg umpire, adjudicating only on run-outs. However, on other very rare occasions I did the full job, religiously moving the six pebbles from one pocket to the other and responding to cries of 'Owzat?' I once gave out LBW a particularly fiery, veteran wicketkeeper of the sugar factory side. To me the ball had struck his pad plumb in front, but he maintained it had hit his bat. He grew apoplectic and had a temper tantrum at the wicket, throwing his bat down, taking off his batting gloves, blaspheming furiously and calling me names not then in my vocabulary. Such was the violence of his emotions that the visiting captain to soothe him agreed to let him stay and asked me to reverse my decision. I should like to say he was out next ball, but he went on to make quite a score. My flickering memory suggests his name, suitably enough, was Pepper, but that might have been a touring Aussie about the same time. In the summers I taught at Ashby County Primary School I played cricket regularly for Scawby in the deepest depths of Scunthorpe and District Cricket Leagues – in Division VI – as the *Brigg Star* duly chronicled our feats, more often defeats. I would cycle over on practice night and for the Saturday matches. Scawby played on an unpredictable piece of turf in

Scawby Park, by kind permission of Colonel Nelthorpe, the local squire and Chairman of Governors at Brigg Grammar School. Here I did play in whites and contributed briefly as a number nine batsman and an occasional slow off-break bowler. I can't remember ever scoring more than fifteen runs or taking more than three fairly expensive wickets, but I enjoyed the exercise and the camaraderie. I managed to hold onto many more catches than I dropped, but to my mother's dismay too frequently returned home with my flannels badly stained not only green, but with patches of greenery-yallery-brown from the crisped cowpats that laid scattered in the outfield and near the playing surface. On match days we drove the bullocks off into a distant corner, but for most of the week they had the cricket area to crop and crap on. We played against Ashby Institute II and a village called Amcotts, that for me was always a romantic, far-off place, as remote as Shangri-La. We travelled by bus for away matches to such venues as Alpha Cement at Kirton Lindsey, Burringham and outlying villages around the Trent. Part of my growing up occurred on these coach trips or in licensed pavilions or village pubs when sometimes rain never even allowed play to start. There were singsongs of old favourites, often with *risqué* lyrics ('The Foggy, Foggy Dew'), and new ones were added to my repertoire, such as 'The Good Ship Venus', 'Eskimo Nell' and 'The Ball of Kirriemuir'. And I became accustomed to a half-pint or two in the match's afterglow.

As a very special treat I went with my father to Bramall Lane to see Yorkshire play. I was a more regular spectator later on when I taught at Barnsley Holgate, but I remember the earlier visit well. It was almost a non-event. Matches against the Tourists were always popular, so my father and his friends decided we had to set off early. We went in a borrowed van. It was a time-consuming, awkward journey to Sheffield and there was difficulty in parking. We arrived at the ground to find the gates closed on a sell-out crowd. However, my father persuaded a householder of a terraced house that partly overlooked the ground to let us view the match from an upstairs bedroom. We could see the wicket in the considerable distance, brought closer by the pair of binoculars we shared around, but not the whole of the outfield. Although the circumstances were far from ideal, we made the most of our day out. The West Indies batted and Yorkshire toiled. Walcott made some lusty strokes and a quick fifty. Eventually he hit out to square leg where we knew the unseen Ted Lester was fielding. At last a relieved and loud cheering told us that the catch had been held. The West Indies declared, having batted nearly all day, then Yorkshire lost two early wickets. However, the papers later recorded an epic fightback to save the game the next day.

❖❖❖

Leisure pursuits of a more cultural nature were inevitably of a home-grown sort. Around Brigg there was no professional theatre and no professional orchestra. A third-rate repertory company, bearing the name of some aged and failed thespian I had never heard of, struggled through a season or two at Scunthorpe's Savoy Theatre, but I rarely went because the usual offering was a dramatised Agatha Christie or some quasi-psychological drama like *Black Chiffon*. People in Brigg made their own music and drama and the townsfolk dutifully went along to support these efforts in the Girls' High School Hall or at the Corn Exchange. There were the Glandford Players who performed either a trio of one-act plays or some supposedly popular play from pre-war. The cast rarely varied from a tight nucleus of seasoned, local veterans. The Johnsons, who lived across the road from us, were mainstays. As a family we regularly went along to their productions. I preferred comedies in which vicars lost their trousers amid hilarious confusion of motives and circumstances, but I do remember one which had cast Mr Johnson as an anguished, chalk-faced and remorseful hit-and-run driver on the verge of a breakdown and confession. CEMA (which must have stood for 'Council for the Encouragement of Music and the Arts') would from time to time send a group of touring players for a one-night stand. The play most akin to a classic that I can recall was a production of JB Priestley's *An Inspector Calls*, but it made no great impact upon me at the time.

After I had left school I was persuaded to join a dramatic group that my old infant school teacher, Miss Florrie Kennington, was attempting to form. She fancied herself as a producer, but there was little chance of her executing that role with the tight caucus that was the Glandford Players. She organised some play readings and planned a production. We were a curious but limited group of talentless, would-be thespians. At one time we numbered over a dozen, but people defected or found better ways of using their spare time. With our dwindling resources we had to curb our aspirations. Originally there had been plans to perform Priestley's *When We Are Married*, but that became numerically impossible. However, the High School Hall had been booked and it was decided to do two one-act plays with a concluding dramatic monologue from Florrie herself. As a teenager but the only male member under thirty, I had perforce to fill the young leading role. I think I must have been in both one-acters, but the one I remember in my nightmares is *Villa for Sale*, a purported comedy obviously and literally translated from the French of Sacha Guitry's *Villa à vendre*. There were only five parts – two elderly vendors, their servant and the prospective buyers, a young married couple. I was the husband and a former classmate from Glebe Road School, Janet D, was my wife. It was an utter disaster – completely under-rehearsed and under-prepared with a distinct lack of backstage support. I don't think we even rehearsed on the stage of the actual performance, for which we had mercifully few paying customers. We forgot lines and moves once we were exposed to the unexpected glare of the lights. We stumbled around the stage incoherently, but somehow got through. The only one who merited praise in the local press report was Janet, who was commended for her calm aplomb in the prevailing chaos. Fortunately, unlike my younger son, I never harboured any dreams of being an actor.

There was also a group of dedicated classical musicians that performed as a small orchestra from time to time. The Bradleys, Henthorn, Thumwood, Richards, Rawdin, Rands and Mrs Major Piggott figured among these and were conducted by 'Rupert' Pratt when a conductor was deemed necessary. There was an attempt to improve standards and bring in younger players under the auspices of the County Council and CEMA. A Miss Schroder, formerly a professional musician and now a senior peripatetic teacher, came one evening a week to give lessons. She taught the youngsters for an hour and then devoted her attention to the seniors. I was somewhat reluctantly enrolled, because I scraped my violin in the seconds of the school orchestra. I never reached a sufficiently high standard to enable me to enjoy instrumental music. With Miss Schroder we practised pieces called Airs, Gavottes, Pavanes and Scherzos in G. I duly rosined my bow, tuned my fiddle with help and tried to keep half an eye on Miss Schroder and one and a half on the music stand. At the end of the spring session a public concert was given. I can remember taking part in only one. After the National Anthem, played jointly by both the younger and senior groups, the youngsters were to play some three or four short pieces and then one in the complete group. The remainder of the concert was played by the seniors. We tuned up in one of the High School classrooms and then made our way to the school hall. My abiding memory is of finding my way to a place on the back row and arranging my music on the stand. I was still gazing around at the large audience in blissful ignorance of the rap of the conductor's baton when the others started playing the National Anthem. I reddened with embarrassment, belatedly tucked my violin under my chin and was just in time to send him victorious, which was most appropriate at Easter 1945. My days as a violinist were not protracted.

I enjoyed singing much more and it has been a lifetime's pleasure. For a couple of years before going up to university I was a member of Brigg Choral Society. It was a successful group of some seventy performers: my mother and father were both members and so were many of the town's notable figures. I joined my father in the tenors of the chorus, as did my brother later, though he also performed several solo parts. We sang secular and sacred pieces. I first sang 'Messiah' with the Choral Society both in Brigg and in

Louth and found them uplifting occasions. We also sang concert versions of *Merrie England* and operatic choruses. This was the nearest I came to *Musik Kultur* in my youth. It was with the Brigg Choral Society that I used to go carol-singing at what we called the workhouse (though in the enlightened post-war days this residential centre for the indigent elderly and the disabled had been renamed 'Crosslands') and the War Memorial Hospital. Some thirty of us under the direction of a choir member with a tuning fork would tour the day rooms of the elderly residents, go through our repertoire and then be asked to sing for the umpteenth time 'Silent Night'. Our efforts were not always appreciated or well received, for to some we merely disturbed their slumbers. We were greeted more enthusiastically in the hospital wards where the nurses added their voices to ours. There was a particular satisfaction in singing 'Away in a Manger' to the newly arriveds and their mothers in the maternity unit.

Probably Brigg's most successful group with some aspirations to popular culture was the Operatic Society. They had no pretensions to Grand Opera, but the Brigg public thoroughly enjoyed their annual productions of such favourites as *The Mikado*, *The Desert Song* and *Miss Hook of Holland*. I was never a singing member of this group, although an avid supporter over several years, because my father was very much involved. Pre-war he was a stalwart of the chorus with an occasional bit part; later he took second-line solo parts such as the Mikado himself and General Birabeau. I remember Mother letting out the uniform of a French Foreign Legionnaire in *The Desert Song*, which was probably the first I was old enough to go to see in the evening performance. To my delight Harold Green dragged a real live donkey onto the stage and it made an ineradicable impression upon my mind by defecating. I used to know all the choruses to sing along to and as a youngster enjoyed the opportunity of bellowing *'And to Hell with Burgundy!'* when they did *The Vagabond King*. The shows ran for almost a week and the Corn Exchange was usually full.

◆◆◆

Cycling around North Lincolnshire was one of my favourite activities. During the war and immediately afterwards there was little traffic: even collecting car numbers, an earlier craze, by the nearby cemetery on the main A18 to Grimsby rarely caused much hurried scribbling. From thirteen onwards I cycled alone or with John Rands all over within a fifteen-mile radius. A spare day in the holidays would see us cycling to the low Wolds villages of Bonby, Saxby or out to Greetwell crossroads and the sandy, wooded play area there. Sometimes our purpose would be to do some brass-rubbing at one of the village churches: later Philip Larkin's 'Church Going' would bring these occasions to mind with a sensual thrill. I remember executing a fine rubbing of the brass in Broughton church. In summer we would cycle regularly to local village shows and gymkhanas. These were widespread and there was always something of interest, especially when one of the High School girls I knew was competing – these were my 'Joan Hunter Dunn' moments. The most traditional Feast Show and gymkhana was held at Messingham and if memory is correct on a Monday. It was a fairly long journey on a cycle, and we had to put our dynamos to work on the way back, but fortunately it avoided the steep Mottle Ash Hill. However, that long road back to Scawby seemed never-ending. But in retrospect Messingham Show always seemed to be a vibrant, exciting experience. In those days I suppose all produce was organic: memory conjures up row upon row of prize vegetables and multicoloured exhibits of sweet peas, dahlias and gladioli, all scrubbed, polished and tastefully arranged – far superior to the international offerings in current supermarkets.

For a few years I was a member of the Youth Hostels Association, and the YHA played a particular part in charting my progress through adolescence. Few parents nowadays would allow two callow fourteen-year-olds to go off on a cycling tour, but John Rands and I planned a week's trip to York and the Yorkshire coast. Whatever reservations they may have had they kept to themselves. I did phone on the first night to say we had arrived safely in York, but for the rest of the time we were out of direct contact with home. We had planned our route, overhauled our cycles, bought waterproof capes and a new puncture outfit and added more capacious saddlebags. We had duly read the YHA leaflets for beginners and felt a first stage of some sixty miles was within our ability, though we had not before cycled half that distance. One Thursday morning in early August we set off. There was no Humber Bridge then and we had to make our way over the Trent at Keadby and over the Ouse/Humber at Boothferry. There were also no bypasses or motorways. We pedalled along with thick clouds scudding overhead, but fortunately the rain held off. Our way took us into foreign parts of the East Riding and north via Howden. Here I remember a proliferation of glasshouses as we ate our sandwiches and drank our 'pop'. In the afternoon we headed north and east on B roads and eventually reached our destination in the early evening. So far so good. I can't remember much about the hostel in York, though it was the first I ever stayed at. I do remember we had only two nights there instead of the expected three. They had overbooked and we were pushed out to temporary overflow accommodation. This turned out to be in a picturesque but dilapidated country house at Naburn, not far from the city. Here there were metal two-tiered beds with tired springs and straw palliasses that were arranged in a couple of large, dusty bedrooms. The primitive washing facilities – no hot water – were down a long corridor next to a Victorian loo that had probably been one of Mr Crapper's first installations. We had to rustle up our own meals and perform the usual YHA chores. The owner of the house was a thin, ascetic-looking chap in shorts, sandals and an open-neck shirt. He lived in a small part of his property and allowed the YHA (of which he approved strongly) to use spare rooms in emergencies. No health and safety regulations applied in those days: there wasn't even a fire escape.

We enjoyed our time in York. I was awed by the Minster and its Rose Window, but the abiding memory is of the Castle Museum – that fascinated me. One moment in particular is etched on my mind: I glanced out of a window and was at once transported back in time one hundred years to a street scene in Victorian York with a hansom cab complete with full-sized, stuffed horse standing under a gas lamp while assorted figures of a chimney sweep, a muffin man with bell, schoolchildren and crinolined ladies went about their business. For several moments I was thoroughly disorientated. This was the first of many museums that have made a firm impression upon me and I always approach a fresh museum in the hope of the unexpected and a lasting memory.

On Monday morning we headed for Scarborough, which I knew well, and we visited old haunts such as Peasholm Park, Gala-Land and the South Cliff, all of which were new to John Rands. The next day we took the coastal byways to Whitby, dropping off for lunch in Robin Hood's Bay, only to find the connection with the Sherwood forester to be very tenuous indeed. Whitby recalls images of Captain Cook, jet jewellery and narrow cobbled streets rising steeply from a fish-smelling, seagull-shrieking quay. I think we dragged our cycles up the one hundred and ninety-nine steps for some reason to reach the Youth Hostel. From somewhere I have a distinct memory – possibly hallucination – of waking up on the top bunk in the dormitory and seeing the sun rising through the stone traceries of the ruined St Hild's Abbey. It is strong and recurring, but I can't guarantee its authenticity. From Whitby we cycled back over the moors and the Vale of Pickering to York, where we spent the final night before returning to Brigg. This first long, unaccompanied trip was a definite rite of passage.

The next year we made our way south for no better reason than John Rands having a long neglected cousin in Sandy, Bedfordshire, and a joint desire to see Cambridge. An added advantage was that the whole route was coloured green on the physical geography maps. I recall making a stop in Peterborough and we reached Bedford, but where we stayed en route remains a mystery. It was an especially hot summer and the sun was bringing up the road surface in soft, gooey blisters. It was all hot, perspiring and seemingly unrewarding toil. We probably had several punctures too. We decided upon what was entirely unacceptable to any right-minded hosteller and took the train from Bedford to Cambridge – there was a line then. Thus we never called upon the Sandy cousin, who presumably felt even more neglected. That first visit to Cambridge has been overlain by memories of countless further visits, since we have lived some twelve miles away down the A14 for the past thirty-odd years. That second cycling tour wasn't a success and it was the last long journey John Rands and I shared.

✦✦✦

In the time I spent at Ashby my social boundaries were further broadened by social gatherings I was included in by my colleagues. Marc Coom had become a friend and mentor with Horace Whickham and Alan Fontaine and I was admitted to their get-togethers. These usually took place at the Whickhams' house, as Horace was married and had two young children. They lived in a council prefab between Ashby and Scunthorpe – later Horace took charge with his wife of a children's home in Market Rasen and we met there. We would gather about seven o'clock. The conversation would roll, often about school, and stories would be recounted over supper and a few beers: impoverished teachers were unlikely to have funds for enough to make them drunk, but our spirits were lifted. We attempted the crossword in – it still had its full title then – *The Manchester Guardian*, for Horace was not a *Daily Telegraph* person. I was not usually much help with the cryptic clues, but on one memorable occasion I made the vital breakthrough for the final, elusive word. The clue involved smoked fish and after hours of unsuccessful puzzling and dictionary searching, I suggested that it might have something to do with the French word *fumer*, 'to smoke'. The dictionary revealed 'fumade' as a smoked pilchard. However, our main occupation was playing cards – whist and rummy – and it was in this agreeable company that I was introduced to 'Three-card Brag'. Stakes were small and no-one ever lost more than ten shillings (50p), but fervour ran high. Alan and Marc would have the manic glint of gamblers, but it was usually Mavis, the quiet wife of Horace, who would secure the most winnings. We often played into the early hours and then I would sleep over, kipping down on a 'put-u-up' in the lounge. We probably played once each half-term, always on a Friday or Saturday night and very occasionally for longer sessions in the holidays. To me this was living life on the edge!

✦✦✦

Time rarely seemed to hang heavily in my childhood and I can't remember complaining, as I hear children nowadays, of having nothing to do and being bored. There was little money for expensive diversions, so we made our own pleasures. We were able to come and go without much hindrance or fear of bring molested – 'paedophile' was unknown as a word or a threat. It was a slower, gentler but more active childhood, in which we were free to create our own leisure pursuits. Television and computers played no part and commercial and peer pressures were not a factor. No doubt it is a rose-tinted view, but I enjoyed my leisure and took my pleasures thankfully in the thirties and forties.

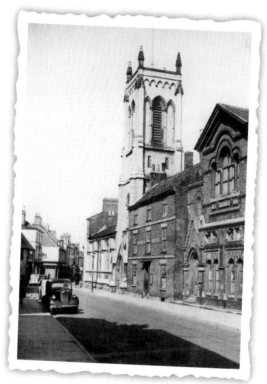

St John's Church and Church House
in Bigby Street, Brigg

13
LINDSEY BLIND

The Lindsey Blind Society played an important part in my growing up. It certainly gave me an understanding of and a respect for people who (as we say now) are 'visually impaired', but it also showed me that blind people are not immune from the frailties that beset us humans in general. In 1938, with my brother on the way, my father was faced with a very important decision. He had worked for Lacey and Clark's, Brigg's largest department store situated on the corner of the lane leading to the Corn Exchange and between the Angel and the Lord Nelson, for almost twenty years and had been given to understand he would be promoted and made a partner in the business. However, a marriage in 1937 had brought a new son-in-law into the firm. Although the newcomer had no experience of the drapery/furnishing/outfitting trade, the ties of blood seemed stronger than those formed by loyalty and know-how. My father could see that there was now little likelihood of the promised promotion and looked for a change. Thus in the middle of 1938 he was appointed to a post with a new organisation within the LCC (Lindsey County Council). They wanted someone to expand and develop what was bureaucratically described as 'Blind Welfare'. They wanted someone to set up and run a new organisation to collate and sell the products of their blind workers as a commercial proposition. Thus my father found himself at the age of forty with a new and unknown brief – it really was a leap into the dark – and for the next twenty-five years he helped drive the success of the Lindsey Blind Society. He became a local government officer with eventually the grandiose title of 'Trading and Industries Organiser', even if the imposing title was not reflected in the salary.

The Lindsey Blind Society was run by a County Council Committee. Its titular head was probably a County Councillor. I seem to remember first a Canon Roe from Middle Rasen and then a Mr Robert J Blakeborough from Home Farm, Habrough, the epitome of a tall, rubicund Gentlemen Farmer. Both were well down the hierarchy of influential politicians and the society was not of prime importance in the responsibilities of the County Council, but this gave the general secretary and my father considerable latitude in its development. I can only vaguely remember the first general secretary, but my father held him in high regard – Arthur Wilson, who was himself blind and read relevant documents in Braille, did much work on the telephone and dictated shorthand notes and letters to an efficient personal secretary. There was an Honorary Secretary – 'WG Key' appeared on the society's notepaper and in small gold letters on its Bedford van – but Arthur Wilson did the real work. It was a great loss to the society when, towards the end of the war, he was promoted to London to an important position in the Home Office. I believe the members of the committee were a mixture of County Councillors and co-opted notabilities who had the time, desire and social status to attend the monthly meetings in Lincoln. However, they allowed the administrators a reasonably free rein.

In addition to the administrative staff within the County Offices, there were three home teachers and my father, who was responsible for selling the wide variety of goods the blind people produced. There would probably be over a hundred people registered as being blind or partially sighted, but only a small proportion was able to be trained or possessed the skills necessary to produce saleable goods. Their ages varied from the late twenties to eighty plus. Some had been born blind, some had become blind through accident or illness in their thirties or forties and others had developed blindness in their advancing years.

Of the home teachers I best remember Miss Lucy Mumby and Miss Sandwith. Both were maiden ladies: both were in their late twenties or early thirties. Miss Sandwith was more homely and Lucy was good fun and more elegant in dress and manner. Unfortunately the love of Lucy's life had been shot down in the early part of the war. Both ladies were professionals in their job, which involved partly education and training and partly welfare. (Social Services were as then unknown.) They instructed the home-based blind people (predominantly women) in hand and machine knitting and in fine basketwork. They also kept an eye on young people who were away at schools for the blind and they regularly saw them to these distant establishments either by car or on the train. The older men went away for training in such things as seating chairs and stools in cane, rush or seagrass. When they had been trained they worked either at home or in a workshop that was set up at Spilsby.

At first our home at no. 29 Central Square was the 'office' of Lindsey Blind in Brigg and consisted of a filing cabinet kept in an alcove behind the door of our only sitting room. This also meant that for business purposes a telephone was required. Telephones were rarities in the thirties in ordinary council houses and when the GPO of those days installed one our standing in the eyes of the neighbours rose considerably – but for me the chief benefit was that the new telephone pole inserted in the street made admirable chalked stumps for our games of cricket (six and out if the ball went into a neighbour's garden, and the position of the pole put left-handers at a considerable disadvantage). I can't ever remember our family having to use a public telephone before ours was installed, but there was a public call box on the side of Central Square adjacent to West Square. However, this was often out of action, because it had a novelty attraction for all the children over a wide area and attracted curious examination if not direct vandalism, though the results were often the same. There was a distinct thrill in listening to the purring dialling tone or actually speaking to the distant operator: and we were forever hopefully pressing Button B. Thus 'Brigg 3159' gave the Rhodes family considerable kudos and we were called upon in emergencies to summon help or pass on momentous information. Usually the neighbour in distress regarded the telephone with fearful suspicion or almost reverential awe and wanted no direct contact with it at all. My father would have to speak to the operator, ask for the appropriate number and as often as not pass on the information. After some considerable time my mother became sufficiently familiar with this new contraption (of which she too was initially afraid and suspicious) to answer the phone and request numbers for other people. She was never entirely happy with using the phone and her voice would affect a strange intonation: a mixture of nerves and ultra-refinement – Mum's 'posh' voice. We had to keep a strict record of all calls and those deemed private had to be accounted for, so a box for payment was kept next to the phone on the front windowsill. It is almost impossible to realise now in these days, when practically everyone over the age of ten has a mobile and we all use the telephone with automatic ease, how novel and intimidating it was to many people in the late thirties and what magicians the switchboard girls seemed when they actually produced the person you wanted to speak to out of thin air.

Obviously my father required transport for his work and as an eight-year-old I was tremendously impressed when one day he drove into the Square and parked a brand new Bedford van outside our home. It was a dark Lincoln green in colour with Lindsey Blind Society in medium sized gold lettering on each side, and the address of the Council Offices, Lincoln, and the name of the Honorary Secretary in much smaller letters on the bottom of the passenger's door. But my first desire was to see the speedometer inside. I was delighted to see the figures on the dial went round to 90mph and found it deeply satisfying. Of course, we never reached that speed: I doubt if my father ever drove above 60mph and usually it was 40–50 on the open road and 20–30 in built-up areas, where there was almost inevitably a group of children playing in the street. None of our neighbours had cars and there was not all that many in private ownership in the whole of Brigg then. Certainly no garages had ever been built for our council houses.

Nevertheless this spanking new van required a safe and secure home and storage space was needed for the raw materials and goods that Lindsey Blind was to use and produce. Thus my father came to an agreement with an old friend from his Reading Room days, who had the fascinating name of Zadok Clarke and who lived in an old house off Colton Street, long since demolished but intriguingly called 'Owl's Nest'. (Owls did actually nest in an old tree in the grounds and could be heard plaintively hooting on dark nights.) Mr Clarke owned land and more to the point some twelve lock-ups next to the old woodwork shop on Grammar School Road. At first Lindsey Blind rented two of these – one as a garage and one as a store – but later on it was necessary to rent another for storage. The other lock-ups were rented out to individuals or to firms: the local Co-op used one as a depot for their milk bottles. The garage was the best part of half a mile from home, but the regular walk to and fro was never considered more than a minor inconvenience. Only the rich in their detached houses had integral or adjacent garages. At first the Bedford had no passenger seat and a small stool was placed in the well by the side of the driver, so that all I could see was sky and the left side of the dashboard. If a second passenger were present they would sit in the back on a second stool or on the contents if the van were ladened. There were no seat belts in those days and no health and safety regulations, yet accidents were few because of less traffic and slower speeds.

Lincolnshire then was the second largest county in the country and subdivided in two – the larger, northern part called Lindsey and the rest co-joined as Holland and Kesteven further south. The blind workers lived all over Lindsey, from Louth, Horncastle and Spilsby at the bottom end to Grimsby and Immingham to the east, and from Barton upon Humber, Horkstow and Winteringham to the north to Epworth, Scunthorpe and Gainsborough to the west. A surprisingly large variety of goods was produced. There were fewer women workers and even fewer who worked on a commercial scale. They were chiefly involved in knitting and crocheting. The knitting was done both by hand and on machine.

There was a substantial array of gents' hosiery and socks in general, although Lindsey Blind rarely made school stockings with appropriate coloured rings at the top, for national firms and authorised outfitters had this market sewn up. However, in my mid-teens I wore half-hose in a variety of heather mixtures, browns, fawn, greys and black: only the last two were allowed at school with long trousers and white was unheard of for general use, only for tennis or cricket. All the half-hose was available in longer lengths, because elderly gentlemen liked socks up to their knees. There were also thick stockings to go with knickerbockers beloved of the landed gentry. Lindsey Blind also had a contract to supply knee-length hospital stockings in thicker white four-ply, though whether they were really bedsocks to keep patients' feet warm in those un-centrally heated days or served some hygienic purpose I can't remember. Hundreds of pairs were produced and my mother earned a few shillings of pin money by ironing and packing them. After the war Scunthorpe United repeatedly ordered several sets of green football stockings for training purposes and it was arranged on one occasion that they should be delivered on the Saturday afternoon when Scunthorpe, then a Midland League club and nicknamed 'The [Pig] Iron', was playing the mighty Tottenham Hotspur in the FA Cup. My father and I duly presented ourselves at the Directors' entrance bearing parcels of stockings and were squeezed into the stand without tickets. I enjoyed the match, chiefly for seeing diminutive Tommy Harmer parade his repertoire of footballing tricks. Spurs won convincingly, but 'The Iron' had given a good account of themselves.

Of the women workers I particularly remember Evelyn Spacey, who lived with her parents at Grayingham, a small village off the A15 to Lincoln. She was the star both for quantity and quality. She was completely blind and her parents had to verify the colours of the wool, but otherwise she managed entirely on her own. She was a young woman, probably in her late twenties when I first knew her. She had been trained to knit on a machine and she produced quality knitwear – sweaters, cardigans, gloves, hosiery and scarves. Evelyn was a remarkable young woman, cheerful and sociable, active and adventurous. She later made the acquaintance of a man who was, I think, partially sighted and the relationship developed so well that they became engaged. Marriage duly took place and the newlyweds set up home – in America. I cannot remember the details but Evelyn's new husband must have had strong connections in the States and there Evelyn was to make her new life. I do remember that my parents attended the wedding and my father took the newlyweds to the airport for the start of their great adventure. I do hope Evelyn found happiness and contentment on the other side of the Atlantic. All this happened in the mid-fifties, but more germane to me was the fact that in 1951 she knitted me a cricket sweater in my Oxford College colours and incidentally raised false expectations when I occasionally turned out for Scawby in the lowest depths of the Scunthorpe and District Cricket Leagues, for the Wadham colours were the same as Yorkshire's: she also knitted a scarf in the different College colours for winter associated sports. I still wear the scarf regularly in cold weather and the cricket sweater has been passed on to my daughter, whom it nowadays keeps warm on her rowing excursions. Lindsey Blind made things to last.

This was especially true of George North, who lived with his sister or daughter at Immingham. George was over seventy when I first met him and he continued working well into his eighties. He specialised in seating chairs and stools in cane, rush or seagrass and was a fine craftsman. The frames were bought in, probably from Fred Aldous, stored in Brigg and then taken out to Immingham as required. Sometimes people had their own favourite chairs and stools that needed re-seating. These would be stripped down and taken to George to see if he could do anything with them. It was very rare that he was found not to be up to the challenge. He could fashion the rush in two or three patterns and the seagrass in various multi-hued formats, and the cane he wove carefully into the evenly spaced holes in the frame. George's products were legendary for their neatness and their tautness – none of his seats ever sagged. As a wedding present we ordered a double stool with Queen Anne cabriole legs in plain seagrass and it has been one of our cherished and much used possessions: a year before our Golden Wedding Anniversary it needed re-seating – and fittingly we managed to have it done by the local Blind Society in Huntingdonshire.

Other male home workers (such as Percy Knipe at Winterton or Winteringham) were cobblers. Most of their time was spent in soling and heeling heavy work boots: only occasionally were ladies' shoes cobbled. The footwear came from the Council-run old people's homes scattered around the county, for the County Council found it economical to pass trade on to its own Blind Society where it could. My father would regularly collect sacks of boots and shoes for repair, distribute them to his cobblers, collect the re-soled and re-heeled footwear and return it to the old people's homes. The cobblers could tell by touch what required doing and would cut out the soles and heels from the large bends of leather (which were stored at Brigg and distributed individually) or select from the bought-in rubber soles and heels. The blind cobblers were well able to add the segs and hobnails for longer wearing when they were needed. I have to say that we as a family never used the services of the Lindsey Blind cobblers because they were better with boots than shoes, and Doc Martens were unheard of as a universal fashion accessory. We used Billy Porter, who had a shop in Wrawby but lived down Grammar School Road in Brigg: we would take the shoes that needed attention to his house and he would deliver the repaired footwear as he cycled home, collecting payment when he called.

In addition to those who worked at home there was a workshop where brush-making, basket-making and some cobbling were carried on. This was situated in the southern area of Lindsey at Spilsby and up to a dozen blind workers were based there. They didn't all come from Spilsby; some were in 'digs' in the town and went home on the bus each weekend. The workshop had a foreman and later a general handyman, both of whom were sighted. The foreman was an elderly Scot called Mr Fraser, who was responsible for quality control, checking and recording the output of each worker, boring holes in the wooden brush-heads and ensuring that all the workers had the requisite raw materials to hand. In particular he had to see the bitumen burner was alight, constantly replenished and working properly for the six brush-makers. These were seated on high stools around a circular bench in the middle of which was a circular burner that melted the large chunks of bitumen into a molten bubbling tar about an inch thick in the circular pan. The bristles, already cut to the correct length, were in trays alongside each worker, who would by touch select a small handful of bristles, wrap thin twine around them to form a small cylinder and then dunk the twined end into the molten tar. This was then inserted into the brush-head, which was already bored out with some thirty or forty holes. The process would be repeated until all the holes were filled. The thickness and type of bristles would depend upon the type of brush being made. They were thick and stiff for yard brushes, not so thick or stiff for lavatory brushes and of varying degrees of softness for sweeping brushes and hand brushes. This was, of course, long before the days of plastics and synthetics, so all were of natural fibres. Once all the holes had been plugged it remained for the foreman or handyman to give the bristles a final trimming with a large pair of shears, permanently fixed to a bench. One blade was static and you raised one handle, shearing as you closed the blades. The brushes were then tied together in dozens or half-dozens.

When road-sweeping lorries were introduced – incidentally forcing a substantial number of elderly road-sweepers like my maternal grandfather out of business and into retirement – Lindsey Blind gained the contract for supplying and servicing the brushes of one or two conurbations in North Lincolnshire. The various cylindrical heads were different from any other brushes and the old, worn-out bristles and the tar had to be cored out before they could be re-brushed. The wooden stocks could be re-brushed some dozen times before new stocks were needed. However, the blind workers rose to the challenge and it became a lucrative if rather fiddly contract, because the sets of ten or so brushes for each lorry had to be kept carefully as a unit.

Brush-making was the main product from the workshop at Spilsby, but three or four men were employed in making baskets of all kinds. Potato baskets were made from osiers, which had to be kept in a water tank outside to remain pliable. Lindsey Blind made thousands over the years – I even used some in my own potato-picking days. They were strong and serviceable. The men sat on inclined boards with the osiers in lengths of some six feet about them. These were woven into baskets after the base had been formed with about a dozen uprights protruding. The handle was then formed by twisting some stouter pieces into a rope's thickness and attaching. Willow and split cane were used for shopping baskets of various shapes and sizes. Later a plastic thread was introduced for decoration into the handles and along the sides. Children's baskets were also made as well as a special line in flower-arranging baskets, fruit baskets and wastepaper baskets with raffia decoration. Garden trugs could be commissioned as special orders. In addition to baskets these workers were able to make cane-sided trays on glass or plywood bottoms and include a beaded decoration. One sideline of those who specialised in basketry was to make besoms for sweeping and larger, flatter models for beating out fires. There was a war on at this time and it was not unknown for the Jerries to drop incendiary bombs on woodland deliberately, so most afforested areas had racks of fire-beating besoms at strategic points. The workforce at the workshop was completed by a cobbler, who mended the boots and shoes from the old people's homes around Lindsey, which were still called by the rather derogatory term 'workhouses', where in fact no work was done by these elderly residents who had no family to care for them and who were those formerly consigned to Poor Law institutions.

One day there was a serious fire at the workshop, stemming from an accident with the bitumen burner used in brush-making. Fortunately all the workers were evacuated without serious injury, but the fire brigade could not save the building from extensive damage. This caused many problems until temporary premises were arranged and eventually a new, refurbished workshop erected on the original site. The fire necessitated rather more regular visits to Spilsby than the usual fortnightly visits. During the school holidays I would accompany my father in the Bedford van, sitting unstrapped first on a small stool in the well and later on the upholstered passenger seat. I used to enjoy these trips to the distant parts of Lindsey: not so much for Spilsby which I considered a somewhat nondescript town, even though it had sent Sir John Franklyn sailing to the far corners of the globe, but we also called at Louth and it was a stimulating journey over the Wolds in all seasons. Petrol, of course, was rationed, but commercial organisations had an allowance and Lindsey Blind had its share. However, it meant that journeys had to be carefully planned and were determined by the number of calls that could be made – either to service the blind workers or to drop off orders at farms, individual homes or public institutions. There was a fortnightly cycle to different points of the compass: Scunthorpe and the surrounding villages were usually on a Wednesday; Barton upon Humber and the Ancholme villages on alternate Tuesdays; and Immingham and the northeast district on Mondays. Thursday was market day in Brigg and often when all the local jobs were done. Fridays were for rather longer journeys.

Each month on a Friday my father would attend a management committee at the Council Offices in Lincoln. This was a trip I looked forward to. We would call at some of the villages like Grayingham, Hibaldstow or Waddingham to do business along the way and be at the County Offices by midday. My father would have preliminary meetings with officers before the main committee meeting was scheduled for two o'clock. I therefore had some four hours to savour the delights of Lincoln – a city, no less; the only one in Lincolnshire, whereas the slightly larger Yorkshire boasted at least five. I would wander up Steep Hill to the Cathedral and eat my sandwiches in that area or down in the river basin. In particular the myriad of small second-hand bookshops along Steep Hill fascinated me and I would spend hours in their dusty corridors and labyrinth of rooms browsing and dipping into the far-ranging stock in the early days of the war. I came across cheap second-hand copies of GA Henty or school stories by the admired Talbot Baines Reed, though they had nothing in common with my present or future schooldays. I also found bundles of paperback stories about Larry the Lamb by SG Hulme Beaman. I had been a devotee of Uncle Mac, who read these stories on *Children's Hour*, and I could persuade myself that they would eventually interest my younger brother – after I had relived my earlier pleasure. Later when I was at Brigg Grammar School I was intrigued by cheap Latin texts for schools of books we never came in contact with in 'Tiger' Richards' Latin lessons. I picked up Caesar's *De Bellum Civili* or individual books of Livy or two books of Virgil's *Aeneid*, all with helpful notes and vocabularies and all for threepence or sixpence. On dull, drizzling days of the holidays I sometimes set about making my own translations in the kitchen, for that was where the only fire was until the embers were precariously carried into the room and used to make the fire there about five o'clock for the evening. I would seat myself at the portable, green-baized card table that was the most versatile piece of furniture in the house (and which we still use in our house today) while my mother cooked or baked and was duly impressed. I was by no means an intellectual, but I did find Livy's accounts of Hannibal interesting and there were few alternatives on dreary days.

Also in Lincoln I used to visit the Usher Art Gallery, particularly if it were a rainy Friday. At that time the Usher was one of the most impressive pieces of architecture that I knew, omitting the Cathedral and churches around Brigg where I sometimes went brass-rubbing on my trusty cycle, equipped with cobblers' wax and remnants of rolls of wallpaper. It was at the Usher that I added to my miniscule knowledge of sex, for I never had any parental instruction and Biology was not then taught at Brigg Grammar School. I used to study the genitalia of Greek gods and heroes in their proud nakedness and admire the goddesses and nymphs with their smooth marmoreal limbs and sweetly curving breasts. I soon realised that an acanthus leaf was not an indispensable attachment and gazed curiously at the varying sizes and shapes of the human penis. I was first made aware of the attractiveness of nipples at the Usher, but remained ignorant of vaginas and pubic hair for they were never shown. It was here that I first came across the paintings of Peter De Wint, whom I grew to admire, and realised that pictures could come larger than three feet by two feet. The Usher did not have a particularly fine collection and there were few old masters, but there was an interesting variety of local and classical landscapes, much florid still life, some porcelain and portraits of notabilities among the local landowning classes, military men and clerical or legal worthies. Anyway, the Usher has a warm place in my heart notwithstanding later visits to the National Gallery in London, the Rijksmuseum, the Hermitage, the Vatican, the Prado and many other more illustrious collections. It was my introduction to real paintings and sculptures – whose female posteriors I would occasionally furtively caress.

Back at the County Offices I would wait till my father was finished and then we would drive back along the Ermine Street in winter blackout or the soft roseate hues of a summer's evening. Often by the time the Bedford had been garaged and we had plodded home, it was time for Henry Hall and his *Guest Night*, to which we listened while eating the home-cooked fish and chips that were our usual Friday night fare.

Travelling around Lincolnshire with my father made me appreciate the often disregarded delights of the county. There is a surprising variety in Lincolnshire, from the chalk uplands of the Wolds to the richly fertile river valleys, from the wild, solitariness of some of the beaches or rather shorelines to the hustle and bustle of market days in the towns or of Saturday nights when in my youth aircrew and squaddies from the many air stations clustered around the county would descend upon their nearest settlement and wreak havoc. There were clear days to enjoy the many ripening crops and the quietly grazing herds and flocks with sights and sounds of harvesting and planting. There were also dreary, dull days filled with blustery rain – remember Dickens set his *Bleak House* in Lincolnshire, but he was a prejudiced southerner! However, I do recall homeward journeys to be negotiated carefully in thick fogs that rolled in off the Humber or drifted wraithlike in the hollows and dips of the Wolds. In the first half of the forties there were no signposts to confirm position and weak headlights were largely masked by slatted covers that were required by law.

Travelling around Lincolnshire – or rather the important bit, Lindsey, for the other parts, Holland and Kesteven, remained obscure and unregarded – was a pleasure to be cherished. I particularly enjoyed driving through Tennyson country with its bucolic and romantic sounding village names – Bag and Mavis Enderbys, Old Bolingbroke, Hagworthingham and Ashby Puerorum – little realising then that for more than a hundred years my ancestors had lived and worked not far away. Around Somersby I always expected to encounter Maud in some Lincolnshire country garden and further afield to flee some irate knight-errant from Tattershall. This area was still completely unspoilt. In other areas we came across pillboxes and anti-tank defences. We were sometimes stopped by coils of barbed wire and our credentials examined by armed guards protecting the many airfields of wartime Lincolnshire.

Even in nostalgic memory it was not all picture-postcard prettiness, for I could never find anything complimentary to say about 'long, lazy, lousy Ludford', though I let the alliteration roll round my tongue. However, even Wragby's Highways Depot and Gainsborough's Workhouse, which we visited regularly, had charms, as did the occasional seaside run to 'Skeggie' and up the coast to Mablethorpe. We would often stop and eat our sandwiches near some small hamlet and I would quickly explore this and enter the old parish church, relishing the curious, hassocky, damp odour and examining ancient tombs and brasses of long-forgotten knights of old with their ladies. Nevertheless Lincoln and Louth were my favourites. I spent less time in Louth, but I found it an attractive place and used to enjoy the area known as Hubbard's Hills, where incidentally I became engaged years later. It was in Louth that my father would call at Mr Bagguley's, though I am not sure about that second 'g' and the following 'u'. As previously mentioned he was a tobacconist and also dealt in stamps. My first stamp album came from him with its incipient collection, to which I added as well as sparse pocket money and avid swopping would allow. In term time my father would bring home a selection on approval from his Friday visit and my friend and I would spend hours during the week agonising over purchases. I recall with quivering senses Mr Bagguley's shop pre-war with its exotic ambience of fine cigars and displays of rare stamps, both completely out of my reach. But those early stamps of Spanish galleons, wild animals, aircraft and ships together with many crowned and uncrowned heads and with such enticing names as Herzegovina, Suomi, Sverige, Liechtenstein and the Gold Coast enlarged my horizons and still remain in the mind. Another favourite port of call on the Spilsby/Horncastle run was the Massingberd Arms, where some female cousin several times removed was licensee. This was then an unpretentious but picturesque country pub where I quenched my thirst on home-made ginger beer and later had my first, underage half of bitter. Ah, nectar – and a rite of passage!

◆◆◆

From his earlier time working at Lacey and Clark's my father had a wide circle of acquaintances who were former customers and continued to buy things made by the blind. He also had a host of country cousins, for the Rhodes family had lived for almost four hundred years in Lincolnshire and, though they sometimes weren't on speaking terms with each other, there were offshoots of the family (of whom I knew nothing) dotted around the county. He would call, do business and then enjoy a cup of tea and very occasionally be given a 'pig's fry', a superb Lincolnshire delicacy, if a family pig had been recently slaughtered. In wartime these were worth their weight in gold and savoured with veneration. Potato peelings, leftovers and edible scraps were scrupulously saved and delivered to neighbours who had space to keep a pig in the hope of a few sausages when it met its ordained end.

One of the things that the society somewhat curiously sold was tea, for it provided a small source of income for elderly blind people unable to work. It had done this from its earliest pre-war days and thus Lindsey Blind had an allocation throughout the war. Supplies came in heavy tea chests that were stored in one of the lock-ups on a pallet-like structure that was a couple of inches off the floor to avoid rodents. The plainly wrapped quarter pounds of loose tea had a square sticker on one end that proclaimed proudly 'Lindsey Blind Society' around a larger central price, which I think was 9d – or 4p in current terms. There were two colours of stickers, green and blue, and the price may have differed slightly, but I cannot remember what was the difference in quality or taste. The individual packets were encased in brown-paper packs of a dozen packets, which were a bit bigger than the present reams of copying paper. The tea was distributed among blind people, who in turn dispensed it to neighbours who bought one or two packets at a time. Anyway, we consumed Lindsey Blind tea throughout the war and thereafter. It wasn't a vast trade, but it was time-consuming. It was a real effort to stack the tea chests two or even three high in the lock-up. Of course, during the war tea was rationed – adults had two ounces per week – and this meant the complication of collecting and checking the weekly coupons that the blind had collected from their customers. It was a miracle that it all tallied each month, but I can't remember any adverse comebacks from the offices of the Ministry of Food, where presumably it was rechecked by clerical staff.

◆◆◆

Even in wartime Lindsey Blind's business expanded and it accelerated after the war. A third lock-up had to be leased from Zadok Clarke to house more goods, raw materials and finished products that were due for consignment to the purchasers when the van was next going in the right direction. Potato baskets were piled high and yard brushes stacked in dozens up to the roof. There were strong-smelling bends of leather measuring some eight feet by three. I delighted in the aroma and the smooth touch of these shiny, light bronze bends. Clutches of broom handles were stacked up in corners and thick bunches of willow and canes were stood on end. Along one wall were fixtures with compartments for smaller and more delicate items, such as skeins of knitting wool and the larger cones of four-ply used on the machines. Here too were stored the boxes of rubber soles and heels used by the cobblers. The larger items were delivered by lorry from the railway station by arrangement. So often it fell to my mother to receive the goods. She would walk down to the lock-ups, open up, check the leather bends, tea chests or bunches of willow or hanks of seagrass that were delivered and sign for them before locking up and returning home. She couldn't move the larger items and sometimes an unhelpful railway lorry driver would refuse to put the goods inside the lock-up and leave them in the yard, but I can't remember any thefts. Most people were honest in those days. When this chore was delegated to me in my mid-teens, I felt grown up and signed the railway chitty with aplomb.

After some five years, the administration outgrew our front room and its filing cabinet and there were just not enough hours in the day for my father to do all the paperwork, because after a full day on his rounds he was due for regular night duties as a Special Constable. Thus an office was opened in Brigg in a small, single room building not far from the old school rooms that became the library in Bigby Street. In this room was a solid mahogany table that was the desk, on which stood a well-used Royal Imperial typewriter. An old cumbersome safe was installed to hold ledgers, stock books and petty cash, for larger sums were banked regularly. There was an old gas fire and now three filing cabinets. There was no toilet, but there were public conveniences a hundred yards away. Neither were there any tea-making facilities, so flasks were taken. A part-time secretary was appointed and eventually at the end of the war a telephone was installed. There was a succession of secretaries, some more decorative than efficient who didn't last long; I chiefly remember Mrs Drury, who was of an age with my mother and most dependably served the society for several years. In my mid-teens I was given minor clerical jobs to do in the holidays, like totalling the postage book and reconciling it with the stamps purchased. I never could make things tally the first time, so it was a good job I was never entrusted with making up the pay packets of the blind workers at Spilsby and others from the various bits of paper recording individual output. This was done by my father or Mrs Drury and I can remember very few disputes. The blind workers knew to within threepence what they expected to receive.

After the war Lindsey Blind expanded its operations further. It opened a retail shop in Scunthorpe at no. 18 Cole Street. This was a terraced house with a shop front and not too far from the town centre. In setting up this retail arm my father was deeply involved and his earlier retail experience proved most useful. In addition to the items made by the blind workers and those at Spilsby other products were bought in from other Blind Societies and from commercial wholesalers. Those products made by the workers in Lindsey now had an official trademark and what we would now call a 'logo', though the word was unheard of in the late forties. This was an outstretched hand, palm uppermost, with an eye in the middle and the text 'Blindsey product' around it. It was generally recognised that 'Blindsey', a clever combination, indicated high quality. Thus hosiery, gloves, cardigans, sweaters, tea cosies and several other knitted goods were on sale as well as a wide variety of brushes and basketry. A considerable number of smaller, allied items were bought in to provide variety and extra profits: these included dressing table sets and hairbrushes, hand-painted condiment sets in the new plastic and in pottery, fancier woollen goods and more exotic basketwork. Some of these, it has to be admitted, were rather 'naff' (such as condiment sets featuring flying ducks or forget-me-nots) and quite garish, but they sold. However, two-thirds of all sales were still of 'Blindsey' products. Someone was hired to run the shop and no. 18 Cole Street also became the base for the local home teacher, Miss Sandwith. In addition it became what would now be called a 'drop-in centre' for blind people and their carers, again not a term in use at the time.

My father became more and more involved as manager/administrator and a general assistant was appointed. He was a local Brigg man, Charlie Sambrook, who now drove the Bedford van or its successor – was it another Bedford or one of the new Fordsons? (In any case it was long before Transits.) My father still used the van occasionally, but he needed his own transport and thus in the late forties he bought a new small Standard 8 in the usual utilitarian grey, for which he was paid a mileage allowance. The advantage was that it was available for pleasure motoring at his own expense. It also meant that travelling to the monthly meeting in Lincoln was much more comfortable and that much longer, out-of-county journeys were possible, for it is inconceivable today how restricted travelling was for ordinary people in the late forties. My father was a County Bowls player and the car made matches much more accessible even for such far-flung places as Whitley Bay.

It also made it possible for my parents to holiday with friends in unknown areas like Ross-on-Wye and on one occasion to visit me for the weekend when I was up at Oxford, a visit full of apprehension for my mother in prospect but in retrospect full of happy memories and satisfaction. However, in those days long car journeys were special occasions and had to be carefully considered. Fewer than one in ten had a car and no-one used one for taking children to school or going to the shops.

◆◆◆

It was through the Lindsey Blind that my limited horizons were slightly widened. The society had a marquee at the Lincolnshire County Show held both on the Carholme and then at the Show Ground newly created off the A15 near Scampton. It also exhibited and sold at the Scunthorpe Show then held in Quibell Park. I attended both and thoroughly enjoyed visiting all the trade stands and exhibits, but lingering over the prize farm stock, especially the Lincoln Reds and the Lincolnshire Longwools – for I was and remain proud of the county of my birth. Then I would spend all my time in the marquee serving and selling. I came into regular contact with handicapped people and came to recognise something of the difficulties they encountered, but also to admire their indomitable courage. In addition I realised something of their frustrations, their loves, lusts and fantasies. They were individuals – some were married with families, some were elderly and had accepted their condition, whereas others, younger, had yearnings and ambitions. In addition to their manual skills, they had a surprising number of other skills and gifts. The chaps from the Spilsby workshop played in a dance band and were well known locally. Two of them formed an accordion duo and played with gusto. They entered the *Carol Levis Discovery Show*, then a very popular radio show and the forerunner of *Opportunity Knocks* and *Stars in Their Eyes*. There was a series of local and area competitions before a Grand Final in London with all competitors longing to be discovered by Carol Levis. There were amateur entertainers of all kinds – from singers and instrumentalists to monologue reciters, from stand-up comics and dancers to animal acts and memory men. Sidney Millard and Reg Todd won a local heat in Spilsby and came to an area competition in Scunthorpe. This was held at the old Savoy Theatre (home of third-rate repertory companies and good local amateur groups). They came for tea at home and stayed overnight. I went with them to the Savoy and actually guided them onto the stage and placed them strategically in front of the microphone. I remember they played a medley of popular tunes and ended with a rollicking version of 'Blaze Away'. They were placed in the first three of some fifteen acts and progressed to the regional final to our great pleasure. My father accompanied them to this, but they did not reach the Grand Final in London to be acclaimed one of Carol Levis's 'Discoveries' and actually perform on the BBC.

I was a fairly regular guide to blind people, taking them to catch buses or trains, escorting them on organised days out along the promenade at Skegness or Cleethorpes and taking them home from the Scunthorpe shop. I suppose the cheerful Evelyn Spacey was the first youngish woman I ever walked arm in arm with. You had to be carefully restrained when guiding a blind person, for it doesn't do to be too forward or forceful in leading. They like to follow with a hand lightly resting on your arm. Once at the beginning of term I remember taking a young blind person back to his School for the Blind in Sheffield.

Thus I owe a great debt to the Lindsey Blind Society: it widened my horizons and taught me a lot, especially that I had much to be thankful for and a certain humility in front of blind people. Through my father's job I was enabled to travel widely in Lincolnshire even during the war years and came to share his delight in the county of our births with its inimitable beauty during the varying seasons.

14
TEENAGE ANGST AND THE SAP RISING

It was Philip Larkin who wrote:

Sexual intercourse began / In nineteen sixty-three
(Which was rather late for me) –
Between the end of the Chatterley ban / And the Beatles' first LP.

He was right on the mark: it was much too late for me. I was born twenty years too soon. It is impossible to conceive how naive and sexually innocent teenagers of the 1940s were and what an asexual existence was ours. There was no mention on the wireless and the *News of the World* (which was apparently far from explicit) never invaded our house, even as fish and chip wrapping. There were no commercial pressures and little overt peer pressure. We had no formal sex education at single-sex Grammar Schools and the subject was never raised by my parents. Why, I failed to see or realise my mother was pregnant until I saw my newly arrived younger brother in her bed and he could have easily been discovered under a gooseberry bush in the garden for all my knowledge. There was a recognised desire to learn more as you moved on to secondary school, but it was not a paramount need. Among my contemporaries it was a case of the visually impaired leading the blind in our quest for enlightenment. We sniggered over imperfectly understood innuendoes and retailed 'dirty' jokes with incomprehensible punch lines in hushed and furtive voices. One such that I remember was of the boy who was sent to the shop for a pint of peas. (These of course were not frozen or fresh, but hard, wizened and bullet-like, which we used also in peashooters.) His parents, making the most of their opportunity, were supposed to be 'on the job' in their bedroom when he returned to shout up the stairs, *'Split or whole, Dad?'* We vaguely understood the pun on 'split 'er 'ole', but had no clear anatomical perception.

As for same-sex relationships, they belonged to a completely alien world. I don't think I heard or read the word 'lesbian' until I was nearly twenty. The words 'queer' and 'shirt-lifter' I had come across, but a 'queer' was a chap who surprisingly did not like women and the word was simply an informal synonym for misogynist. I couldn't conceive a purpose for lifting shirts. Looking back I think I was once subject to a half-hearted homosexual advance from a *News of the World* stereotype, but I was much too innocent in my late teens to recognise it. It was also rumoured that a shop manager in the town had a collection of dirty postcards (including some of women committing curious and unnatural acts with donkeys) which he showed on occasions to favoured paperboys: I never delivered papers.

At home we took *The Daily Telegraph*, which never contained pin-ups of scantily clad young ladies or cartoons such as that which featured Jane in the *Daily Mirror*. I do remember cutting out a picture of a Hollywood starlet (Evelyn Keyes, I think) in revealing pose dressed in some diaphanous material: I rescued it from newspaper wrapping the family fish and chips one Saturday lunchtime and carefully smoothed it out, before secreting it in a book in my bedroom. A little later on such pictures were plentiful, for being a film fan I subscribed to *Picturegoer*, which often featured nubile young ladies inadequately clothed. The front cover of one issue depicted Jane Russell in enticingly provocative pose in the hay, advertising *The Outlaw*: I don't think I went to see the film, but the actress left an indelible impression upon my youthful imagination. Occasionally one of my friends would pass round a grubby, well-thumbed copy of *Health and Beauty*, but there was something chaste and unexciting about these naked bodies often posed with beach balls or doing physical exercises, rather like school PE. My closest acquaintance with sexual activity came from literary sources. In the mid-forties there was nothing like the explicit passages found in much of contemporary fiction, but one author titillated my imagination. I had read about the adventures of Baroness Orczy's Scarlet Pimpernel and picked up a seemingly similar historical romance, Dennis Wheatley's *The Launching of Roger Brook*. This was a raunchy eye-opener and filled in a few blanks in my knowledge. I went on to read anything I could by Wheatley and thus came across my first inklings of the occult, which was an ephemeral fascination.

◆◆◆

Sex with its yin and yang remained on a literary plane on the periphery of my experience, but there was also a more personal, darker and more guilt-ridden side. Our teenage male bodies were telling us of physical changes, charges and discharges. They were new, embarrassing and largely out of our control, causing much surprise, torment and furtive covering up. We never voiced these experiences and neither did our closest friends discuss such matters. Nocturnal emissions – even today the phrase 'wet dreams' seems too explicit – were fairly regular and if they awakened you from slumber involved messy clutching, squeezing and throbbing. Then there was lying on the damp patch in an effort to dry it out and afterwards a feverish, secret rubbing of the offending areas to reduce the stiffness of sheet and pyjamas to disguise the telltale signs. My mother always made my bed and must have been aware, but no mention was ever made. Guiltily I expected some reference. Even more guiltily I discovered 'the joys of masturbation', a phrase that surfaced in a small repertoire of 'dirty' songs, which I lustily bellowed later in male singsongs on coach outings. The period did not last long, but it seemed to have unpleasant effects that were connected in my mind with the dimly understood but alarming references we saw to venereal disease, which appeared on posters in surgeries and clinics: the habit was also believed to cause blindness. For months I became a pimply, spotted youth and, like Chaucer's Summoner, no ointment (not even 'Valderma') could cleanse me of my spots. They did nothing for my appearance or self-confidence and I felt they completely inhibited whatever chance I might have of attracting girls. Girls and the attraction of sex played only a limited part, unfortunately, in my Yeller-belly Years, even though I may have wished for a more intimate association. I had no knowledge of their minds or their bodies. Names of girls flicker through my memory. From the very early years there was Margaret C, who lived three doors away but left Brigg before infant school days, and Ellen T, who lived next door. We certainly played together from time to time and shared a clothes-horse tent one afternoon, playing parents and house. Memory hints at a certain sexual precocity of 'I'll show you mine, if you show me yours', but not clearly and Ellen was more inquisitive than I. At Glebe Road School girls were either avoided as far as possible or admired from afar for their intellect like Margaret B. Nor did they register as important in the early Grammar School years. I had a youthful crush on Peggy B and I would mark her progress along Woodbine Avenue from an upstairs window as she returned home from an after-school piano practice. High School girls like Peggy, Caroline H and Ruth P in their green gingham school dresses and white ankle socks were hardly sex objects, but they first stirred faint, uneasy longings in the loins. There was no opportunity for physical contact, for the social mores of the day were based on a strict segregation of the sexes. Church and school activities allowed no scope for hanky-panky. These young ladies were as unattainable as Hollywood stars like Betty Grable, Maria Montez and Donna Reed, or Marlene Dietrich with her disturbing but exotic/erotic aura. Another girl was Gwendoline – as far removed as possible from Oscar Wilde's heroine: she was a simple-minded lass from Scawby Brook older than I, whom I met at church. She caused me huge embarrassment among my peers by appearing frequently at Jack Clark's, Brigg Grammar School's semi-official tuck shop, when we were buying our buns at morning break and claiming close acquaintance with her husky *'Hello, John'* and manic smile.

◆◆◆

Parties were rare events in my life at this time. Pre-war there had been a small succession of birthday parties among four or five friends' and neighbours' sons, but these were usually boisterous, all-male occasions and Sunday School parties were mixed but decorous affairs. During the war rationing allowed only family entertaining to mark the great church festivals of Christmas and Easter. Entertaining friends in any formal manner was just not a social custom among our stratum of lower middle-class society. My parents never had acquaintances round for a meal or drinks, nor did they dine out. The thought of holding a dinner party never occurred and, anyway, dinner was a meal eaten between noon and one o'clock. Sherry parties, even cocktail parties, might be held in the big houses on Wrawby Road, but not in Central Square. Church and other organisations to which we belonged had 'Social Evenings' after the war, but these were relatively staid affairs in age groups from mid-teens to mid-eighties. I once did have a Party – it deserves a capital 'P' – to mark my twenty-first birthday, but that is outside the scope of this memoir.

Thus invitations to parties, where all of those attending would be teenagers and some of them girls, were extremely cherished and eagerly anticipated for weeks. Peggy B's parties were the only ones to which I was invited. Peggy was an only daughter and somewhat indulged by her parents. For two or three years after the war she had a party in January and probably seventeen would be invited. A male cousin and a couple of friends from Sheffield were included and they brought a heady metropolitan presence to the rustic gathering of lads and lasses from Brigg Grammar and the High School. Before tea we played paper-and-pencil games, including 'Consequences', with the opportunity of making some veiled and *risqué* allusions, some based on fact and some the result of lurid imaginings. For this game you each had a piece of paper on which you wrote your answer to a question, folded the answer over and passed the paper on to the next person before writing your answer to the new question on this piece of paper: who met whom, where, when, what did they do, how were they dressed, what did they say and what was the consequence. The resultant hybrids were read out aloud. Then we tucked into egg and cress, crab paste or potted meat sandwiches, and jellies, trifles, macaroons and Christmas cake. The drink was usually cups of tea, lemonade and a dark brown, effervescent liquid, new to me, called 'Tizer'. But one year there was a highly sophisticated addition we drank out of wine glasses: it was called 'Fruit Cup'. It was served with a scoop from a large bowl into which tins of fruit cocktail had been added to lemonade and Tizer and topped off with several glasses of port. It was an innocuous brew but definitely an adult drink. You should remember that in 1947 teenage drunkenness and binge drinking had to wait another fifty years to be discovered – and there was no Coca-Cola. No-one raided parents' drink cabinets – these existed only in Hollywood films – and any furtive filching from the bottle kept in the pantry would have been instantly noticed.

After tea we played traditional games of Pass the Parcel, Musical Chairs and Charades, but then someone, probably the cousin from Sheffield, would make the suggestion we boys – and possibly the girls too – had been waiting for with almost painful anticipation: Postman's Knock. However, letters, stamps and rappings from employees of the Royal Mail had been abandoned in the version conducted by the Sheffield cousin. We paired off by drawing names out of a hat, boy with girl. There was, by design, an odd number invited to the party and the odd one was handed a torch. The couples found a suitable chair or part sofa with the girl on the boy's lap. The lights were switched off and the couples were expected to 'snog', though that inelegant word was not then current in our vocabulary. The person with the torch had to make sudden flashes upon the various pairs to try to discover two *not* in an osculatory embrace. You had to time your sudden illumination carefully by switching back to a pair who might have paused to draw breath. When this occurred, the girl/boy with the torch changed places with the girl/boy found in dereliction of their duties. This was my height of passion in my youth, but it consisted of little more than faint-hearted fumblings, careful clutches and pursed lips jammed against pursed lips. The eagerly awaited sexual frisson never really developed, though some may have been more tactilely adventurous than I and encountered that mysterious zone known as 'stocking tops'. The boys were unusually reticent about what had happened in the dark and anyone who boasted was held to be lying. But the girls might be overheard clucking in a mixture of alarm and excitement: *'Do you know what he did? He squeezed me hard – here.'* – *'Where?'* – *'Here.'* – *'He didn't.'* – *'He did!'* – *'Oooooh!'*

After a final glass of Fruit Cup and a further piece of Christmas cake and an attempt at the Hokey-Cokey, we dispersed at the dangerously decadent hour of eleven o'clock. Those girls who were not staying over were collected by parents, so there was no-one to escort home. I had only a few hundred yards to go, but there was lightness in my step: by the standards of those days, I had partied. How different from the party habits and expectations of today!

The high spot of the Brigg social calendar at this time was the New Year's Ball organised by the Bowling Club and held in the Angel Hotel Ballroom. For years my father was treasurer of the Bowls Club and Alf Rands ('Uncle Alf') secretary and thus were much involved in the preparations before the event and on December 31st. Neither my mother nor Aunt Lil ever attended, but in the last years of the forties I went together with John Rands. I had gone to a few private dancing lessons at what was called a 'studio' in Scunthorpe and had some half dozen half-hour sessions with an ageing teacher to the sounds of a scratchy, wind-up gramophone. I could never lose myself in the music nor effortlessly glide round the floor in a quickstep or a foxtrot and the samba rhythms were utterly beyond me. With hard concentration I could get along the floor by diligently counting '1–2–3' for the waltz or the veleta and '1–2–3–STAMP!' for the St Bernard's. When we came to a corner, I often had to stop and disentangle my feet. At none of the dances I went to was there any of the new-fangled jiving or jitterbugging. I never grabbed my partner roughly or flung her around, but decorously placed my hand high upon her back. Instead of gazing adoringly into her eyes, mine were fixed on the floor watching anxiously what my feet were doing. I was too busy counting to murmur sweet nothings.

The Bowling Club Ball was a formal event. It was popular and usually a sell-out. The important people of Brigg society were there – civic leaders, local farmers, the big shop owners and the professional classes – all in their rarely used dinner jackets with their tightly corseted, coiffured wives in voluminous brocade evening gowns. I had no dress suit, but wore my best suit and for the first time a bow tie to give an indication of formality. Finding a partner was a bit of a problem, but I plucked up my courage and asked Caroline whom I knew well from church and who was intimidatingly the daughter of my History master and housemaster from school. She appeared dressed in a long, close-fitting satin dress in a checked green and yellow design, which exposed several more square inches of fair white flesh below the neck than did normal school wear. I complimented her and we set out to enjoy our evening. We managed to secure more than one refill from the punch bowl and felt even more euphoric. We attempted such energetic and unknown dances as the Eightsome Reel and Strip the Willow. We took part in progressive dances. I bravely clasped the whale-boned sides of elderly ladies and galloped them through a few bars of the Gay Gordons. The buffet supper introduced me to *vol-au-vents* for the first time, but all too soon we were welcoming in the New Year and then standing together in a circle for 'Auld Lang Syne'.

Going to the ball was an important point in my social education. It also meant collecting Caroline in Sid Whelpton's taxi and having a taxi back as far as Westrum Lane, then a bare, unadopted way beyond the level crossing on the outskirts of Brigg. The taxi departed, Sid paid but untipped, and we stood awkwardly in the gateway, making polite and dutiful conversation. Then after a clutched embrace and a peck or two – with me gazing apprehensively over my shoulder at the darkened house to see if there were any parental observation – we broke off and parted. Caroline put her key in the front door and I trudged through the mud and slush in the lane back to Central Square. However, with a greater elasticity in my stride: this was growing up.

◆◆◆

My Yeller-belly Years had brought me to the brink of the fifties safely, happily with few traumas and no major tragedies. They may seem tepid and unexciting in comparison with these sensation-seeking and self-indulgent times. I feel I was lucky not to have had to withstand the commercial pressures and material expectations faced by today's teenagers. I was certainly unaffected by anything like the contemporary fixation with the celebrity culture of minor, self-serving non-entities. As we reached the midpoint of the twentieth century, I had negotiated most of the perils of adolescence and had developed some small sense of worth and social maturity. Now I looked forward to Oxford and beyond.

15
ASHBY COUNTY PRIMARY SCHOOL

At the beginning of 1949 I was in limbo. I had finished my time at Brigg Grammar School at the end of the previous Christmas term, having stayed on an extra term in a wildly over-optimistic attempt to win an Open Scholarship at Oxford and had not been too dismayed to have failed. I had already gained a place to read English at Wadham College and was due to take up that place in October 1950. I had anticipated having to do my national service in the interim. However, the army took one look at the outrageous hammer on each of my little toes and scrutinised the perforations in my ears (a relic of scarlet fever) and decided that it would be better off without the benefit of my services. This was a jolting disappointment. 'Gap' years and VSO were as then unthought of and anyway I was far too unadventurous and parochial to think of spreading my wings at that time when I was just over eighteen. Thus I faced the prospect of filling in some eighteen months locally and, if possible, profitably. My career intentions were vaguely of being a teacher. I had enjoyed my schooldays and revered most of my teachers and it was accepted as a secure and satisfying profession, if not particularly well paid. There was no careers officer then or even family friend to suggest wider horizons as an alternative.

◆◆◆

In 1949 education was in an even bigger mess than it is today. There was no money available to replace school buildings, sadly neglected during the war years, or to refurbish the stock cupboards, and a shortage of materials of all kinds. But the biggest shortage was in teachers, whether qualified or not. And this worked in my favour. I read in the local press that teachers were urgently required in the Scunthorpe Division, part of Lindsey, one of the three administrative areas of Lincolnshire. I wrote to the Scunthorpe Office and quickly received instructions to present myself before the headmaster of Ashby County Primary School at ten o'clock the following Monday morning. Ashby was an outlying suburb of Scunthorpe and some eight miles from where I lived.

I didn't get off to a very good start. I was four and a half hours late for my appointment. I had a prior appointment for nine o'clock at Scunthorpe Hospital, as the army doctor had written to my family GP that my ears should be looked at and so an appointment was made. I was at the hospital in good time, but because of administrative delays and my own ignorance of procedures I wasn't seen till after lunch. (Things don't seem to change.) Anyway, it was decided that nothing could be done, or needed to be done, so it wasn't a very productive experience. I hastened by local bus to Ashby and presented myself to the headmaster just before half past two. He was the long established and redoubtable Charles Bramley, but more of him later. Such was the serious staffing shortage that I think anyone deemed capable of standing in front of a class would have been accepted with alacrity. I was told I would be taken on and was asked to be at the school by quarter to nine on the Wednesday morning, less than two days thence. It may have helped that Charles Bramley, like me, had been educated at Brigg Grammar School (where he had long played the piano at Old Boys' Dinners) and he also knew of my father through local choir and operatic circles.

Thus on the Wednesday morning I got off the early bus from Brigg to Scunthorpe via Ashby and entered the school as a putative and tyro teacher. I was dressed in a well-worn suit with clean shirt and tie and with shiny black shoes (burnished by my mother, who prided herself on her skills in black-leading grates and bringing shoes to a beautiful shine). The school was an aged Victorian building with a small front yard, directly abutting onto the busy Ashby High Street at its lower end. There was a main door for staff and visitors and separate entrances for 'Boys' and 'Girls' on each side. The main door opened onto a fairly wide corridor with a wood-blocked floor. The head's room was immediately on the right: there was no secretary's room, nor even a secretary, for heads were expected to do all their own paperwork – or get an ambitious colleague to do it out of classroom hours, which is what Charles Bramley often did. I can't remember a staffroom as such, nor any facilities for making hot drinks: instead we took flasks of hot tea or the ubiquitous Camp coffee and drank them on duty in the playground or in one of the classrooms.

There were four classrooms on either side of the corridor, with the largest classroom partitioned off with a high screen to form a separate third which housed the 'special' class. The rudimentary cloakrooms and washbasins with cold taps were at the rear and the toilets were outside. There was no staff toilet as such inside and I can't remember clearly what arrangements were made. The males could use the boys' urinals outside, but what the ladies did I have no idea. Possibly in an emergency they made use of the facilities at the head's house, which was on site – but it would have had to be a dire emergency.

There were nearly four hundred children in this building, aged between nine and eleven. There were three classes in the top year and four in the other year group, with the special class of about twenty children spanning both years. However, this was just over half the school. Some five hundred yards up the High Street and housed in Church Hall premises was the more junior element and the infants department. The whole school comprised some six hundred and fifty children, which was large for a primary school in the mid-twentieth century, though primary schools in Scunthorpe tended to be larger than the norm, until new schools were built some ten years later and eased the pressure.

I can vividly remember my colleagues in the main building with whom I was in daily contact, but those up the High Street were less well known and remained somewhat shadowy figures, for they rarely had cause to venture down to the main school. There was no equal pay then and there was underneath in the whole teaching profession a simmering resentment among some staff and this was reflected in membership of the National Union of Teachers (NUT) or the National Association of Schoolmasters (NAS), then the two main teaching unions for primary teachers. The NAS was a male-orientated organisation and opposed to equal pay for women, since they did not have families to support, as the men did. The NUT had primary school members of both sexes (as well as some secondary members) and was the largest union and campaigned for equal pay for women. There was also status rivalry among those who had done the full teacher training course of two years at such prestigious establishments as The City College, Sheffield, Chester or St John's, York, and those who had changed careers and become emergency-trained teachers, whose post-war course had been for only one year at such places as Padgate, the former initial training base of the RAF. However, at Ashby any latent antagonism rarely erupted in overt bitterness or recrimination and generally staff relations were most amicable.

❖❖❖

Over the whole school brooded the somewhat alarming presence of Charles Bramley. He was an institution and had been head of the school for well over twenty-five years. He was about sixty and not in the best of health. He suffered badly from asthma and was subject to hacking coughing fits. He always had an inhaler ready to hand, either on his desk or in his capacious jacket pocket. It was unlike present-day models, being like a giant's scent bottle with a spray protruding on one side and with a huge rubber ball attached by a rubber tube on the other. He would raise the whole contraption in one hand, clamping the other round the bulbous rubber end and squeeze. He would spray the contents into his widely open mouth for some time, heaving and groaning, and then sink down in his chair, gradually recovering his breath in large, slobbering gasps. It was quite unnerving when this happened in the midst of a conversation or when he had come into your classroom. The children would sit as if hewn out of stone if an attack occurred during a visit to their room. It wasn't a matter for levity and Charles Bramley was a noted caner, with a well-deserved reputation for a strong right arm. Most of the parents of the present children had attended the school during his long headship and proudly regaled their children with stories of how they had been chastised by Chas B. The children got no sympathy at home if they complained that they had been caned unjustly at school.

Charles Bramley was a character who would have been comfortably at home in a Dickens novel, for he was a mixture of Wackford Squeers, Mr Micawber and Mr Bumble the Beadle. His large frame was declining, but he remained corpulent and his large belly overhung the top of his trousers, shirt showing in the sizeable gap between waistcoat and braced trousers. He was somewhat untidy in appearance and there were always food stains from fallen gobbets on his jacket and waistcoat. He had large features with a prominent, bulbous nose and red-rimmed, watery eyes. He had scant grey hair untidily combed across the top of his head with overlong fringes round his ears and the back of his neck. He was not very active at this time, remaining for long periods in his room with infrequent sallies to patrol the school corridor. He would shamble along, cane in hand and inhaler bulging in pocket, to peer through the glass panes in the upper part of classroom doors. If the whim took him, he would push open the door, whereupon the class would shoot to their feet in utter silence and face the front of the classroom, expressionless save for flickers of apprehension. He would ignore the teacher, chide some unfortunate girl for not standing straight and cuff a boy who dared glance at his neighbour. He might then slam his cane on a desk and snarl out well-tried questions: *'How many days in a ye-are?'* followed by *'How many days in a leap ye-are?'* or *'Six sevens?'* These were sometimes answered en masse or by an individual if the cane were pointed in that direction. If the individual were unable to answer the question, his neighbour was invited to help. On a bad day an arm would be grasped, a hand held out and a smart blow from the cane administered. Then with critical comments about the class's general ignorance, he would shuffle off like an irritated grizzly. But just as he got to the door to leave, he would catch the teacher's eye and disconcertingly give a sly grin and wink. By such methods he perpetuated the Charles Bramley mythology. He certainly was no monster, though larger than life, and he was held both in awe and affection by generations of Ashby scholars. He was a most accomplished pianist and well known in local musical circles. He had also been a fine choir trainer and his school choirs won many trophies at local festivals. Even in my day he would thump out tunes on the piano and the children's voices would soar to angelic effect.

A few years later Charles Bramley came to a memorable end when he had a fatal heart attack while enthroned on the outside toilet of the head's house with his trousers around his ankles. Chas B was not one to go out with a whimper but with a big bang. I owe him a debt of gratitude, for he supported and helped me and oversaw a period of growing maturity in my callow youth.

✦✦✦

The other teachers and colleagues were an interesting and varied group. There was no official hierarchy in primary schools in those days and duration at the school was the main yardstick for deciding seniority. Bessie Wrigley, then a spinster in her late thirties, was the most senior. She was a Methodist lay preacher and a delightful, kindly lady. From her I had valuable support and quiet advice. She was a dedicated teacher and worked tirelessly for the benefit of her classes: at that time each teacher's efforts were exclusively aimed at their particular class, for there were no pastoral responsibilities over a whole year or any overall responsibilities for part of the curriculum. Mrs Chantry was a farmer's wife from Messingham and had come back to teaching during the war. I had a connection to her, for I found she had been a pre-war customer of Lacey and Clark's when my father worked there in the thirties and when he had often made deliveries to her in Messingham, so she was kindly disposed to me in a vague, motherly way. Another female teacher who had taught for a few years in the school was Freda Pollard, who was the daughter of a well-known local builder and whose husband, a former member of the RAF, worked in the family business. She was probably the most affluent member of staff. She was under thirty, attractive and always smartly dressed with carefully modelled hairstyles and make-up. She had no children then and the head tended to allot better classes to her. I thought she was quite something. The other female teacher was not long out of college and in her very early twenties, Sylvia Butterick. Despite being closer to my own age than any of the others, she was the one I had least to do with.

I came to have much closer acquaintance with my male colleagues. Marc Coom (or Marcus to give him his full name, as Charles Bramley always did) came from a teaching family. His father taught Woodwork and Metalwork at Scunthorpe Grammar School and his sister was also a primary teacher. Marc had a large moustache, a gruff voice and a fine sense of humour and drove an impressive motorcycle with sidecar. He was devoted to teaching and the children were fond of him. During my time there his motorcycle combination was involved in a bad accident in the middle of Scunthorpe and as a result he had a leg amputated. However, he survived the traumatic event with both fortitude and determination. He returned to teaching, drove a specially adapted car and later became headmaster at the school in Ashby. Horace Whickham had served in the RAF during the war and had then trained as a teacher. He brought a touch of the outside world to his teaching, but felt he was under-remunerated. He found difficulty in providing for his wife and family in the manner he would wish. Marc, like myself, still lived at home, but Horace had rent to pay and a family to support. He resigned later to become a housefather at a children's home elsewhere in Lincolnshire, where his wife Mavis was also employed. It eased their financial position considerably and Horace was still able to do some teaching too. The other one who completed a social quartet of sorts as well as a pedagogical one was Alan Fontaine. He was a local lad who changed from being a post office engineer to a teacher after service in the RAF. He later married a local girl and they lived at nearby Bottesford. He had a questing mind and eclectic tastes. He was also an able musician, playing the piano and the viola to a good standard. The piano was useful at school and various orchestras and operatic societies made use of his services. I think he remained in teaching in the Scunthorpe area for many years. The odd man out in many ways was Frank Hymers, the other teacher in the main school. He was also a musician and one who dressed in an artistic manner, reminiscent of a character in Gilbert and Sullivan's *Patience*. He had charge of the special class and was dedicated to their welfare, though because of scant resources significant successes were limited. Frank seemed to live on an emotional knife-edge.

I rarely came in academic or social contact with colleagues from the other part of the school, but there were two exceptions. RJ Mitchell was in charge of the annexe and was also responsible for the school teams that competed in local schools' leagues in football and sometimes athletics. I helped and ran the second football team under his direction. 'Mitch' was an all-round sportsman, playing cricket for Scunthorpe Town in the Yorkshire League and occasionally keeping wicket for Lincolnshire. He had a certain air and he too became a local primary head. Joan Tutty was the other teacher I came to know quite well. She taught in the annexe and took the younger children. She came from Scawby and we often travelled on the bus together. Her brother was a 'biker' before there were such things and competed in TT races in the Isle of Man and at Cadwell. Joan was something of a tomboy with great energy and we sometimes played tennis together. It was through her that I played cricket for Scawby in the nether regions of the local leagues for a couple of years. She later married Graham Robertson, who came as a teacher in my second year there. He was a competent footballer and his family ran a well-known fish and chip business in Scunthorpe. Another who joined the staff in my second year was Alan Skinner, an ebullient character straight from his training at St John's, York. He played cricket for Appleby-Frodingham and was a boisterous St Bernard of a teacher. The final one I remember was with us for only a short time on, I think, two separate occasions and, like me, was unqualified. She was taken on in staffing emergencies while 'resting' between acting engagements. The daughter of the editor of the *Scunthorpe Evening Telegraph*, she had curiously been born three doors away from where I lived in Brigg. Her name, one that can still fill London theatres, was Joan Plowright. She also, of course, became Lady Olivier and more recently a Dame – though not of the pantomime variety. These were my colleagues with whom I spent my working hours over the next eighteen months as well as considerable social time at parties and at sporting events.

◆◆◆

However, this was all in the future. On that bleak Wednesday morning either towards the very end of January or in the first days of February I was introduced and it was decided that for the rest of that week I would help out in various classes to get the feel of the school and would spend one morning up at the Church Hall annexe. I first spent half a morning with Bessie Wrigley, who had the 'scholarship' class. These were well-behaved and well-motivated children. I sat through Bessie's RE lesson, tested spellings and then helped individuals with their sums. After break I assisted Mrs Chantry in the period set aside each day for reading and then after lunch I was with Marc helping in the handicraft project he was doing, before finally I read the class a story before home time. I had been relatively busy and had quite enjoyed the experience. The next morning was spent with younger children up at the annexe. I observed Kit Cousans, Joyce Cross and Joan Tutty use all their undoubted skills and patience upon the reception class and the six-year-olds, but I have never taught at that level – and would never have had the patience. In the afternoon I was back at the main building taking a group of boys for PE and Games. On Friday I spent time with the special class, where Frank Hymers gladly accepted my help. I was placed on a small chair at a table with some half dozen children with – to use more modern euphemisms – severe learning difficulties and behavioural problems. It was quite shattering, for I had never been in contact with such children in the course of my own school education. In my class at Brigg Glebe Road there had been slow learners, but nothing like this. I had gaily coloured counters of various sizes (more suited to Tiddlywinks than serious education) and dog-eared reading books with boys in sailor suits bundling hoops by a pond with nursemaids in attendance. Later Frank played the piano and I sang along in some simple songs, even helping to produce a respectable round of 'London's Burning'. The Friday afternoon was spent with other classes who were engaged upon varied activities and for the final hour they could play with their friends at board games they had brought from home.

The following Monday morning I arrived to find a crisis. A new teacher who was expected couldn't come and was not now expected to come at all. I would have to take the class. Colleagues ensured that I had chalk and a board rubber, that the inkwells were well supplied and that there were enough pens in one box and pencils in another. A register was pushed into my hands and I was propelled through the door of a classroom to find fifty-odd faces turned expectantly toward me. I drew a deep breath, took out my trusty fountain pen and called the register.

The primary curriculum had not changed since my own days at what was then called elementary school. After the calling of the register there was some RE. There was no area suitable to hold a school assembly, even with part of the school, so we never met as a whole body. After RE there was time for spellings and then for sums before the morning break. Then there was reading practice and grammatical exercises. The afternoon sessions were also broken by a short break and were spent in written English with a long period for Art once a week. Time after break on Friday afternoons was given over to playing games or reading books brought from home. Since many of my class did not possess books at home, a separate pile of ancient silent readers had to be kept in readiness. It was into the afternoon sessions that PE and Games and Handicraft or Sewing had to be accommodated. This was done by pairing classes of one male and a female teacher, the lady taking the girls of both classes for PE and the man taking two lots of boys. Similarly two sets of girls were gathered together for Sewing and two lots of boys for Handicraft. Music or rather Singing was also on the timetable and sometimes two classes were joined together in a large classroom that had a piano in it, as long as one of the teachers could play. Alternatively a teacher could take over the special class temporarily, while Frank Hymers took the vacated class for Singing. It all seems so very uncoordinated now set against current primary practice and, of course, it could all be put into disarray by staff illness, for there were no extra supply teachers then.

I found myself in charge of a class of ten-year-olds, who in a rigorously streamed situation were regarded as the lowest of four mainstream classes in that year group. There were fifty-four children in that class, slightly more than in the top 'scholarship' class, for in 1949 the Eleven-Plus dominated primary education. A school was judged on how many scholarship passes to Grammar School they achieved. The overall rate was under 20%, so a school that could claim a quarter of its pupils went on to Grammar School was held in high esteem. In Scunthorpe there was Scunthorpe Grammar School and a Technical High School for those who were not quite good enough to get into the Grammar School. The rest went on to secondary modern schools, though this term wasn't used then. The majority of our children went to Ashby Girls or Ashby Boys according to sex and left at the age of fourteen. These schools were situated at the upper end of the High Street. Because of the kudos attached to passing the Eleven-Plus (as well as the hundreds of new bicycles added to the equation by anxious parents), the 'scholarship' class had the pick of what scant resources were available. Most of the teachers accepted that as the preordained order of things.

I soon settled into a routine with my class. Because of bus times I was always at school just after eight and was able to write up the blackboard with the day's spellings and with examples of the 'sums' that were to be attempted later. After calling the register – and my class were a hardy lot, so there was precious little absenteeism for illness and even less (except for Paul B) for truancy – we would embark upon the spellings. These were arranged in groups, such as five words ending in '–eam' and five words ending in '–pt' (wept, leapt, kept, except and inept). We pronounced the words, I explained the meanings, giving examples, and the class wrote them down in their spelling notebooks. There was no real link or context. At other times we would collate 'i-before-e' words and then 'e-before-i' words and later words ending in '–gh'. I could choose the combinations at will. There was a weekly test on the spellings each Friday.

The religious part could come either before or after the spellings. I had been brought up to go to church, having been to Sunday School and was still in the choir, so I didn't mind taking RE. Other colleagues, however, were not altogether happy in teaching this subject. I regret that even my efforts were similar to what I had been subject to when I was at elementary school. There was a class set of the Shorter Bible and from this we read sections dealing with Old Testament stories of Moses or the parables from the New Testament and occasionally we attempted to re-enact them. There was little spiritual enlightenment.

In Arithmetic there were three sections – Mental, Mechanical and Problems: all three deserve their capitals! The first was practised in the mind, explained and then tested verbally. There was considerable chanting of tables and learning by rote how many stones there were in a hundredweight and how many pennies in a pound. In Mechanical the working out was on paper and I attempted to instruct them in how to add, subtract, multiply and divide in whole numbers and later in fractions, in pounds, shillings and pence, in hours, days and minutes, and in tons, hundredweights, pounds and ounces. Rods, poles and perches were deemed defunct at that time, though parents and grandparents took this as further evidence of how 'soft' contemporary education had become. The problems involved reading a set of circumstances and deducing the right formula to reach a correct solution. Many were hypotheses concerned with various numbers of men mowing meadows of given acreage or children buying sweets at differing prices or of different colours. But the main problem was many of my class could not read the questions.

The readers were old and dog-eared. A substantial number featured the aforementioned little boys in sailor suits, bundling hoops or sailing boats on ponds with a pram-pushing nursemaid in attendance. There was a list of words at the top of the page and these were incorporated in anodyne sentences below. Often the words had a similar sound – rain, train, sprain and again – but there was little continuity or context. The new *Janet and John* books were not for the likes of my class and Spot or Dr Seuss were as yet unheard of. There was some attempt at grading the readers by their difficulty and you were supposed to progress up the scale, though my class was not expected to move further than the foothills. I would hear groups read in turn, while the other groups rehearsed a section silently. I would also have individuals out by my desk for one-to-one attention. We did some whole class work on phonics to build up a basic vocabulary. We also had sessions of silent reading when the children could select a book from the well-worn pile of silent readers. One of the favourite choices was the Toytown series by SG Hulme Beaman with Larry the Lamb and Dennis the Dachshund, whom they knew from *Children's Hour* on the radio. These paperbacks were always well illustrated.

Some children in the class still couldn't write in a meaningful way. They had more or less mastered the shapes of individual letters, but couldn't join them together and putting the right shapes in the right order to make recognisable words was beyond them. Those who were more proficient copied out whole sections from the reading books, but the less able furrowed their brows and laboriously copied out words or simple sentences.

Much of the written work was involved with mechanical accuracy, such as knowing the right plural for 'knife' or 'fox' and the correct past participle for 'swim' or 'bring'. The class did its best to turn singulars to plurals in given sentences and change from the present tense to the future. We spent time on finding out where to put full stops or question marks and which words always needed a capital letter. There were attempts at creative writing, but too often these were a regurgitation of a folk or biblical story or an account of what they had done in the holidays – usually not much! The highlight may have been a day trip to Cleethorpes, for there were no organised play schemes in those days and certainly no foreign holidays.

So much for the famous three Rs. In Art we used crayons and sometimes powder paints that had to be mixed carefully in large jam jars and then dispensed into smaller containers to each double desk. The water had to be brought in large jugs from the cloakrooms. The paper we used was wallpaper scrounged from all available sources or large sheets of grey sugar paper that were cut into manageable portions roughly ten inches by twelve. Some children elected to bring their own paint boxes from home, but there were relatively few who possessed them. The subjects for painting were hackneyed – the family at tea, the scarecrow, a sunny day. The paint powder was expendable, but not so the paintbrushes. These were carefully counted out and even more carefully counted back in, rather like a reporter in the Falklands War. Sometimes we would devise geometrical shapes and colour them. Very occasionally we could borrow a set of compasses from the 'top' class. These too had to be scrupulously counted out and then back in. I had at least three boys who had to be watched carefully, for they were apt to push compass points into other pupils' posteriors. The time set aside for Art was the most anarchic session of the week.

PE and Games took place in the tarmacked playground and we tried not to let inclement weather conditions prevent us. We wore no special clothing for PE, neither children nor teacher. I took off my jacket and tie and put on a pair of 'daps', as we called sandshoes or plimsolls in those days – trainers were forty years ahead in a much more affluent age. I retained my normal shirt and suit trousers, held up by rather garish braces. The boys took off their sweaters and jerkins and the girls their cardigans. Many but by no means all wore 'daps': there were a considerable number of hobnail boots. It was regimented PE. The boys were in lines and there was a complicated manoeuvre with arms outstretched facing forward and then sideways to ensure the correct spacing. We then proceeded in a ritual of exercises in running on the spot, raising arms above heads, bending knees, touching toes, twisting the body with arms outstretched and swinging both arms windmill fashion. We also performed a combination of these in 'Underneath the Spreading Chestnut Tree', as we had seen His Majesty George VI perform at a Scout camp on pre-war newsreels. I also incorporated a games session which involved team relays of various kinds. Sometimes it consisted of the team leader zigzagging through the line of his team and then touching the next in line, who then zigzagged his way through the team before setting off the next member. The team that completed the full sequence first won.

That game relied upon no accessories, but there was some limited apparatus stored in a small wooden shed by the outside toilets. There were wooden markers like small, modern traffic cones and there were coloured sashes of braid to distinguish different teams. There was a maximum of five footballs for a group of fifty – if luckily all were inflated and had no punctures. Team relays were devised which necessitated passing the football over heads and then between the legs of the team. When the back marker received it he had to rush to the front and start the whole process again. This was sometimes amplified by having the boy with the ball bounce it basketball fashion up to the school wall and back again. The boys enjoyed best a boisterous game in which one team of about a dozen would be surrounded in a largish circle by the other three teams and the ball was then hurled at the team in the middle. When one of its members was hit supposedly below the waist, he was out and the game continued, timed by the teacher's watch, until all the team had been eliminated. Then another team would take its place in the middle and the winning team would be the one who survived longest. It was difficult to control fifty jostling boys with bloodlust in their eyes armed only with a whistle, but they all seemed to enjoy these sessions and they did release surplus energy. Such were the simple joys of primary school PE in the late 1940s.

Handicraft involved much cutting out of cardboard, colouring, gluing with paste and covering with more surplus wallpaper. We made cutout trains and carriages and we glued covered matchboxes together to form small sets of drawers. At Christmas we cemented a candle to a firm cardboard base, glued on a further covered matchbox, stuck a small fir cone on the box and scattered snow-like glitter over all. Pipe cleaners were fashioned in more or less approximations of animals and innumerable calendars were devised. I suppose we were starting what *Blue Peter* carried on, but our efforts were of the palest and most ineffectual hue of blue.

I enjoyed reading and telling stories and story-time was a period I extended whenever possible. Somehow Winnie the Pooh had missed me in my own childhood and I was delighted to make the acquaintance of Christopher Robin and his friends at this belated stage. The Ashby children loved the stories too and I have found (as Walt Disney did) that they have universal appeal. I read them to my own children and then grandchildren, to various 'A' level English students at the end of term and introduced them to my Polish trainee-teacher students when I was lecturing there in the mid-1990s. They all loved Pooh and gloomy Eeyore and satisfying the hunger of bouncy Tigger. Mark Twain's Tom Sawyer and Huck Finn were also among my favourite stories to read dramatically and they held the children's rapt attention. One day I was reading the passage in which Tom is terrified by the sudden appearance of Injun Joe with a candle in his hand when trapped in the cave with Becky. I had the full attention of the class and pointed towards the door where Injun Joe was. Unfortunately, as they followed the direction of my pointing, the headmaster chose that moment to peer through the small window in the door to the classroom. Instead of Injun Joe with a candle there was Chas B with inhaler. There was an involuntary gasp, a frisson of fear and then someone giggled. The whole class dissolved in nervous laughter to relieve their moment of panic. This must have been the first time Charles had been laughed at and I had much explaining to do.

◆◆◆

For all the eighteen months or so I was at Ashby I taught a class that numbered over fifty. The double desks were crowded into the Victorian-built classroom and there was never much room to move about. The girls sat together and so did the boys, but they were not arbitrarily divided into boys on the left and girls on the right. The tall teacher's desk, from at least the turn of the century, had one capacious compartment and was placed on a raised podium. I sat at it on a high stool. Across the front of the desk lay my symbol of authority – the cane, which was about four feet long, relatively pliable and could have been used by any gardener to stake their plants. I didn't use it very often and never on girls. Some four or five boys were the ones who were chastised for insubordination, for bullying other children or blatant inattention. I don't think it made much difference to their behaviour, but it did help to keep in line other boys who might have been tempted to transgress. I did not have to keep any record of any beatings I carried out and my authority to wallop was never questioned by parents, children or colleagues.

However, I don't think they bore me ill will for the occasional whacking. Though it was a large class it was relatively docile and there was always the threat of Charles B in the background as the pervading genius loci to dissuade further any potential disrupters. In one sense it is difficult to place the children socially: they were not village or rural children, nor were they by any stretch of the imagination city slickers. They were almost exclusively children of the artisan class in a semi-industrial town. The complex of steelworks in adjacent Scunthorpe provided employment for many of the fathers and 'the works' was the magnet that drew in the few families that had not been born and bred in this part of North Lincolnshire. Some fathers worked in local businesses such as bakers or ironmongers and others worked for the Scunthorpe Borough Council. Only a few mothers worked and these largely served in local shops. Practically all the parents had left school at fourteen and had few academic aspirations for their children. The

Eleven-Plus dominated primary education at that time, but these parents were realistic enough to know that the children in my class had no chance of passing for Grammar School, since they were in the bottom stream. (In my own elementary class at school, we were the only class in the year group and it was hoped that ten or in a good year twelve might pass for Brigg Grammar School or the Girls' High School.) So there were low expectations of my group in Ashby. The children would pursue the compulsory education course until they were fourteen and then find jobs.

Few of the class after almost sixty years stand out clearly in the mind and it was difficult to get to know over fifty children as individuals, even though I was with them all day and every day in term time. There was a certain lumpen biddability about most of them, who perhaps could see the faint glimmerings of light at the end of this educational tunnel in the form of a job and greater independence.

Four of the children who stood out from the general sea of faces were all incomers. Two were twins, Brenda and Doreen C, who were from London and had the greater alacrity and energy (frequently misplaced) of the city-born. They were identical and I could never with absolute certainty distinguish one from the other even when they were apart, which was rarely. They had mischievous grins and black hair cut in a rough Eton crop. They invariably wore dark pinafore dresses. They were livelier and took longer to settle to more mundane tasks such as learning tables or basic spellings. Paul B was another incomer with an obscured background. He was small and psychotic, yet he could turn on the most bland expression of angelic innocence. In my mind he was categorised as similar to a gangster known as 'Baby Face'. He had the lowest IQ in the class and seemed destined to cause trouble. It was therefore not surprising to learn later that in his late teens or early twenties he had been involved in crime and was charged with taking another's life, though whether the charge was murder or manslaughter, I don't recall. Curiously the other incomer was also later arraigned for manslaughter. In over forty years of teaching I can't remember ever having heard of any other former pupils having taken another's life and yet here were two in the same class. This last incomer, Jacques U, had come from across the Channel and I never did know how he came to be at Ashby County Primary School. His English was poor, insufficient to enable him to survive easily in an English playground. He was different and hence an oddity. He was sullen and had an uncertain temper; whether this was his natural temperament or forced upon him by his predicament, I don't know. He was very much a loner and some years later circumstances led him to defend himself or exact revenge with a fatal knife. Paul and Jacques were the two I caned most, but it doesn't seem to have had a salutary effect.

Three local boys remain in the memory. John B was one of the more athletic with animal energy, but not many brains. He was amiable and played for the School Second XI football team. Alan W was probably the tallest in the class and one of the strongest, and too often got into fights in the playground. I also chastised him several times a term. The saddest of all was Alan D. He was the one child in the whole class who had an exceptional talent. He could draw with scrupulous accuracy and paint and colour in a fluent and mature style. He produced some wonderful paintings. Alan too was different. In contrast to the ebullience and earthiness of the other boys, he was a pale, almost elfin creature. He had semi-transparent skin with long, artistic fingers and had difficulty coming to terms with the rough and readiness that was Ashby County Primary. His parents were more elderly than the norm and more middle-class. They had high hopes for their only son, who was probably touched with autism – though I didn't even know the word at that time, let alone be able to recognise the symptoms. He received no special help, though he drew like an angel. Unhappily he died in his early secondary schooling when his cycle was in collision with a car.

There was a great similarity in dress among the boys – boots, short trousers, grey shirt (buttoned, but usually tie-less) and home-knitted pullover or jerkin, which was a woollen garment that had long sleeves, was pulled over the head and had three buttons to fasten the slit in the front of the neck. The girls' clothes allowed a little more for individuality: dresses (often various gingham checks) in summer; blouses, cardigans and thick skirts in winter. Most of the clothes were home-made and with the poorer families many were obviously hand-me-downs. Hairstyles were the best barometer to maternal care. Some girls had basic, square cuts with an often grubby ribbon tied simply around one arbitrarily chosen lock, but with others you could see the hair was regularly washed, brushed and plaited and braided with ribbons carefully tied.

On the whole the girls were more biddable, more industrious and had better brains than the boys in the class. Compared with the local Ashby-born girls, the Cockney twins seemed to be worldly wise, yet the Lincolnshire lassies had a quiet, dependable common sense and you anticipated that these qualities would find full expression when they later became wives and mothers of families. Zena L had an exotic name and was an attractive, active girl. Linda P had blonde hair in becoming plaits and persevered. Little Dorothy P was kindly, considerate and hard-working. She always tried her best, but was never going to pass the Eleven-Plus.

These are the ones who remain in the memory. They also figured in the Nativity play I attempted with them in the approach to Christmas 1949. Dorothy P was Mary, Linda P the Archangel Gabriel, while John B was the leading shepherd, Alan D one of the Magi and Paul B a shepherd hanger-on with no speaking part. They did their best and with the help of Bessie Wrigley we managed to dress them in some approximation to their roles by rummaging in an old clothes box and the children bringing items from home. They were very proud, with towels bound round heads, swathed in old curtains or clad in best white dress with gold paper wings. The Nativity story was told and two other classes were invited to join our class to hear it. I didn't feel, however, we could expose our efforts before the parents. This experience did convince me that I was never likely to be a Trevor Nunn and this was the only play I ever directed in over forty years as an English teacher, though I was connected in other ways with scores of productions.

Primary schools in Scunthorpe and District competed against each other in those days at football and athletics and there was intense rivalry. This competitive spirit was encouraged fiercely by headmaster, staff and parents, and the children responded with increased efforts. I was put in charge of 'Ashby II' as we appeared in the league tables of schoolboy football in the *Scunthorpe Evening Telegraph*. We wore red shirts and sometimes used a pitch loaned by Ashby Institute, the local semi-professional team. In those days there was no training and specific coaching. We trotted around the pitch, practised heading and trapping and played mini practice games. For away matches we used the local bus service to venture across Scunthorpe to such strange and exotic venues as Henderson Avenue, Brumby and Crosby. We even went as far as Messingham. When we played at home I refereed and when we played away I cheered and exhorted from the touchline. If it were a crucial league match or a cup final, we tried to find an impartial and locally qualified referee and the teachers of the opposing schools were the linesmen. For such matches there would be a goodly smattering of parents, who were most partisan. Curiously it was the mothers in headscarves and wellies who most vociferously questioned the lineage of the referee and his assistants. The boys expended a great deal of energy, kicked heartily at the ball (which they avoided heading if they could) and tended to run about in packs. The balls then were made of thick leather, which became heavier and heavier as the water on the pitch soaked through the dubbined cover. It was a brave and foolhardy lad who headed clear in the second half. Matches were sometimes stopped because the inflated rubber inner case had punctured. And at half-time it was often necessary to undo the lacing and pump more air into the ball. The scores now seem strange, as the attackers always seemed to get the better of the defenders and 4-4-2 formations were unknown. It usually was more like 1-1-8. Frequently games were won or lost by scorelines such as 8-5 or 9-7, but sometimes we were outclassed by an opposing First XI and would maybe lose heart in the second half with a temporarily chastening 13-0 defeat. Such scores were quickly shrugged off and hopes of an improbable victory in the next match returned.

While I was at Ashby a new and enterprising travel firm started up in Scunthorpe and persuaded the local authority to support day trips by special train of whole year groups from the various primary schools in the area. It involved some thousand children, scores of staff and meant leaving from Scunthorpe railway station before 7am and returning late at night. I remember one outing was to Norwich and incorporated a boat trip on the Broads. The logistics seemed to work smoothly, for I can't recall any traumatic experiences and we brought all the children safely home. Another trip was to London. How we negotiated our way around the city with over a thousand ten-year-olds in tow I can't remember. Surely we didn't use the Underground. I do remember the endless counting of heads and the fact that the twins (who were the only ones with London experience) had been told on no account to leave go of teacher and I had one clamped to each hand the whole time we were in London.

However, such breaks in routine were rare and remained in the minds of the children because of the rarity. The five terms I was at Ashby followed each other in the approved order of things. It was a formative experience for me, though not well paid – £15 a month before a few deductions. (I gave my mother £5 a month and managed my social life and travelling expenses on the rest, even amassing a small balance in my TSB account.) Ashby did, however, show I could hold my own in a classroom and I spent nearly the next fifty years teaching and being taught.

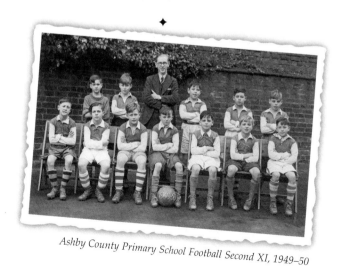

Ashby County Primary School Football Second XI, 1949–50

199

On holiday in Scarborough, c. 1934

Cricket in the street:
myself and John Rands

In the clothes-horse tent: myself,
Ellen Thacker and John Rands

St John's Church Choir,
c. 1943

Me as a Cub, c. 1938

Speech Day, Brigg Grammar School, 1948

*Brigg Grammar School
Cricket Second XI, 1948*

*Brigg Grammar School
Football Second XI, 1947–48*

*Charles Bramley, headmaster,
Ashby County Primary School*

Staff of Ashby County Primary School

EPILOGUE

In *A Midsummer Night's Dream* Duke Theseus refuses to countenance an epilogue from the 'rude mechanicals' and opts for a 'bergomask dance': I have two left feet and dancing has never really been a pleasure, but I do feel that here an epilogue could be useful. In writing about my twenty Yellerbelly Years in Brigg, Lincs, I wished initially to describe to my grandchildren how different childhood was some seventy years ago. They are far more self-confident and widely travelled and have many more material possessions than I had, but they have to contend with many more pressures and blandishments from commercial organisations and from their peers. I was unlikely to be knifed for 'dissing' someone's trainers as our light, canvas gym shoes (called 'plimsolls' or just 'daps') all cost 2s 11d (15p) from Woolworths. I hankered for no designer labels or logos – the only one I knew was the utility mark '**CC**ⁿ'. I wanted to show how life was simpler then and relatively unpressurised, for the realities of war and the threat of invasion did not really impinge upon me. I was free to grow up in a smaller, more cocooned world, content with my place in that world and having respect for those I accepted as my elders and betters.

However, although my place in the world was fixed in a niche as the elder son of Frank and Min Rhodes, I find I have written about my first twenty years with the self-absorption of youth. I have placed myself in the foreground and filtered all my experiences through my own eyes. I have never felt I was conceited or self-important, yet I fear it may appear so. I have not given my immediate family its rightful place or due importance. I do believe I was 'well brought up' and owe a debt to my parents I was never able to repay. My mother may seem a shadowy figure, always in the background, and this is true. She did not push herself forward but was content to stay away from the spotlight, helpful and of service – she was baking for and serving at old people's teas in Brigg when she was over seventy and older than many of the guests. More importantly she was always there at home for me. I was cleanly turned out, slept in a warm, laundered bed and was well nourished by wholesome home cooking of a high standard, despite wartime restrictions. Mum tended my injuries and ailments and loved me through all my faults and shortcomings. Though she was never openly critical, I was able to sense her disapproval and altered course accordingly. She was modest, loving and supportive and took a quiet pride in the achievements of her husband and two sons, playing down her own success as a County Bowls player. In contrast with these days of aggressive feminism and career women, she was content to be a homemaker – and more are needed nowadays.

My father was more extravert and had he had the educational opportunities available to my brother and myself he would have been an even more important figure, for he had a keen mind and much common sense. He was a valued member of many organisations in Brigg and was prepared to put in that extra effort. As a father he was gently firm and just occasionally reinforced the correction of a fault or wrongdoing by applying a long-handled hairbrush to my backside. There was never any ill-treatment or abuse, apparently so common in some of today's memoirs and so highlighted by contemporary media. I knew the standards he expected and tried not to let him down. He had aspirations for me, hoping I could enjoy an education he had never had and use the opportunities this would open up. He somehow maintained these hopes, despite the inauspicious omens of my early secondary education: I think his proudest moments must have been to see both his sons receive the accolade of Bachelor of Arts in the Sheldonian Theatre, Oxford. With surprising Rhodesian versatility I graduated in English and David in Physics – and he with a First.

I note that there are very few references to my younger brother, David, in these twenty years, but our joint memorable experiences in this period were few. His arrival did have an unsettling effect upon me, for it was unexpected and disturbed the normal tenor of my life. The difference of over eight years in our ages was highly significant, for it meant that in my first twenty years we did not often do things together. I had all the advantages of eight years' superiority, mentally and physically, and did not want to be encumbered by a baby brother in my social activities. He had his circle of friends and I had mine. Moreover, at the time when he might have become more interesting and worthy of social consideration, David (who usually enjoyed robust health) contracted a most virulent combination of pneumonia, tuberculosis and pleurisy, so much so that prayers were offered in St John's for his survival. For almost a year he was away from home and a patient at the Branston Hall sanatorium on the other side of Lincoln. Open air and spartan conditions seem to have categorised sanatoria in the late forties and he also had to contend with the long and bitter winter of 1947: it is a wonder he survived – but I'm thankful he did. I do remember making a few visits with Mum and Dad in the Lindsey Blind van on Sundays to see him at Branston and adding my contribution to the treats we brought, but no clear memories remain. Anyway in 1948 I had other things on my mind, such as Oxford Entrance and Higher School Certificate. David made a full recovery and went on to excel academically and athletically at Brigg Grammar School, attaining such heights as *Victor Ludorum*, utterly beyond my capabilities. It is outside the scope of my first twenty years, but I was later able to bask in his successes as a scientist and a singer. He was the best man at my wedding in 1957 and, though in our working lives we have always been separated by two hundred miles or so, we have kept in touch and see each other once or twice a year. The Rhodeses have never been a family to live in each other's pockets, but the family ties are firmly in place and the dedication at the beginning of this book is sincere.